PIONEER

Edited by

Mildred Tanner Andrews

Introduction by Leonard Garfield

Contributions by Karin Murr Link,

Marc Blackburn, and Dana Cox

Pioneer Square

Community Association

in association with

University of Washington Press

Seattle & London

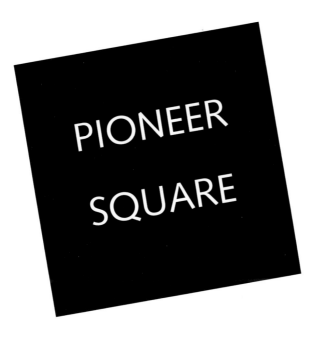

PIONEER SQUARE

Seattle's Oldest Neighborhood

University of Washington Press
PO Box 50096, Seattle, WA 98145
www.washington.edu/uwpress

Library of Congress Cataloging-in-Publication Data

Pioneer Square : Seattle's oldest neighborhood /
edited by Mildred Tanner Andrews ; introduction
by Leonard Garfield ; contributions by Karin Murr
Link, Marc Blackburn, and Dana Cox—1st ed.
    p.   cm.
Includes bibliographical references and index.
ISBN 0-295-98503-8 (pbk. : alk. paper)
    1. Pioneer Square (Seattle, Wash.)—History.
2. Seattle (Wash.)—History.   I. Andrews,
    Mildred Tanner.
F899.S47P566   2004
979.7'772—dc22   2004025999

For **GEORGE ANDREWS**

The Seattle Motorcycle Club revs up in Pioneer Place for its June 4, 1911, "Endurance Run to Vancouver, B.C." Photo by Webster & Stevens. ColorOne Photographic and Digital Imaging

CONTENTS

Preface   ix

Acknowledgments   xv

Introduction
LEONARD GARFIELD   3

1 A Change of Worlds
MILDRED ANDREWS   7

2 Urban Frontier Years
MILDRED ANDREWS   25

3 Rise of the Urban Center
KARIN LINK   42

4 Railroads: Premier
Entrance to the City
MILDRED ANDREWS   61

5 Prospectors and Patriots
MARC BLACKBURN   80

6 Skid Road
MILDRED ANDREWS   94

7 The Era of Booms and Busts
MILDRED ANDREWS   118

8 Left Bank
MILDRED ANDREWS
WITH "OUT OF THE CLOSET"
BY DANA COX   142

9 Preservation and the
Era of Civic Revival
KARIN LINK   174

Bibliography   207

Contributors   215

Index   217

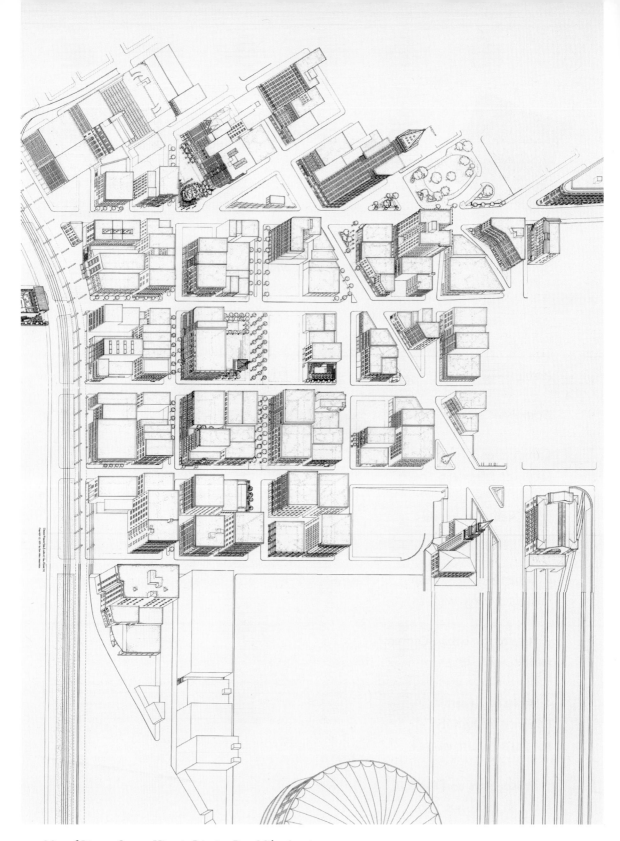

Map of Pioneer Square Historic District. Don Miles Associates

When we walk along Pioneer Square's tree-lined streets and marvel at its picturesque, Victorian- and Romanesque-style architecture, we often wish the place could tell its stories. In recent years, the district's historic buildings and projects to preserve them have been the subjects of well-researched articles and books, but documentation of the neighborhood's social and economic legacies has not kept pace. The guiding philosophy of the Pioneer Square History Project is that historic preservation should be about preserving community as well as architectural landmarks. My coauthors and I have endeavored to make the buildings and the place "talk," by bringing to light stories of people and events that link today's neighborhood with its colorful past.

Pioneer Square is the birthplace of downtown Seattle and its constantly evolving soul. From its roots as an ancient Duwamish Indian homeland to a pioneer settlement, through booms and busts in the nineteenth and twentieth centuries, to its emergence as a center of arts, sports, transportation, and urban living, Pioneer Square presents the story of our region in all its color, diversity, and spirit. Told on a human scale, the district's social and economic history is as significant as its architectural heritage.

Today, Pioneer Square's Klondike Gold Rush National Historical Park, Seattle Unit, and the Underground Tour Museum focus their exhibits on people and events that with few exceptions are more than a century old. Other venues that display historic photographs concentrate on the same period or on more recent restorations of the district's historic buildings. Most published histories and guidebooks are similar in scope. The historian Murray Morgan's acclaimed *Skid Road,* first published in 1951, is a notable exception, with rich detail about the district's social history. Unlike Morgan's classic, which he calls a history of Seattle "from the bottom up," this book unfolds the drama, keeping Pioneer Square at center stage from past to present.

Our goal is to present players and acts from that drama in the contexts both of Pioneer Square's heritage and of Seattle's and the region's history. Pioneer Square is historically a cultural mosaic that has been home to a predominantly male population of blue-collar workers and the struggling poor. Here, ethnically diverse groups of immigrants clustered in enclaves, where they retained their cultural traditions while trying to gain a foothold and begin the process of assimilation into the American mainstream. Adding to the mix, Pioneer Square's business proprietors have spanned the socioeconomic spectrum. In its heyday, the district made national headlines as a center of gold-rush fervor, transportation and trade, labor unrest, vaudeville, and vice.

Pioneer Place, looking southeast, 1911. Museum of History and Industry, Webster & Stevens. 15694

Pioneer Square has weathered transformations from the city's most vibrant business and cultural center to notoriety as the nation's original Skid Road. It was home to Japanese-American families who operated small businesses and working-men's hotels until the U.S. government forced them to leave during World War II. Prior to Pioneer Square's rebirth as Seattle's first designated historic district, artists and galleries moved into abandoned warehouses and lofts. The Bohemian arts community paved the way for a variety of one-of-a-kind small businesses. As the district's business community revitalized, property owners and developers undertook projects to restore historic buildings for residential and business use.

Today, in what some call the "new gold-rush era," a development boom in and around Pioneer Square has sparked a period of transformation and rebirth. Gentrification has displaced many older pensioners and low-income workers, prompting a concerted community effort to promote low- and middle-income housing that spans the gap between missions and upscale residences. Community activists want to strengthen their neighborhood's economic base but simultaneously preserve its character as a cultural hub for artists, galleries, bookstores, and other unique small businesses. As sports stadiums, transportation systems, and office complexes make the district an economic cornerstone of Seattle, the historic buildings remain as protected landmarks.

It is a critical time to bring to light the district's complex social and economic heritage, so that the neighborhood and the city can understand its significance. By exploring links between former times and the present, we endeavor to create a sense of historic context that will undergird planning, development, and public art as Pioneer Square navigates its way toward the future. An appreciation of the district's social history has the potential of transforming it from a monument to the past into a living treasure that illuminates Seattle's ongoing heritage and gives it a unique identity.

In summer 1998, Leonard Garfield, then head of the King County Cultural Resources Division, and I met in his office in the Smith Tower, where we conceived the idea for this book. We outlined a research methodology that included both academic and community-based perspectives. Our plan was to draw on published works and archival resources, along with extensive interviews of people who would tell us their stories. Collecting significant photographs was a top priority. When we made our proposal to the Pioneer Square Community Council (since merged into the Pioneer Square Community Association), we received its enthusiastic endorsement and sponsorship. Our project fit into the Arts and Legends component of the new Neighborhood Plan, offering scholarly historical research and interpretation that would provide a foundation for a host of outcomes.

As chair of the Pioneer Square History Project Advisory Committee, I worked with Renee Tanner, who served on the PSCA board, to recruit dynamic, dedicated, and knowledgeable members. The committee helped shape the contents of the book, identified community resources and interviewees, and designed a stream of advance projects to engage the community and the general public in the process of exploring Pioneer Square's cultural and built heritage. Tanner and I shared the responsibility of raising funds and coordinating the production of a touring photographic exhibition, an interactive Web site, public lectures, guided tours of the historic district, a discussion guide, a richly illustrated walking-tour booklet, and a photographic archive for researchers. In addition, History Project staff worked as consultants on related projects, including a guidebook for future public arts projects in Pioneer Square and historic photographic exhibits that are installed on the base of the Occidental Park pergola and in the Frye Hotel and Merrill Place lobbies.

When Garfield accepted the position of executive director of the Museum of History and Industry, he remained actively involved on our project's advisory committee but had to reduce his planned coauthor role to writing the book's introduction. We were fortunate to find well-qualified coauthors—Marc Blackburn, Dana Cox, and Karin Link—among the members of the advisory committee. My thanks to each of them for careful research, patient revising of drafts, camaraderie, and unflagging good humor.

Members of the project advisory committee, some of whom served for the duration and others for shorter terms, helped make the book and related projects a reality. Those not already mentioned are Cary Atlas, David Brunner, John Chaney, Gary Hartnett, David Ishii, Lee Keller, Angela Mack, Angie McCarrel, Jennifer Meisner, Kathy Nielsen, Mark Nielsen, Cynthia Rose, and Michael Young. Other board and staff members on the former Pioneer Square Community Council and current Pioneer Square Community Association who have provided significant administrative support include Holly James, Casey Jones, Heather MacIntosh, Craig Montgomery, Suanne Pelley, Rosemary Rice, Sunny Speidel, and Doug Vann.

In the course of our research, my coauthors and I conducted numerous interviews, along with archival and on-site research. We also profited from casual conversations with architects, business owners, developers, historic preservationists, residents, artists, homeless people, community activists, social workers, visitors, historians, people whose roots date back to earlier generations in Pioneer Square, and others who shared their insights. Many of the interviewees are cited in the book for specific contributions, while others helped provide context and contributed to our interpretation of themes, events, and political, social, and economic issues. While I unfortunately cannot name them all, some who deserve special acknowledgment are Kenny Alhadeff, Ralph Anderson, Sid Andrews, Alan Black, David Brewster, Kirby Brown, Cath Brunner, Meta Buttnick, Morrie Buttnick, Ron Chew, Howard Clifford, Dorothy Cordova, Walt Crowley, Kevin Daniels, Paul Dorpat, Michael Fajans, Polly Friedlander, Kay Harai, Gary Hartnett, Ilze Jones, Grant Jones, Bob Kaplan, Billy King, Marleen Koob, B. J. Krivanek, Larry Kreisman, Greg Kucera, David Label, Donald Lachman, Greg Lang, Jim Leong, Jimmy Manolides, Ed Marquand, Lorraine McConaghy, Esther Mumford, Tim O'Brien, Charles Payton, Mike Peringer, James Rasmussen, Larry Reid, Rosemary Rice, Robert Roblee, Rick Simonson, Rod Slemmons, Greg Smith, Sunny Speidel, Frank Stagen, Mayumi Tsutakawa, Catherine Vandenbrink, and Warren Wing.

As photo editor, I am grateful to our many contributors, especially Paul Dorpat, Rod Slemmons, Karin Link, Carolyn Marr of the Museum of History and Industry, Anne Frantilla of the Seattle Municipal Archives, Ilze Jones of Jones & Jones Architects and Landscape Architects, Dorothy and Fred Cordova of the Filipino American National Historical Society, and Sunny Speidel of the Seattle Underground Tour, all of whom went the extra mile to help me locate and interpret historically significant photographs. Ilze Jones, G. Craig Thorpe, and Greg Smith of the Major Property Owners Group graciously provided renderings of their visions for future development in Pioneer Square.

As chapters took shape, members of the advisory committee read drafts and gave feedback. In addition, several of the interviewees read and critiqued all or parts of our work. My coauthor Karin Link was especially helpful in the process of revising and editing.

I am grateful to all of the above and to the staff at the University of Washington Press, notably Marilyn Trueblood for shepherding the manuscript through production, Kris Fulsaas for copyediting, and Audrey Meyer for the design.

Finally, on a personal note, a very special thanks to my husband, George Andrews, for reviewing my drafts, for helping me with the photo selection, and most of all for six years of patience and encouragement that enabled me to complete this project.

On behalf of all of the authors, I invite you to join us on our journey through Pioneer Square's history and toward its future.

Mildred Tanner Andrews
Project Director,
Pioneer Square History Project

ACKNOWLEDGMENTS

The Pioneer Square Community Association is proud to partner with the University of Washington Press in publishing this book, which is the culmination of a six-year project. A host of individuals and organizations have been involved, sharing their enthusiasm, professional expertise, and financial contributions. First of all, our thanks to the former Pioneer Square Community Council, which had the vision to establish the Pioneer Square History Project and integrate it into the Arts and Legends Program, a primary component of the 1998 Neighborhood Plan.

The History Project could not have happened without financial support from many generous donors. Our thanks to the following for making it possible: Paul G. Allen Charitable Foundation; Hugh and Jane Ferguson Foundation; Leonard Garfield; Goodman Financial Services; Jones & Jones Architects and Landscape Architects; King County Landmarks and Heritage Commission, Hotel/Motel Tax Fund;

National Trust for Historic Preservation; Nesholm Family Foundation; No Boundaries, Inc.; Northwest Interpretive Center and Klondike Gold Rush National Historic Park; Pendulum Creative; Pioneer Square Properties; Seattle Department of Neighborhoods; Gregory Broderick Smith Real Estate; Martin Smith, Inc.; Museum of History and Industry, Seattle; South Downtown Foundation; the Underground Tour; Thomas Street History Services; Vulcan Northwest; and the Washington Commission for the Humanities. In addition, we wish to acknowledge the following, who undertook related projects and engaged History Project staff as consultants: Alliance Management, Inc.; Elderhostel; the Frye Apartments; Nitze-Stagen Corporation; Pals of the Pergola; and the Seattle Arts Commission.

The book is enriched by a wealth of illustrations, each of which is acknowledged by a credit line. Major photographic donations came from Manuscripts, Special Collections, University Archives (MSCUA), University of Washington Libraries, and from the Museum of History and Industry, Seattle (MOHAI). We are grateful to them and to the following for permitting us to reproduce their photographs and illustrations: Kenny Alhadeff; Mildred Andrews; Meta and Morrie Buttnick; Color One Photo Lab; Paul Dorpat; Michael Fajans; Filipino American

"Pioneer Square" by Frank Kunishige, ca. 1920. Born in Japan, Kunishige became active in the Seattle Camera Club in the 1920s and worked in the studios of acclaimed local photographers Edward S. Curtis and Ella McBride. Here, he suffuses light and shadow into a technically created illusion of mist, giving a melancholy tone to his photograph of the pergola. Collection of David F. Martin and Dominic Zambito

National Historical Society; Jones & Jones Architects and Landscape Architects; Billy King; Karin Link; Low Income Housing Institute (LIHI); Major Property Owners Group (South Downtown/Pioneer Square); David F. Martin and Dominic Zambito; Dany Mitchell; Esther Mumford; Northwest Gay, Lesbian and Transgender History Museum Project; Mary Randlett; Ross Rieder; Robert Roblee; Seattle Department of Neighborhoods; Seattle Municipal Archives; Seattle Public Library; Rod Slemmons; Bill Speidel—The Underground Tour; Sound Transit, G. Craig Thorpe; Washington State Archives—Puget Sound Regional Branch, Washington State Historical Museum, Washington State Office of Archaeology and Historic Preservation; Washington State University Library; and Doug Vann.

Finally, a special thank-you is in order to the coauthors. Mildred Andrews is the driving force that pulled the book together and kept the vision in focus. Her initial chapters set the stage with overviews of the district's ancient Native American and pioneer history. Drawing on her previous work, she expands into more recent periods, exploring multicultural areas of social, economic, and cultural aspects that have shaped Pioneer Square. Karin Link expertly describes the architectural significance of the district, the histories of individual buildings, and the politics of historic preservation. Marc Blackburn contributes an incisive summary of the Klondike gold rush and its impact on Pioneer Square. Dana Cox discusses roots of the regional gay and lesbian community in the district, and Leonard Garfield's introduction places the chapters in a general context.

We are grateful to all of the above and many others who have contributed to this project.

Craig Montgomery
Executive Director, Pioneer Square
Community Association

PIONEER SQUARE

Introduction

Leonard Garfield

It has been more than 150 years since the intrepid settlers in the Denny Party came ashore in 1852 at the foot of what is now known as Washington Street in Pioneer Square. What they saw as a forested wilderness was the ancient homeland of Duwamish people, who made them welcome—neither group knowing how dramatically their worlds were about to change.

To the first American settlers, the shores of Elliott Bay were an incipient urban center, a future metropolis. And from the start, Pioneer Square served as their trade and manufacturing center. That very first year, Henry Yesler's mill was processing timber from nearby hillsides, while ships from San Francisco were calling on the small settlement. Although fewer than a hundred settlers had made this their home, Seattle was already engaged in the basic economic activities of much larger places, assuming the urban form that would distinguish it for years to come.

While we often think longingly of the slower pace of an earlier time, we would be hard-pressed to find relief in nineteenth-century

For decades the Smith Tower reigned as the tallest building west of the Mississippi. In this contemporary view from Occidental Park, it peeks over the Interurban Building. Photo by Bruce Reichert. ColorOne Photographic and Digital Imaging

Seattle. Granted, the first decades were more gently paced, slowed by the Indian wars and economic downturns of the 1850s and 1860s. But by the 1880s, the city's population boomed in an unprecedented way, and it continued to explode throughout the next few decades.

From 1888 to 1890, the population more than doubled, from 19,000 to 43,000; it doubled again to more than 80,000 by 1900; then it almost tripled in the next decade to 240,000. By 1910, Seattle was the twenty-fifth-largest city in the United States.

Just as distinctive as the city's rate of growth was its demographic character, and the most compelling characteristic was that Seattle was a man's place. Throughout the nineteenth century, the population of the Seattle area was more than 60 percent male. According to some estimates, the ratio in Pioneer Square might have been as much as fifteen men to every woman.

Many of these men were single, general laborers—working in the mills, warehouses, and canneries and on the docks. In addition, thousands of single men came to Seattle from remote lumber and mining camps or from ships to spend free time, the off-season, or time between jobs. They came from other parts of the United States as well as from Japan, China, Italy, Greece, and northern Europe.

The fact that Seattle was predominately male,

transient, and working class was important in shaping its character. It is not coincidental that Seattle became a center of theater circuits devoted to entertaining their male audiences, a town of battles between sin and propriety, a stage for major labor clashes, and even the site of an unprecedented general strike.

Pioneer Square was indelibly shaped by the population, rapid assimilation of newcomers, and rapid change that would characterize Seattle for the next 100 years. The district became a microcosm reflecting the overlapping phases of Seattle's growth as a city as it took its place on the world stage.

The first embryonic period, which accurately can be called the Urban Frontier Years, generally includes the years from settlement to the Great Fire of 1889. Built initially around Yesler's mill, the town grew densely but stayed close to its roots. Even during the boom years of the 1880s, 12,000 inhabitants clustered within ten blocks of Mill Street, now called Yesler Way.

The second stage of growth can be called the Rise of the Urban Center, a sustained boom time that stretched from the postfire years through the first decade of the twentieth century. During this period, Pioneer Square was a hub of many aspects of the civic and economic life of an expanding metropolis. The Square was the region's central business district, home to everything from grand mercantiles to hotels, from warehouses to blue-collar entertainment.

During this phase, the urban center was so fast growing that it bounded back from the Great Fire of 1889 stronger than ever. The building

The tiny Triangle Hotel and Bar, built in 1909 near the waterfront. With only eight rooms on the second floor, this home for working men was said to be the smallest hotel on the West Coast. Photo by James Patrick Lee. MSCUA, University of Washington Libraries, Lee 541

frenzy rivaled anything in Seattle history and stimulated a new awareness of architecture and construction technology evidenced in buildings that still stand today.

The urban center was enriched by two other seminal events in the 1890s. When James J. Hill's transcontinental railroad finally arrived in Seattle in 1893, it spurred development in Pioneer Square, and the Klondike gold rush, begun in 1897, brought wealth to the district at a time when the rest of the nation was still struggling out of an economic depression.

Yet by the early twentieth century, the urban center outgrew the confines of Pioneer Square. Retail and financial activities increasingly moved north, warehouses and industry south, and residential districts east. In the end, it was these areas outside the Square that would become more economically powerful than the district that served as their incubator.

The third overlapping phase, from 1900 through World War II, can be characterized as the Blue-Collar Years or the Era of Booms and Busts. As engineering feats of regrading and tidelands development opened the city to further expansion, and as population growth forced residential expansion beyond downtown, Pioneer Square assumed a special role as a workers' hub, an area of laborers, immigrant hiring halls, working men's hotels, and bawdy houses. During this phase, land and rents were cheaper than elsewhere in the city. Entertainment (often of a rowdy nature), warehouses, and transient hotels dominated. It is during this era that Pioneer Square assumed its permanent Skid Road image (though the name came earlier, from the moniker for Yesler Way when logs were skidded down the hill to Yesler's mill).

The fourth phase of Pioneer Square history, from 1945 to 1960, might be called the Era of Neglect, when the larger community had mostly forgotten Pioneer Square as anything other than an old, dilapidated neighborhood waiting to either die or be transformed. The earthquake of 1949 literally and figuratively shook the district to its foundations; through the next decade, more businesses left and buildings were boarded up.

But from the late 1950s through the 1990s, the Square entered a new stage—the Era of Civic Revival—when the neighborhood became a battleground of sorts for the soul of Seattle, a symbol of what could be and what should be. A debate raged between advocates of urban renewal and those who envisioned a restored district of handsome buildings, outdoor cafes, and an easy mingling of artists, merchants, and the down-and-out. Some civic leaders proposed tearing the district down and replacing the historic buildings with parking lots—an urban renewal vision that gained some momentum in the 1960s.

But architects such as Victor Steinbrueck and Ralph Anderson, gallery owners including Richard White, activists including Bill Speidel, and many others recognized that Pioneer Square was not only a place of beautiful buildings but a place of spirit as well. When the first large parking structure was built, replacing a grand Victorian building that was demolished in 1961, it became suddenly clear that the district's past held valuable and irreplaceable tools for its future.

By 1971, the City of Seattle formalized what the visionaries and entrepreneurs had already begun, by creating a thirty-block historic district, the first in the city and one of the first in the West. Over the next two decades, millions of dollars were invested in protecting and preserving the buildings of the district. At the same time, Pioneer Square became an active center for the arts, and entertainment and cultural tourism have been predominant themes in the district ever since, especially since construction of the Kingdome in 1976. The Square is still an incubator but has never lost its Skid Road identity.

What will the future bring? Over the past ten years, a revival in Pioneer Square created the largest wholesale renaissance since the heady days of the 1970s, with entire blocks being converted to new uses during restoration of much of their architectural character; by the late 1990s, Pioneer Square had even attracted a significant number of high-tech industries. Entertainment and tourism continued to fuel the economy with development such as Safeco Field in 1999 and Seahawks Stadium in 2002. But the future is far from clear. The Nisqually Earthquake of 2001 and the changing nature of the region's economy have both had profound impacts.

Whatever happens in Pioneer Square, it will likely serve as a harbinger for the larger community, a barometer of its health, and an incubator for the trends that will characterize the city as a whole as we move into the future.

1 A Change of Worlds

Mildred Andrews

At night when the streets of your cities and villages are silent and you think them deserted, they will throng with the returning hosts that once filled and still love this beautiful land. The White Man will never be alone. Let him be just and deal kindly with my people, for the dead are not powerless. Dead—did I say? There is no death. Only a change of worlds!

—*Chief Seattle, 1855 (translation by Henry Smith, October 29, 1887,* Seattle Star*)*

Chief Seattle gave his now-famous speech when, in sorrow, he relinquished the Duwamish and Suquamish homelands to the U.S. government in 1855. Although historians ponder the validity of this translation (discussed later in this chapter), the message and its grandeur seem sound. Today, the speech is valued as a regional treasure, frequently quoted in religious services and political and environmental debates.

In the eyes of most early explorers and pioneers, the Pacific Northwest was an uncivilized wilderness. Settlement progressed rapidly in the habitable Puget Sound region, making the Duwamish one of the first Northwest tribes to face near obliteration. The site of a deserted Duwamish village became the birthplace of the City of Seattle's downtown, now the Pioneer Square Historic District. In today's metropolitan community, some three hundred descendants are all that remain from the original Duwamish population that once numbered in the thousands.

As explorers, fur traders, and settlers came into contact with the Duwamish, the Pacific Northwest's economic, social, and political opportunities were transformed from what the region's original peoples had experienced.

Duwamish People and Culture

For centuries, the Duwamish people lived in clearings along the banks of the Duwamish River and its tributaries, on the shores of Lake Washington, and on bluffs and beaches along Elliott Bay—now the downtown Seattle waterfront. Vast tracts of old-growth forest extended from their homeland eastward to the peaks of the Cascade Range, crowned gloriously by Mount Rainier. Looking west across Puget Sound, which they called Whulge, they could see distant silhouettes of the craggy Olympic Mountains. Their homeland centered near the mouth of the Duwamish River, which flowed through a saltwater marsh into the depths of Elliott Bay. Historian David Buerge says that they were known as DuwAHBSH, because they paddled their canoes upstream and downstream to the bay.

At the time of settlement, Chief Seattle

Edward S. Curtis staged this photo of Puget Sound Indians, with a portable reed shelter and dugout canoe used for river travel. The clothing is made of woven cedar bark and skins. Museum of History and Industry, 18837

led both the Duwamish and neighboring Suquamish peoples, whose home was across Puget Sound from what is now Seattle's waterfront and on islands in between. As part of the Puget Sound Salish group, they shared linguistic and cultural traditions with the larger Coastal Salish group.

In the mild Puget Sound climate, the Native people developed a complex social and material culture, whose life rhythms were in harmony with the seasons and the natural environment. Women used the shredded inner bark of red cedar to swaddle infants and weave robes, rain capes, and mats for bedding and shelter. Their hand-woven baskets that included intricate traditional designs were used for gifts, trade, and storage and as sturdy utilitarian vessels for gathering and hauling. Cooking baskets were tightly woven to hold water, so that fire-heated rocks

could be tossed in to boil food. Men carved dugout canoes and split cedar into planks to construct longhouses. They used the most suitable kinds of wood for making bows, tools, and harpoon shafts and for carving ceremonial masks and dishes.

During the warm months, the Duwamish moved from place to place, navigating their snub-nosed, flat-bottomed canoes along the rivers and shores, and lived in temporary shelters to fish, hunt, and gather seasonal roots and berries, which they dried and preserved for winter. Their seminomadic lifestyle was possible in part because of abundant natural resources and the mild climate and in part because they did not have farms or livestock.

During winter they lived in villages, including several in or near what is now Pioneer Square. Permanent longhouses built of cedar planks and peeled bark housed several related families. This was the time for bonding with each other and with previous generations and their mythical forebears, including animals, stars, rivers, mountains, and boulders. Everyone joined in the rhythmic "power sing," helping the host call back supernatural allies. Children and grandchildren gathered around to learn from elders, who told ancient stories that they had heard long ago from their grandparents. In the richly symbolic Lushootseed language, the elders invoked the power of myth and humor to teach their tribal history and traditions of living wisely with the earth and with each other.

Because the longhouses were made of wood, none of them survived into modern times. A variety of sources, including archaeological excavations, memoirs of early pioneers, and myths and family histories that Duwamish elders have handed down to younger generations, provide clues about the traditional lifestyle. Ethnographic historian David Buerge has determined that there were some twenty-six winter villages in the Duwamish homeland. Two of them were located near today's train stations on land that bordered a saltwater marsh. A more important one was at what is now Pioneer Place, where the pergola and the Chief Seattle fountain now stand. Buerge cites this as the sole example of a Duwamish village that has managed to remain a gathering place for Native people (as well as the larger community) and a living link with the ancient past. He has found that some contemporary Duwamish, like their ancestors, still call the place Djijila'letc (djee-djee-LAH-letsh), an old Lushootseed name that translates as "little crossing-over place."

In the historic landscape, a sandbar emerged at low tide at what is now the intersection of First and Yesler, connecting the quarter-mile-long island on the south with high ground to the north. East of the island was a marshy saltwater lagoon. Buerge writes:

Eight large longhouses, each measuring approximately 60 by 120 feet, were said to have stood there, housing a population of as many as 200 people. These made their living spearing flounders in the lagoon, fishing in the bay, digging clams on the beach, and hunting in the dense surrounding forests. They were the most important group living on Elliott Bay, and their winter village was said to have been the site of a large "assembly hall," possibly a potlatch house, at which people from all over the area gathered for important business and ceremonies. A fort, apparently a palisade of cedar slabs built to protect the people and their neighbors from the attacks of raiding parties, was also said to have stood on a high point of the island. At certain times of the year when the salmon were cleaned and hanging by the thousands on huge racks to dry, the people of Djidjila'letc and their friends gathered on the sandspit that marked the southern boundary of the lagoon and held boisterous gambling matches called slah-HAHL, "sing gambles," that commonly lasted for days.

Events such as these were sometimes incorporated into a potlatch, held in celebration of a wedding, a child coming of age, or another special event. The host took pleasure and pride in giving away gifts to all of the invited guests. The extent of his generosity was seen as evidence of his power to amass wealth.

Along with singing, traditional dances, and gambling, the potlatch might include athletic competitions. It was an opportunity to develop trade with guests from faraway tribes and to strengthen mutually protective alliances against common enemies. From ancient times, the Duwamish had had to defend themselves against hostile tribes, who sent raiding parties to plunder their villages and take slaves. But a more formidable threat emerged with the arrival of explorers and traders.

Exploration and Invasion

European and American expeditions had explored the Northwest Coast for decades prior to 1792, when Captain George Vancouver sailed the British ship *Discovery* through Admiralty Inlet into Puget Sound. In the same year, U.S. Captain Robert Gray discovered the fabled "great river of the West," which he named the Columbia, after his ship. This marked the beginning of a fifty-year rivalry between the British and American governments for ownership of the Native peoples' land.

Commissioned by President Thomas Jefferson for the "Voyage of Discovery," Meriwether Lewis and William Clark brought the first overland expedition to the mouth of the Columbia in 1805. In 1841, the American expedition led by Charles Wilkes was the first to survey Elliott Bay, which he named for a member of his crew.

From Furs to Farms

Beginning in the eighteenth century, merchant ships had dropped anchor in inlets along the Northwest Coast, where they traded blankets, trinkets, and liquor to Indians in return for beaver and otter pelts that were in demand in Europe and China. Mountain men from America and Europe ventured across the West as trappers and traders. The British Hudson's Bay Company built trading posts at Astoria, Oregon; Vancouver, Washington; and, in the 1830s, on the Nisqually delta near today's Olympia, Washington. On July 17, 1833, the Nisqually post's *Journal of Occurrences* noted

a trade of excellent beaver and leather by the "Nuamish tribe."

A social pattern developed wherein friendly tribes made some of their women available to the newcomers. There were abusive relationships but also common-law marriages that engendered mutual respect. Indian wives of white men wore wool and cotton dresses, learned English, and raised their children in accord with their husband's culture. At the same time, they remained valuable liaisons with their tribes. But contact with early explorers and traders exacted severe tolls on the Native peoples. Previously unknown diseases, including smallpox, tuberculosis, measles, and syphilis, spread rapidly from tribe to tribe. Highly esteemed medicine men and women were helpless against fatal epidemics that, according to historians, claimed the lives of 60 to 90 percent of the Northwest's Native peoples. Years before the first settlers arrived, the Duwamish deserted several of their winter villages, including Djidjila'letc.

By the 1840s, the natural resource of furbearing mammals—beavers and otters—was severely diminished. As the fur trade dwindled, the Hudson's Bay Company encouraged former trappers as well as newcomers to take up farming and settle near its posts. New on the scene were Protestant missionaries and Roman Catholic "Black Robes," who came to the frontier to Christianize the Native peoples and teach them farming and settlement skills.

At first their efforts met with marginal success, but they left significant legacies by bringing their religion to the frontier and founding settlements. Their letters, published in church newspapers, spoke glowingly of the land of opportunity that was here for the taking. Along with explorers, they planted seeds for the great westward migration of settlers from the United States during the 1840s and 1850s. Devastated by white man's diseases, many of the tribes were ill equipped to resist the growing stream of pioneers, who would spell the demise of their semi-nomadic way of life and much of the primordial environment.

The vast territory north of the Columbia River was opened up to settlers, thanks to the Treaty of 1846, which established the border between British Columbia and American territories in the Pacific Northwest. Two years later, Congress established Oregon Territory. To entice settlement in the area, the American government enacted the Donation Land Law of 1850, permitting each male citizen to claim 320 acres of land. If he were married, his wife could claim an additional 320 acres. Settlers were required to "prove up," which meant that to gain free title, they had to live on and make improvements to the property for four years.

Locally, Chief Seattle was witness to and participant in the transition. Christened Noah Seattle, he was baptized as a Roman Catholic, which to him did not seem incompatible with ancient tribal teachings. His mother was Duwamish; his father was a Suquamish headman. By his own account, Seattle was born on Blake Island, and in his childhood, he witnessed Captain Vancouver's arrival off Bainbridge Island. Records from Fort Nisqually show that he traded pelts for blankets and other imported goods.

Seattle distinguished himself as a warrior in his youth. In about 1806, he ambushed a raiding party of Upper Green and White River people and their relatives from east of the Cascades, whose intent was to plunder Duwamish villages and take slaves. As the raiders' war canoes raced down the Green River, Seattle instructed his men to fell a tree across rapids in their path. When the canoes crashed into it, Seattle's men attacked from the shore and successfully protected their people. Buerge says that according to Samuel Coombs, an early pioneer, Seattle

A bronze bust of Chief Seattle, sculpted by James A. Wehn in 1909, tops a public drinking fountain at Pioneer Place. Photo by James A. Wehn. MSCUA, University of Washington Libraries, neg. NA4025

rose to chief of both the Suquamish and the Duwamish following his Green River victory. He secured his dominance not only by defending his people, but also by participating in attacks against other tribes.

By the time the first settlers arrived in 1851, Seattle had undergone a transformation. A respected elder, he had freed his own slaves and changed from a war leader to a diplomat and peacekeeper.

Duwamish Make Settlers Welcome

As pioneers began making their way into the Puget Sound area in the mid-nineteenth century, the Duwamish people welcomed them with enthusiasm. Buerge says that Chief Seattle encouraged them to come, since he wanted the

American trading presence to break the monopoly of the Hudson's Bay Company. In addition, they would deter the threat of raids from hostile tribes. James Rasmussen, a contemporary member of the Duwamish Tribal Council and owner of Bud's Jazz Records in Pioneer Square, concurs with Buerge that the Duwamish were pragmatists who realized that cultural assimilation was inevitable. At the same time, they felt they had nothing to fear, since they fully expected their people to remain in the majority.

There were some five hundred Duwamish living in villages around Elliott Bay and hundreds more in their homeland that extended from what is now Renton to Shilshole Bay. In an interview with the *Seattle Times* on May 27, 2001, Rasmussen says that the Duwamish were probably thinking, "How are we going to work with these people? How can we make it a profitable endeavor? How can we get more wealth and get to be more important?" From the start, they traded labor, salmon, and berries in return for pieces of cloth, coins, iron pots, and tools that would influence the way they lived. Both settlers and Natives quickly learned to communicate in sign language and Chinook, a trade jargon that combined French, English, and Indian words.

First Settlers Arrive

In June 1851, the region's first white settlers staked their claims on the banks of the Duwamish River in the vicinity of today's Georgetown. Led by Luther M. Collins, they planted his seed potatoes before returning to Fort Nisqually for the rest of their party and the livestock that they had driven overland from the Midwest. In all, the homesteaders included Henry Van Asselt (age thirty-one), Jacob Maple (fifty-eight), his son Samuel (twenty-two), Collins (thirty-four), his wife,

Diana (thirty-two), and their children, Lucinda (thirteen) and Stephen (seven).

In late September, David Denny, John Low, and Lee Terry arrived at the mouth of the Duwamish River just in time to see the strange spectacle of a scow filled with fruit trees navigating its way upstream on the incoming tide. On board, Diana and Lucinda, who had cultivated the nursery stock at Nisqually, conversed in Chinook with Indians. While the Collins party saw agricultural potential in the river valley's rich bottomland, Denny and his companions were looking for a place to found a city. They envisioned the head of the Duwamish River as a trading center for agricultural produce and natural resources.

Low and Terry engaged Indians to take them on a dugout canoe tour of the upper river. At the same time, Denny trekked along the western shore of Elliott Bay, where Chief Seattle extended his personal welcome. The newcomers chose a clearing on a West Seattle beach for the site of their settlement. Low and Terry quickly staked their homestead claims (at age nineteen, David Denny was still too young to qualify for free land). When Terry, a failed gold prospector, suggested naming the place New York after his home state and its seaport metropolis, his companions agreed that their future city would be nothing less. A more circumspect Arthur Denny soon modified the name to New York, Alki (a Chinook word meaning "by and by"), and so the spot became known as Alki.

David Denny was the younger brother of Arthur Armstrong Denny, the leader of an extended family group that had come west by covered wagon from Cherry Grove, Illinois, with the intent of settling in Oregon. En route, they had teamed up with the Lows, the William Bells, and later the Terry brothers. But on arriving in Oregon, they found that the best lands in the Willamette Valley were already claimed and that Portland, Oregon, with 2,000 residents, was becoming crowded and expensive. David Denny and his companions had ventured north as scouts for the party to look for a land of opportunity in the Puget Sound area.

Low returned to Portland with the note that David had written to Arthur: "We have examined the valley of the Duwamish River and find it a fine country. There is room for 1,000 settlers. Come at once." Terry set out for the Hudson's Bay Company post at Nisqually to buy badly needed tools. Alone, David began building a log cabin. Three weeks later, a group of ten adults and twelve children came ashore at Alki Point from the schooner *Exact* in a cold, drenching rain. David hobbled forth from the still-unroofed cabin with a festering ax wound in his foot. Feverish, hungry, and disillusioned, he said, "I wish you hadn't come, but I'm glad to see you. The skunks have gotten in and eaten all my provisions."

"Grandma" Fay, who remained on board the *Exact,* recalled the scene:

I can't never forget when the folks landed at Alki Point. . . . I remember it rained awful hard . . . and the starch got took out of our bonnets and the wind blew, and when the women got into the rowboat to go ashore they were crying every one of 'em, and their sun bonnets with the starch took out of them went flip flap, flip flap, flip flap, as they rowed off for the shore, and the last glimpse I had of them was the women standing under the trees with their wet sun bonnets all lopping down over their faces and their aprons to their eyes.

Friendly but curious Natives gathered nearby in their winter camp. For decades they had seen explorers, trappers, and traders, but a community of families with women and children was new. The Indians gave the settlers woven cedar mats to cover the roof beams of the small cabin.

The entire party, along with several Natives, gathered inside, savoring the heat from Mary Denny's cookstove.

Following are the names, ages, and family affiliations of the Denny party, half of whom were small children: Arthur Armstrong Denny (twenty-nine), his wife, Mary Boren Denny (twenty-nine), and their children, Louisa Catherine (seven), Margaret Lenora (four), and Rolland Herschel (two months); David Thomas Denny (nineteen); Louisa Boren (twenty-two); Carson Dobbins Boren (twenty-seven), his wife, Mary Boren (twenty), and their child, Gertrude Lavinia (one); John Nathan Low (thirty-one), his wife, Lydia Colborn Low (thirty-one), and their children, Mary (nine), Alonzo (seven), John (four), and Minerva (two); William Nathaniel Bell (thirty-four), his wife, Sarah Ann (thirty-six), and their children, Laura Keziah (nine), Olive Julia (five), Mary Virginia (four), and Lavinia (ten months); and Charles Carrol Terry (twenty-one) and his brother, Lee Terry (nineteen).

The Dennys and Borens were interrelated. Arthur and David were brothers; Mary Denny's siblings were Louisa Boren and Carson Boren. A romance had already blossomed between David and Louisa, who would soon celebrate the community's first wedding.

In a short time, the Denny family had their finished log cabin to themselves. The Indians showed the pioneers how to split cedar logs into boards, which they used to construct the Bell and Boren cabins. Still suffering from the effects of ague, Mary Denny was unable to produce milk for her baby, Rolland. A Native woman recognized the problem and introduced her to clam nectar, which proved a satisfying and nutritious substitute. The Indians brought gifts of shellfish, berries, and edible roots and showed the pioneer women how to prepare them. From the Indians' perspective, the sharing of food and recipes was reciprocal. They thought nothing of reaching into a pot to help themselves to a bite of whatever was on the stove or table. One disgruntled pioneer woman assuaged her irritation by swatting hands with her wooden spoon.

The Alki settlers survived their first winter thanks to help from their Indian neighbors and to potatoes they purchased from the Collins party in the Duwamish valley. During that winter, the Denny party cleared land, chopped down trees, and launched its first industry: selling lumber to San Francisco–bound freighters. But the timber supply was limited and lack of a harbor made it dangerous and sometimes impossible to load logs onto waiting ships. In addition, the soil at Alki Point was poor for crops.

The Birth of Downtown Seattle

Because of the generally difficult conditions at Alki, Arthur Denny, who was trained as a surveyor, decided to look for a more promising location for the city that he envisioned. He set out with Indians in a dugout canoe to explore nearby bays. Using horseshoes tied to his wife's clothesline, he plumbed the depths of Puget Sound in search of a harbor. Elliott Bay was

ideal, with deep water close to shore and protection from the winds and waves.

The landscape as Denny and his fellow pioneers found it would be almost unrecognizable today. Steep, densely forested hills ran north and south between Lake Washington and Elliott Bay through what would become downtown Seattle. To the south, vast tide flats sprawled across the site of today's sports stadiums and cement factories, and the mouth of the Duwamish River widened into a saltwater marsh (now manmade Harbor Island and the East and West Waterways) that teemed with wildlife. First Avenue approximates downtown's original shoreline, where steep bluffs stood above the beach below.

Near what is now First and Yesler, the pioneers came ashore. They explored the island that they named Denny's Island and discovered the sandbar that connected the island to the mainland at low tide. Looking toward the site of today's pergola, they spotted an abandoned longhouse, partly overgrown with wild roses. Historian Buerge says that the former residents of the village of Djijila'letc had probably moved to Alki and taken their other longhouses with them.

While the Lows and the Terrys remained on

Louisa Boren (left) and her older sister, Mary Ann Boren, Mrs. Arthur Denny. Louisa married Arthur's younger brother, David, on January 23, 1853, in the settlement's first wedding. MSCUA, University of Washington Libraries

their homesteads at Alki, the Dennys, Bells, and Borens staked their claims on the east side of Elliott Bay, creating the beginnings of what we now know as downtown Seattle. Louisa Boren and sister-in-law Mary Boren were so eager to move to their new home that they hired Indians to paddle them across the bay in a canoe. On the site of today's Hoge Building at Second and Cherry, the two women laid the log foundation for the new settlement's first cabin.

In April 1852, the families moved from Alki Beach to their Elliott Bay homesteads. The Arthur Dennys and the Carson Borens claimed what is now central downtown. The William Bells' homestead, known as Belltown, was north of them. As the settlement's first bride and groom, Louisa Boren and David Denny celebrated their wedding in January 1853, then paddled a canoe to the cabin on their homestead north of the Bells, which now includes Seattle Center.

Commercial and Civic Roots

David S. "Doc" Maynard, a merchant and physician from Ohio, operated a general store in Olympia before coming north at the urging of his friend Chief Seattle. At age forty-four, nearly twice as old as any of his fellow Elliott Bay pioneers, Doc Maynard built the settlement's second cabin. His homestead south of the Borens' included Denny's Island, which became the heart of the community's first commercial district. Located along what is now First Avenue South between Yesler Way and Jackson Street, the island was about a quarter mile long and no more than 1,300 feet wide.

Maynard opened the settlement's first store, the Seattle Exchange, at what is now First and Main. His ad in the October 30, 1852, edition of Olympia's *Columbian* offered "a general assortment of dry goods, groceries, hardware,

etc., suitable for the wants of immigrants just arriving." When his fellow pioneers laid plans to call their settlement Duwamps and register it as Puget Sound's first U.S. post office, Maynard quickly proposed the more euphonious name Seattle in honor of the chief.

Late in the year, forty-two-year-old Henry Leiter Yesler, who like Maynard was from Ohio, embarked on a dugout canoe tour of Puget Sound to locate a homestead and a site for his steam sawmill—the first in the region. In Seattle, he found the settlers industriously cutting timber for shipment to San Francisco. He liked their vision of a city, and they welcomed the idea of a steam-powered mill to enhance trade. However, Yesler resigned himself to continue his search, since all of the waterfront property had been claimed. Unwilling to lose

David S. "Doc" Maynard. Photo by E. M. Sammis. Museum of History and Industry, SHS 15,461

Henry Yesler's lumber mill employed both settlers and Native Americans, shown here at the cookhouse on Mill Street. The pioneers' first public gathering place, it is now the site of the Mutual Life Building at First and Yesler. MSCUA, *University of Washington Libraries,* UW 32372

such a promising prospect, Maynard sealed the deal by adjusting his claim to give Yesler the northern narrow strip that provided frontage on Elliott Bay and extended east to the top of the steep hill. Carson Boren chipped in an adjacent swath. The strip formed a panhandle to the bulk of Henry Yesler's 320–acre homestead to the east, half of which was in the name of his wife, Sarah, who waited in Ohio for him to send for her.

Yesler hired workers to begin preparing the mill site, then went to San Francisco to meet the ship that months earlier had left New York with his engine and saws. By early 1853, the mill's sharp whistle signaled employment and the beginning of Seattle's first industry. Loggers and cattle teams skidded mammoth trees down the skid road on Mill Street (now Yesler Way) to the millpond. In the adjacent shed, sawyers

turned out rough boards and planks. The milled lumber was a boon to the frontier community, which by late summer boasted twenty frame buildings.

From the start, Yesler courted bigger, more profitable markets in California boomtowns. As orders for the high-grade lumber increased, the mill operated around the clock, with laborers working twelve-hour shifts. Workers loaded cargo onto waiting ships from the wharf, which had to be lengthened again and again to meet the demand. During 1854, the major market was San Francisco, but one shipload embarked for Honolulu and another for Australia. Seattle boosters saw the wharf as their gateway to the world.

Yesler's hired hands included transplanted Americans, European immigrants, and Indians. In a letter to Sarah, he described them as "a large number of people of different shapes [and] forms [who] speak all sorts of languages." Historians Linda Peavy and Ursula Smith observe: "An anomaly among Seattle's white settlers, Henry not only treated his native employees fairly, but also found no fault with white employees who lived with 'their squaws.'" In Sarah's absence, Henry Yesler took a mistress of his own, Susan, who was the daughter of Suquattle, the headman of the local Duwamish. Together they had a child, whose later married name is recorded as Julia Benson Intermela.

Before setting up the mill, Yesler had used rough-hewn logs to build the 25–square-foot cookhouse that served as his home and office for six years. Built on pilings at the water's edge, the cookhouse was where mill hands took their meals and where several of them bunked on the second floor. In addition, it was the community's first social and civic center. Pioneers gathered in the dining hall for the settlement's first sermon, first trial, and first public entertainment.

By late 1853, while laborers found lodging at Yesler's cookhouse and nearby boardinghouses, visitors and newcomers of modest means had another option. South of Maynard's store, Captain Leonard Felker built a handsome, two-story frame building with a gleaming white facade that stood atop a low bluff, beckoning navigators from across the bay. Felker House

E. A. Clark's early 1860s image of pioneer Seattle is said to be one of the settlement's first photographs. Notice the elevated water system, made of logs with bored-out centers, that supplied water from a hillside spring. The Pioneer Building now stands on the site of the Yesler's first home, which is in the foreground with Sarah Yesler standing on the porch. She had remained in Ohio for seven years, before Henry sent for her and built the house. Museum of History and Industry, 83.10.6,331, Webster & Stevens, 210–X

offered pleasant accommodations for visitors and temporary housing for several pioneer families, including the A. C. Andersons, the Bailey Gatzerts, and the John Learys. In addition, Felker House employed the town's first prostitutes and served as the setting for sessions of the district court. Its Irish manager, Mary Ann Conklin—also known as Madame Damnable—was notorious up and down the coast for her good cooking, hot temper, and exceptionally salty language.

Maynard Makes His Mark

In December 1852, the Oregon Territorial Legislature established King County, named for the incoming vice president of the United States, William Rufus Devane King, who died before the inauguration. Doc Maynard attended the legislative session in Oregon, and, at his urging, Seattle was named the new county's seat. On personal business, he successfully lobbied the Legislature to grant him a divorce from his estranged wife, whom he had left in Ohio. This freed him to marry Catherine Broshears, a widow he had met on the trail when she and her family were stricken with cholera. Taking pity on her, Maynard had left his own wagon train, doctored her back to health, then accompanied her westward. En route they had fallen in love. The tall, dapperly dressed doctor was an unusual sight as he traveled with Indians in a dugout canoe between Seattle and Olympia to court Catherine, who lived at her brother's home. The Maynards celebrated their wedding in January 1853.

On March 2, 1853, President Franklin Pierce signed the act that created Washington Territory north of the Columbia River. Within days, Maynard, Arthur Denny, and Carson Boren filed the first plats for the "Town of Seattle." Denny and Boren platted their claims with streets parallel to the waterfront, which north of Mill Street (now Yesler Way) runs roughly northwest-southeast. But at the foot of Mill Street, the bay curves southwest. Maynard insisted on a north-south grid for his claim south of Mill Street, with streets also running parallel to the waterfront—which here runs north-south. The divergent plattings remain evident today, with curious triangular-shaped lots and mismatched street grids that meet at Yesler Way. A teetotaler, Denny later wrote derisively that Maynard, "stimulated with liquor," had determined that he was "not only monarch of all he surveyed, but of what Boren and I surveyed, too." The rift extended to the naming of streets. Mill Street was the dividing line between Maynard's Commercial Street (now First Avenue South) and Denny's Front Street (now First Avenue).

Treaties and Reservations

The Duwamish watched without protest as the newcomers staked out claims and cut back the ancient forests. They counted several of the pioneers among their friends, including Doc Maynard and Henry Yesler, both of whom were appointed by the Territorial governor to serve terms as Indian Agent for King County. Maynard gave medical treatment to Duwamish patients, and both men listened to their concerns and helped organize conferences between them and the new government.

On January 22, 1855, Washington Territorial Governor Isaac Stevens held a meeting with regional Indian leaders at Point Elliott (called Muckilteo, "good camping ground," by the Indians). Stevens offered to let them keep 48,000 acres, divided into four reservations, and to pay them $15,000 in twenty equal annual installments in return for title to most of the present counties of King, Snohomish,

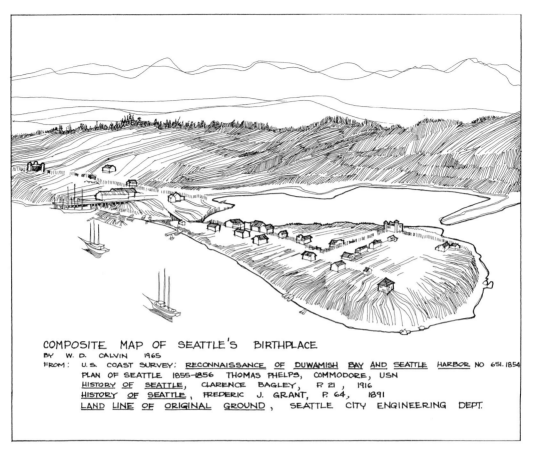

COMPOSITE MAP OF SEATTLE'S BIRTHPLACE
BY W. D. CALVIN 1965
FROM: U.S. COAST SURVEY: RECONNAISSANCE OF DUWAMISH BAY AND SEATTLE HARBOR NO 651.1854
PLAN OF SEATTLE 1855-1856 THOMAS PHELPS, COMMODORE, USN
HISTORY OF SEATTLE, CLARENCE BAGLEY, P. 21, 1916
HISTORY OF SEATTLE, FREDERIC J. GRANT, P. 64, 1891
LAND LINE OF ORIGINAL GROUND, SEATTLE CITY ENGINEERING DEPT.

The settlement's downtown was an island at high tide. Pioneers began the city's decades-long process of recontouring the landscape, using sawdust from Yesler's mill for landfill. This composite map by W. D. Calvin is published in Bill Speidel's Sons of the Profits, *Seattle, 1967. Note the blockhouses at Second (now Occidental) and Main and at Front (now First) and Cherry, where settlers took shelter during the Battle of Seattle. Courtesy of Bill Speidel, the Underground Tour*

Skagit, Whatcom, Island, and Kitsap. Indian leaders gave numerous speeches, expressing sorrow about what they had come to believe was an inevitable transition.

Chief Seattle, while resting his hand on the head of the short, disgruntled governor, delivered the most eloquent oration. Henry Smith, a Seattle physician and poet, was familiar with the Lushootseed language and took notes. More than thirty years later, he wrote his now-famous translation for the October 29, 1887, edition of the *Seattle Star*. The last three lines appeared for

the first time in Clarence Bagley's 1929 *History of King County*. Today, James Rasmussen notes how difficult it must have been for his Duwamish ancestor to explain that "we are the land, the land is us" to people who didn't hold such a concept. He maintains that it's fruitless to argue about how much of the speech is Smith's and how much is Seattle's. His advice is, "Don't pick it apart. Enjoy." Following are excerpts:

Every part of this country is sacred to my people. Every hillside, every valley, every plain and grove

Emily Inez Denny, the daughter of David and Louisa Boren Denny, was three years old at the time of refuge in blockhouses during the Battle of Seattle. Her original painting, based on childhood memories, is on display at the Museum of History and Industry. Museum of History and Industry, SHS 18,380

has been hallowed by some fond memory or some sad experience of my tribe. When the Red Man shall have perished from this earth and the memory of my tribe shall have become a myth among the White Men, these shores will swarm with the invisible dead of my tribe and when your children's children think themselves alone . . . they will not be alone. . . . At night when the streets of your cities and villages are silent and you think them deserted, they will throng with the returning hosts that once filled and still love this beautiful land. The White Man will never be alone. Let him be just and deal kindly with my people, for the dead are not powerless. Dead—did I say? There is no death. Only a change of worlds!"

In sorrow, Puget Sound Indians signed the Point Elliott Treaty and many began moving to reservations.

Battle of Seattle

But later in the year, when Governor Stevens approached tribes east of the Cascades, the Yakamas fought back. Their war spread across the mountains to the White River valley, where several families along with military troops were massacred. Survivors abandoned their homes and fled to Seattle, which at the time had some three hundred residents. Blockhouses stood as emergency shelters at Front and Cherry and at Second (now Occidental) and Main.

According to one account, friendly Indians warned Catherine Maynard of an impending attack by a large war party. On January 26, 1856, women and children took refuge in the blockhouses. Marines and the USS *Decatur,* stationed in Elliott Bay, fired howitzers and cannons to ward off the attackers. The Battle of Seattle ended in a single day. Casualties included two settlers and an unknown number of Indians.

Reprisals followed against the attackers, but Indian wars in King County had come to an end. For nearly a decade, the pace of settlement slowed, in part as an aftermath of the hostilities. Another cause was the American Civil War, which drew a majority of able-bodied young men from both the North and the South, some of whom might otherwise have emigrated west.

Duwamish Roots Remain

Four years after the attack on the settlement, the Duwamish people had not been paid for their homeland, and the U.S. Senate still had not ratified the Point Elliott Treaty. At a meeting with Indian Agent Michael Simmons, the aging Chief Seattle said:

I am and have always been a friend of the whites, Mr. Simmons. . . . I fear we are forgotten and that we are all to be cheated out of our lands. I have been very poor and hungry all winter and am sick now. In a little while I will die. I should like to be paid for my lands, before I die. Many of my people died during the cold winter without getting their pay. . . . Indians are not bad. Mean white people are bad to us. If any person says we do not want our paper [treaty] he lies. . . . I want you to write quickly to your great chief what I say.

The Senate finally ratified the treaty in 1860, but it took three more years before the first

payment was made. Chief Seattle had successfully negotiated for reservation lands on Bainbridge Island for the Suquamish Tribe. However, when the Duwamish people in 1865 petitioned Congress for a reservation in the Duwamish River valley, they met with overwhelming resistance from local citizens, whose economic and political objectives took precedence. Leaders in King County drafted their own opposing petition and submitted it to Arthur A. Denny, Washington Territory's official congressional delegate. There were 156 signatures, representing almost all of the resident citizens, including David S. "Doc" Maynard, David T. Denny, Henry L. Yesler, and others whom the Duwamish counted among their friends. For the tribe, this represented the beginning of a struggle for legal enforcement of their treaty rights that continues to the present day.

Historian Buerge relates a sad tale of a humiliation endured by Chief Seattle on a visit to the young city a year before his death. As he walked down a sidewalk dressed in a coat and top hat, ten-year-old Alice Mercer ordered him to get out of her way, then pushed him into a ditch. Bystanders laughed. Chief Seattle still visited old friends, but public sentiment held that Indians should get out of the way of white people. However, historian Clarence Bagley reports that in 1866, hundreds of whites went to Port Madison on the Suquamish Reservation to pay their last respects at the chief's funeral.

In the same year, the newly incorporated City of Seattle included a provision in its charter that barred Indians from residency. But citizens still wanted their participation in the community. Henry Yesler needed Native men to work at the mill, and he depended on Native women to render oil from dogfish and grease the skids on skid roads, so that loggers could slide trees from the hills down to the bay. City matrons and bachelors hired Native women to

Basket sellers on the sidewalk at Frederick and Nelson's store in downtown Seattle. The designs show that these women were either Makah from Washington's Northwest Coast or Nootkan from Vancouver Island, British Columbia. Instead of utilitarian baskets, Native American women made smaller, more decorative ones to sell to collectors and tourists. Museum of History and Industry, PEMCO, Webster & Stevens, 83.10.7929

do their laundry; local consumers and tourists expected to buy clams, seasonal berries, and traditional baskets from Indian vendors on street corners; and storekeepers were glad to take their money.

From their perspective, the Duwamish wanted to stay in their homeland. Until the early twentieth century, Indians camped on beaches outside the city limits and on manmade "Ballast Island" near the foot of Washington Street, where ship captains dumped their ballast before loading cargoes of coal or lumber. A few, including Salmon Bay Charlie in Ballard, managed to stay in their homes outside the city

limits. According to the 1870 Census, fifteen-year-old Julia, the daughter of Henry Yesler and Susan Su-quattle, resided with Henry and Sarah Yesler. Nothing is known about Sarah's and Julia's relationship, but Sarah most likely had no objections on moral grounds, since the Yeslers were Spiritualists who believed in free love, and since her former female lover had been their house guest.

James Rasmussen, present-day member of the Duwamish Tribal Council, still lives in the Beacon Hill neighborhood in the home of his great-grandmother, Anne Tuttle, whose Indian name was Quitzlitza. He says that she married

Indians camped on Ballast Island, 1899. By this time, land reclamation projects and railroad trestles and wharves had filled in most of the area between the original shoreline and the island. Photo by Anders B. Wilse. Museum of History and Industry, 141

a white man so that she and her children could remain on their ancestral land.

Chief Seattle's oldest daughter, Kickisomlo Cud, a widow, also stayed in the city. When Catherine Maynard heard that her married name was Cud, she said, "Why, you are much too good looking a woman to carry around such a name. I now christen you Angeline." Her two daughters, Mamie and Chewatum (nicknamed Betsy), married white men, but in Betsy's case, her husband's drinking led to abuse and tragedy. When Betsy hanged herself, Angeline took in

her grandson and raised him. As the city grew, she continued to sell clams on the streets, do laundry for matrons, speak Chinook, and live in a waterfront shack at Pike Street. Her pioneer friends gave her gifts and offered assistance, but when she had more than she needed, she gave it away. Unlike her father, she did not tolerate harassment from children. She kept clams in her pocket, which she hurled with deadly aim at any young boy who dared to taunt her.

Late in life, "Princess Angeline" became a favorite subject of visiting journalists and tour-

Princess Angeline. MSCUA, University of Washington Libraries, NA1519

ists who wanted to photograph her. When President Benjamin Harrison paid an official visit in 1891, city leaders proudly introduced her as the daughter of Chief Seattle and the head of her nation. Rising to the occasion, she shook his hand, curtsied, and extended the greeting "Kla-how-ya" in exchange for his "Hello, how are you?" Five years later, Angeline died at age eighty-five. Her friends built her a casket shaped like a canoe, and Seattle schoolchildren collected pennies and dimes for a headstone. Her funeral was held in June 1886, at Our Lady of Good Help Church at Third and Washington, which was packed to capacity. Chief Seattle and Angeline were Roman Catholics, and she had been one of only a handful in the village when Father Francis Xavier Prefontaine built the church in 1870. Under his leadership, the church's membership burgeoned; the Sisters of Providence were recruited to serve the poor and establish Seattle's first major hospital and the Sisters of the Holy Names set up a school. (After the pioneer church's demolition in 1904, the City Council commemorated its founder by giving the name Prefontaine Place to the block between Washington Street and Yesler Way. Father Prefontaine contributed a bequest for the public fountain on the adjacent small triangle at Third and Yesler, which passersby can still enjoy today.) Angeline is buried at Lakeview Cemetery among her friends the early pioneers, in her ancient homeland.

And the settlement? After incorporation in 1866, it began to make a rapid transition from a pioneer outpost to an urban frontier.

2 Urban Frontier Years

Mildred Andrews

While gladly accepting Native hospitality, pioneers in what is now the city of Seattle envisioned their settlement as an urban frontier. The Denny party heralded it as the birthplace of a metropolis and initially called it "New York, Alki" (see chapter 1).

Doc Maynard had his own grand dreams. When he opened the settlement's first general store at Commercial and Main, he proclaimed the place the "Gateway to the Orient" and "the Queen City of the Northwest." Maynard was the first to sell property at cut-rate prices and give away land to help the city grow. His efforts were instrumental in establishing Commercial Street (now First Avenue South) as the heart of the community's original downtown.

Henry Yesler's mill gave the local economy a tremendous boost. Most of the male pioneers worked for the mill or in businesses that catered to mill workers. The mill's cookhouse was the center of the community's fledgling civic and social life.

Historian Roger Sale notes that at this juncture, Seattle could have become a company logging town, such as Port Gamble on the Kitsap Peninsula or Port Madison on Bainbridge Island. He credits Arthur Denny for having vision and leadership that planted entrepreneurial seeds and conditions conducive to economic diversity.

Arthur Denny's Vision

At his store on the southwest corner of Commercial and Washington, Arthur Denny sold merchandise purchased from San Francisco. Unlike Doc Maynard and other pioneer merchants, he bought directly from the suppliers, rather than from ship captains who sold goods on commission. In this way Denny was able to maximize his profits and also "reduce San Francisco's toehold on Seattle."

He entered into partnerships to establish numerous other businesses, including the city's first bank. It began inauspiciously, with Dexter Horton, Denny's partner in the store, putting customers' valuables in leather pouches and stashing them in the coffee barrel or under the floorboards, and later in the backless safe shoved against a wall. From these humble beginnings, Dexter Horton Bank was chartered and eventually grew into Seattle First National Bank, known as Seafirst, Washington State's largest bank (now Bank of America).

Arthur Denny served as postmaster, regimental officer, Territorial legislator, and congressional representative at different times. As a legislator, he helped win the Territorial University (forerunner of the University of Washington) for Seattle in 1861, then donated eight and one-half acres of his knoll overlooking

Interior of the Dexter Horton Bank, 1875. Left to right: Rolland H. Denny, B. F. Briggs, Dexter Horton, Charles Denny, Arthur A. Denny, Norval H. Latimer, and H. Latimer.
MSCUA, *University of Washington Libraries,* UW 4173

downtown. Others provided an additional acre and a half to satisfy the state's ten-acre requirement. Within a year, the University Building stood prominently atop "Denny's knoll" at Fourth and University (now the site of the Fairmont Olympic Hotel). Despite the university's initial enrollment of only sixteen students, Seattle leaders saw it as a symbol of stature, foresight, and promise for the city's future.

Denny worked tirelessly to promote the city's transportation systems and railroad connections. A surveyor, he led an exploring party to Snoqualmie Pass in 1865 and instigated the building of the region's first road across the Cascade Range.

Maynard's Follies

By this time, Doc Maynard had dropped out of the city's political, economic, and visionary leadership. The "Battle of Seattle" and its consequences for his Native friends had so disheartened him that he lost hope in the future of his downtown property. In 1857, he traded 260 acres of Pioneer Square to Charles Terry for a 319-acre farm at Alki. A bonanza for Terry, the deal still holds the record as the city's largest land swap.

The Maynards failed at farming. After their farmhouse burned down, they returned to Pioneer Square in 1861, where they opened the city's first hospital and provided all of its services, with Doc Maynard as physician and his wife, Catherine, as nurse. It was a two-bed ward in their home, located at the present-day site of Elliott Bay Book Company on First and Main.

While there, the couple entertained an unexpected visitor. Doc Maynard's first wife, Lydia, not knowing about their divorce granted by the Oregon Territorial Legislature, came from Ohio to ask for her half of their homestead claim. In the midst of legal discussions, Catherine was hostess to their visitor, and at times the doctor strolled down the street with his ex-wife on one arm and his current wife on the other. Lydia returned to Ohio empty-handed when the courts ruled that she had not met the residency requirement.

Cultural Pursuits and Entertainment

In 1859, townsfolk danced away the night at the grand opening of Charles Plummer's hall, later named Snoqualmie Hall, on the second floor of his dry-goods store at Commercial and Main. It was the city's first venue designed for public assembly. Others soon followed, including Bachelor's Hall, on Front Street between Cherry and Columbia, and Yesler's Pavilion, at Front and Cherry, which featured popular roller-skating nights. Crowds turned out for public meetings and special events, including traveling minstrel shows, boxing matches, and acclaimed seventy-year-old singer Anna Bishop. When Plymouth Congregational Church booked the pavilion for Sunday mornings, someone always had to come early to sweep up the sawdust that absorbed tobacco juice from Saturday night.

The Pioneer Library Association was chartered in 1868 with lawyer James McNaught as president and Sarah Yesler volunteering as the first librarian. As the forerunner of today's public library, the association purchased books and met for readings and literary discussions. Catherine Maynard provided a reading room in her home until 1873, when the association moved its lending library and activities into the pavilion.

Community leaders recognized the need for an outdoor public space in the heart of the growing commercial district. They reserved a small sawdust-covered triangle in front of the Occidental Hotel between James and Mill Streets, which converged on Front Street (now the site of the "sinking ship" parking garage). Historian Willis Sayre writes, "In this tiny space, in the seventies, all the circuses which came to town were held. At other times platforms were built there for dancing and in 1877 crowds of boys and young men played baseball and football there."

First African Americans

Seattle's first African-American resident was Manuel Lopes, who worked his way from New England to Puget Sound as a sailor. In 1852, he opened a restaurant and a barbershop on Mill Street on what is now the site of the Merchant's Cafe. Lopes had ordered the city's first barber chair, which was transported by ship around Cape Horn.

In her book *Seattle's Black Victorians: 1852–1901,* Esther Mumford says that Lopes owned the only snare drum in the settlement and that he beat a tattoo three times a day to signal mealtimes. "Each Fourth of July he headed up a procession of villagers which wound itself through the mud, and among the stumps and shanties of early Seattle."

In about 1860, William Grose became Seattle's second black resident, followed shortly by his wife, Sarah, and their two children. Standing six feet four inches and weighing more than four hundred pounds, "Big Bill the Cook" built Our House Hotel and Restaurant on Yesler's Wharf (on the south side of Mill Street below Commercial Street), where he dished out good food and kindness to newcomers and the needy. One of them, Robert Moran, arrived in Seattle with only a dime in his pocket. When he later made a fortune building ships, he never forgot that Grose had grubstaked him.

Illustrator's rendition of the "Mercer Girls" en route to Seattle, Harper's Weekly, *1866.* MSCUA, *University of Washington Libraries, 68*

Counting prominent pioneers among his friends, Grose became one of the city's largest taxpayers and landholders. He purchased property from the Yeslers on Madison Street (now in Seattle's Central Area), where he gave away land to other African Americans to develop a residential district and community center.

Although they were only a small fraction of the population, Seattle's black pioneers played a significant part in shaping the city. From the beginning, they sought opportunity in a place that was considered racially tolerant: Washington Territory did not adopt Oregon's discriminatory laws that mandated segregation and outlawed interracial marriage. Nonetheless, tolerance was often an illusion in Washington, where prejudice and customs from other parts of the nation often led to de facto segregation.

The Bachelor Problem

By the 1860s, in Seattle men outnumbered women three to one, and most of the women were married. Asa Shinn Mercer, the idealistic young president of the city's new Territorial University and a single man, came up with an innovative plan. After raising funds from other local bachelors, he traveled to economically depressed New England, where women were in the majority as a result of Civil War casualties. If a woman wanted to consider marriage, he could guarantee her a choice of suitors in Washington Territory, or if she wanted a career, there was ample opportunity.

In 1884 and 1886 expeditions, Mercer returned around Cape Horn with forty eligible women (later immortalized in the 1968 TV series "Here

Come the Brides"). Dressed in their best, eager bachelors welcomed them at Yesler's Wharf, and the entire community turned out for a reception at the Territorial University.

All but one of the "Mercer Girls" eventually married. The exception was Elizabeth "Lizzie" Ordway, who rejected several suitors, declaring, "Never shall I give up the life of single blessedness!" On August 9, 1870, she rang the bell to welcome the first pupils to Central School, the city's first public school building, and was a leader in the budding crusade for women's suffrage.

John Pinnell, a San Francisco brothel owner, saw a gold mine in Seattle's "bachelor problem." In 1861, he recruited Indian women to open the infamous Illahee (a Chinook word for "home place"). The city's first bawdy house stood south of Mill Street, where sawdust was reclaiming the saltwater lagoon. Within a few years, Pinnell began importing "ladies of the evening" from his San Francisco establishments. The raucous contingent that cheered them ashore at Yesler's Wharf contrasted sharply with the decorous crowd that greeted the "Mercer Girls."

Townsfolk referred to Seattle's first red-light district as "down on the sawdust" or the "lava beds." From the start, there were attempts to close it down. This was the beginning of a controversy that would embroil local politics well into the twentieth century.

First Railroads

Seattle's business and political leaders geared up for a new challenge after July 2, 1864, when President Abraham Lincoln enacted the Northern Pacific's charter to build a railroad from Lake Superior to Puget Sound. As local communities such as Tacoma and Port Townsend vied for the prize of the terminus, Seattle touted its attributes. It had the Territorial University,

an economic base that included lumber and ship building, and a deep protected harbor.

But on July 15, 1873, stunned townsfolk listened as Arthur Denny read his telegram from the Northern Pacific: "We have located the terminus on Commencement Bay." Because of an economic depression, it would take ten years for the railroad to reach Tacoma. It would take an additional five years to lay track through the Cascade Mountains, so that trains could bypass rival Portland, Oregon, with a direct transcontinental route to Puget Sound ports.

Not to be outdone, Seattle maintained its economic edge and greater population, even when Tacoma had the railroad advantage. In a show of the now legendary "Seattle spirit," local citizens dug into their wallets, then gathered at Steele's Landing near the mouth of the Duwamish River on May 1, 1874. After a picnic lunch prepared by the women, leading businessmen and laborers alike grabbed picks and shovels to begin building the Seattle and Walla Walla Railroad (S& WW), which was intended to lead across the Cascade Mountains and connect with the transcontinental line.

The city was obsessed with the need for a passable route across Snoqualmie Pass that would replace the crude wagon trail pushed through by Arthur Denny's 1865 surveying party. In 1876, a Seattle delegation persuaded the Territorial Legislature to authorize lotteries to fund the road. Sponsors were required to pay 10 percent of the gross receipts to King County.

Henry Yesler saw this as an opportunity. He sold 60,000 tickets at $5 apiece, with his now out-of-date mill as first prize, then reneged when he was accused of running an illegal gambling operation. In court, he was found guilty and fined $25. Nonetheless, he kept the money from tickets that he had already sold.

In the meantime, James M. Colman (namesake for the waterfront's Colman Dock at the

The Seattle and Walla Walla's first locomotive, the A. A. Denny, *steams along the narrow-gauge track that ran to Renton. Photo by Webster & Stevens. Museum of History and Industry,* PEMCO, W & S *83.10.6,275*

foot of Columbia Street) took over management of the financially troubled Seattle & Walla Walla Railroad and issued a labor contract to Chin Gee Hee for a crew of Chinese workers. Although it fell short of its goal, the S & WW reached Renton and later Newcastle, which was far enough: there was abundant coal in the surrounding hills. The trains opened up a lucrative industry, transporting "black gold" to bunkers on the King Street dock and San Francisco–bound freighters. Workers in Pioneer Square built coal cars, cast-iron wheels, and woodwork for regional railroad and mining companies.

In 1881 Henry Villard, a wealthy German immigrant and owner of the Oregon Improvement Company, bought out the S & WW, which he renamed the Columbia & Puget Sound Railroad. The company extended the tracks south to Black Diamond, Franklin, and Ravensdale, where it invested heavily in the coalfields. The Oregon Improvement Company improved and expanded its docks on the Seattle waterfront

and added passenger service with a small clapboard depot near the site of today's King Street Station. Laborers transferred coal from railroad cars to giant coal bunkers and waiting ships on the bustling pier at the foot of King Street. Coal soon surpassed lumber as the city's major export.

Indirect Transcontinental Connections

Without divulging his plans, Villard secured $8 million from eastern capitalists. Through his famous "blind trust," he stealthily gained a controlling interest in and assumed the presidency of the Northern Pacific, which was scheduled to reach its Tacoma terminus via Portland, Oregon, and Kalama, Washington. On September 8, 1883, he hammered the final spike at Gold Creek, Montana.

A charismatic promoter, he visited Seattle within a week and promised the jubilant city its own long-awaited transcontinental connection.

Seattle rolled out the welcome mat when Villard and his entourage of governors, senators, and railroad officials arrived—not by rail, but aboard the steamer *Queen of the Pacific*. Thomas Prosch, editor of the *Seattle Post-Intelligencer,* wrote:

Citizens made extraordinary preparations for the reception. . . . The streets had been adorned for miles with evergreen trees, arches, bunting and appropriate emblems and sentiments. . . . When the Queen came in sight, she was met by . . . the firing of guns, the ringing of bells, the blowing of whistles, the music of bands, the shouts of the people and every other imaginable expression of welcome and exultation. . . . It was a fine day.

As promised, Villard built a spur line from Seattle to Stuck Junction (now Auburn) but then ran into financial difficulties. The Northern Pacific's board demanded his resignation. New directors were Tacoma stalwarts who vowed that "a locomotive would never turn a wheel into Seattle." The track was nicknamed the "orphan road," with grazing cows taking the place of trains.

Undaunted, Seattle leaders once again took matters into their own hands. In 1885 the Seattle Lake Shore and Eastern (SLS&E), owned by local boosters Judge Thomas Burke and financier James Gilman, began laying tracks from the downtown waterfront to Ballard, then along the shores of Lake Union, Lake Washington, and Lake Sammamish to the coalfields at Gilman (now Issaquah). The city granted the line a 30–foot-wide swath along the waterfront next to the Northern Pacific's tracks. Railroad Avenue (now Alaskan Way) was widened with a planked surface, supported on concrete piers, and flanked by waterfront wharves. Trains jockeyed for position while longshore workers transferred coal, lumber, and agricultural produce to waiting ships.

With a revenue stream in hand, Burke and Gilman hatched a scheme for a transcontinental connection. They laid plans to extend their line north to the Canadian border, where it would link with the newly completed Canadian Pacific (see chapter 4).

Chinese Immigrants Build Railroads and Communities

Regionally and across the West, railroad construction was inextricably linked to Chinese immigration. In 1868 Chin Chun Hock opened the Wa Chong Company, on Mill Street, which manufactured cigars and sold imports, including tea and then-legal opium. His business partner, Chin Gee Hee, arrived in 1875. As a labor contractor, the Wa Chong Company imported men from China to work in logging camps, coal mines, and canneries and to help grade streets and build railroads. A few were employed as house boys (domestics) for white matrons. Thousands worked on the S&WW, the SLS&E, and the Northern Pacific and its branch lines. As transcontinental routes were completed, many of the Chinese workers stayed to form permanent communities.

Seattle's Chinatown grew between Mill and Main Streets from Commercial Street to Fourth Avenue South. By 1880 the overwhelmingly male community had six hundred to seven hundred residents, along with a transient population of laborers who migrated from work camps to purchase supplies or find a new job. Three other Chinese merchants had established labor contracting businesses in addition to the Wa Chong Company. Laborers saved their money to open their own small businesses, including laundries and restaurants that served a mixed-race clientele. There were Chinese-operated truck farms north and south of downtown. Wearing characteristic straw hats and sandals,

In February 1886, Seattle's Home Guard formed a protective square around the city's Chinese at Commercial and Main and fought back a vigilante mob. Drawing from Harper's Weekly, Museum *of History and Industry, 3130*

some two hundred fifty peddlers carried baskets of fresh fruits and vegetables up and down the streets, hawking them to consumers.

As economic conditions worsened in the 1870s and 1880s, whites across the West began to see the industrious Chinese as a threat. They would work for less pay than white workers and do jobs that nobody else would do. Economics fueled racism. In response, the U.S. Congress enacted the Chinese Exclusion Act of 1883, which prohibited further immigration of working-class Chinese and denied naturalization rights to those who were already here. Not

appeased, white agitators demanded expulsion of the Chinese. Violence spread across the West. Vigilantes killed three Chinese on a hop farm in east King County, and others were driven out of mining towns. On November 3, 1885, a mob drove the Chinese out of Tacoma.

Seattle's Chinatown Survives Anti-Chinese Riot

Yesler's Pavilion was the scene of an impassioned meeting of the anti-Chinese Congress, a regional organization that decried the fact that nearly 13 percent of Seattle's working males were Chinese. At the same time, Mayor Henry Yesler called a meeting of moderates, who met uptown to organize the Home Guard, an armed force that would put down violence. In February 1886, Seattle's anti-Chinese marched into Chinatown to roust its 350 residents from their homes and herd them to the dock and a waiting steamship, the *Queen of the Pacific*. A crowd of militants passed the hat to raise the $7–per-head fare.

But before the Chinese could leave, Chief Justice Roger Green of the Territorial Supreme Court issued an order requiring the ship's captain to appear in court. The Chinese were housed in a warehouse for the night. The next day, citizens lined the street to watch the Home Guard escort them back to their homes. When a violent vigilante mob stopped the procession at Commercial and Main, the Home Guard formed a protective square around the Chinese, who huddled on the ground. Shots rang out; one of the anti-Chinese was killed and four more were wounded. The standoff ended with the arrival of a company of armed militia and Governor Watson Squire's declaration of martial law.

The anti-Chinese swore out warrants for the arrest of four leading citizens, including Judge Thomas Burke, on charges that their actions were illegal and had perpetrated the shooting. Since martial law was in force, the warrants could not be served under civil law. After reviewing the evidence, a grand jury dismissed all charges against the accused. Intimidated, most of Seattle's Chinese left the city, but those who wished were allowed to stay. Chinese houseboys remained in the homes of Sarah and Henry Yesler, Louisa and David Denny, and others. A few merchants, such as Chin Gee Hee and Chen Cheong, remained and kept their property. Within the next two years, the local economy recovered, laborers were in demand, and many of the Chinese who had left returned to the revitalized Chinatown, centered around Second and Washington.

The Lynching of 1882

The Chinese escaped bloodshed in 1886 in part because of previous mayhem that was not racially motivated. At the beginning of the decade, the "lava beds" south of Mill Street harbored thugs and thieves who perpetrated violent crimes throughout the city. At about 6:00 P.M. on January 17, 1882, George B. Reynolds, a popular clerk in a local store, was on his way to work when two transients held him up at Third and Marion and demanded his money. He reached for his pistol, but the thieves shot first, fatally wounding him.

When someone rang the fire bell, two hundred men responded and fanned out in patrol squads to capture the killers. Four hours later, they found two men hiding in a haystack on a waterfront wharf. One of them had a revolver with an empty chamber that still smelled of burnt powder. The patrol squad reluctantly turned them over to a policeman, but kept their shoes, which they matched to a footprint at the murder site. Men who had participated in the search and others who gathered

with them were convinced that they had the killers.

Shortly after the arrest, a bloodthirsty mob descended on the jail in an alley off Mill Street. Sheriff Louis Wyckoff held his ground, vowing that if anyone took the prisoners, it would be over his dead body. The mob backed off until the next morning's arraignment in Yesler Hall. Justice of the Peace Samuel Coombs heard testimony from twenty-eight witnesses before ordering the accused back to jail to await trial. From the back of the hall, someone shouted, "Let's get 'em!" The vigilantes overpowered police guards, grabbed the prisoners, and dragged them out the back door to the alley and down to two maple trees at Front and James Streets, where long railings had been secured high in the branches with ropes tossed over them. As soon as the prisoners were noosed, many hands grabbed hold to string them up. Chief Justice Roger Green of the territorial Supreme Court slashed at the ropes with a pocketknife, but the mob shoved him aside. A large all-male crowd, including many prominent citizens, gathered to witness the grisly hangings.

With vengeance at a fever pitch, someone suggested going after Benjamin Payne, who awaited trial for the October 1881 murder of Seattle policeman David Sires. Vigilantes stormed the jail, broke down the doors, seized Payne, and dragged him to the gallows. While putting a rope around his neck, they demanded a confession. Payne cried out: "You hang me, and you will hang an innocent man." His captors quickly hoisted him aloft between the other two bodies.

In the afternoon, the coroner's jury met, deliberated each case, and issued its verdicts, which were published that evening in the *Seattle Chronicle*: "We the jury summoned in the above case find that [name of deceased] came to his death by hanging, but from the evidence fur-

The hanging of William Howard, Benjamin Payne, and William Sullivan on January 18, 1882. Sarah and Henry Yeslers' home is behind the maple trees, which they planted in 1860. Several in the crowd can be identified, including William Grose and Henry Yesler whittling a stick in the foreground. Drawing by A. W. Piper, published in Harper's Weekly, *February 4, 1882.* MSCUA, *University of Washington Libraries,* UW 12055

nished we are unable to find by whose hands. We are satisfied that in his death substantial and speedy justice has been served."

Two days later, Sheriff Wyckoff died of a heart attack. His friends said that he was overcome by the inability of his police force to protect its prisoners. The community, including many of the vigilantes, mourned the sheriff's death, but few citizens had remorse for the executed men. A grand jury later refused to indict anyone for the lynching.

When the national press published the story, editorialists depicted Seattle as a lawless town with vigilante justice. Many who had taken part realized that they had erred and that the consequences of their actions could have a negative impact on the city's future. A growing coalition

maintained that henceforth, citizens who took the law into their own hands should be treated as criminals.

Today, visitors to Pioneer Square can tour a model of the pioneer jail cell and delve deeper into the intriguing history of local law enforcement at the Metropolitan Police Museum, located north of South Jackson Street at 317 Third Avenue South.

Women Win, then Lose, the Vote

In 1853, at the first session of the Washington Territorial Legislature, Arthur Denny proposed a bill to grant the ballot to white women. Some surmise that the motion lost because at least one dissenting lawmaker resented the exclusion of his Native American wife. In 1871 Susan B. Anthony and Oregon's Abigail Scott Duniway brought the national women's suffrage crusade to the Northwest. In Seattle, they addressed crowds at Yesler's Pavilion and at the Methodist Episcopal Church. They were guests of Sarah Yesler, who subsequently served as temporary president of the new Washington Woman Suffrage Association. Men in the city's Law and Order League voiced support, maintaining that women would "vote moral." In 1883, Washington Territory enacted women's suffrage, making it the third territory in the nation (after Wyoming and Utah) to enfranchise women.

Most respectable women were married, and caring for home and family was their major role. Outside the home, they worked as teachers, milliners, cooks, and nurses; through their churches they strove to make their communities more livable. The vote gave them an unprecedented public role, which included serving on juries with men. They banded together in newly organized women's clubs and units of the Women's Christian Temperance Union to crusade against vice and the demon rum. In Seattle, newly enfranchised women cast their ballots in the 1884 election and tipped the balance for law and order.

Charles J. Woodbury observed in the New York *Evening Post:* "Whatever may be the vicissitudes of women suffrage in Washington Territory in the future, it should now be put on record that at the election, November 4, 1884, nine-tenths of its adult female population availed themselves of the right to vote with a hearty enthusiasm." Of Seattle, he wrote: "Even the bars of the hotels were closed; and this was the worst town in the territory when I first saw it. Now its uproarious theaters, dance-houses, squaw brothels [which employed Native American women] and Sunday fights are things of the past. Not a gambling house exists."

Seattle's major source of revenue for the city government had been the "sin" tax for liquor, gambling, and prostitution. City coffers diminished as loggers and miners squandered their paychecks in more liberal communities. Seattle weathered its purity for only a year; at the next election, voters threw proponents of law and order out of office, repealed anti-vice laws, and welcomed back the madams, pimps, and saloon keepers.

The tide turned quickly against women's enfranchisement. A powerful saloon lobby gained allies on the Territorial Supreme Court. In 1887 the justices overturned a lower court's decision by ruling that it was unconstitutional for women to serve on juries. The Territorial Legislature revised the law accordingly, but ensured that women still had the right to vote. Then in 1888, the Supreme Court based a new decision on a technicality and ruled women's suffrage unconstitutional.

Sarah Burgert Yesler. MSCUA, *University of Washington Libraries,* UW 2439

In 1886, Sarah and Henry Yesler moved from their small pioneer home up the hill to their new forty-room Victorian mansion, which replaced Sarah's orchard at Third and Jefferson, now the southwest corner of the King County Courthouse. The building survived both Yeslers and Seattle's Great Fire of 1889. Sarah served as librarian for the Pioneer Library Association and was a prime mover in the Ladies Library Association that kept it going. On Henry's death, he deeded the mansion to the city for its public library. When it burned down in 1901, philanthropist Andrew Carnegie came to the rescue with grant funds to build the stately downtown library that served the city for decades. Courtesy Seattle Public Library

Although they could no longer go to the polls, women had learned to participate effectively in public process. They continued to promote social reform, founding day-care centers, homes for unwed mothers, and orphanages. An example is the Ladies' Relief Society (now Seattle Children's Home), founded in 1884 by fifteen women, including Sarah Yesler, Caroline Sanderson, Mary Leary, and Babette Gatzert. Their purpose was "aiding and assisting the poor and destitute, regardless of creed, nationality, or color." At first the board members opened their homes to provide immediate and temporary assistance to indigent people. Due to the overwhelming need, they soon narrowed their

focus to children. They successfully persuaded King County commissioners to allocate funding for "The Orphan Home," which was built at today's Seattle Center on a lot contributed by David and Louisa Boren Denny.

In the cultural arena, women organized the Ladies' Library Association to perpetuate the work of the earlier pioneer organization. The library was commonly regarded as "among the luxuries of civilized life," and in the rapidly growing city, most men were too busy with business and politics to be involved. In 1890 the newly ratified Seattle City Charter included a public library department with a provision that at least two of the board members be women.

This bird's-eye view of Seattle and its bustling harbor was drawn by E. S. Glover of Portland in 1878. In the center, Yesler's Wharf, lined with businesses, extends into Elliott Bay. On the right, trains from Renton deliver coal to bunkers on King Street Wharf. Lithograph by A. L. Bancroft, San Francisco. Museum of History and Industry, SHS 11.2.40

Boomtown

Seattle's population exploded from 3,500 in 1880 to almost 43,000 in 1890. It was a time of unprecedented transformation.

In 1880 Yesler's Wharf extended some 900 feet into the bay, the biggest and busiest pier north of San Francisco. On it were warehouses and shipping firms, a machine shop, a saloon, and a stable for horses and mules that hauled freight. The Oregon Improvement Company's coal bunkers claimed the city's second-largest wharf, located four blocks south at the foot of King Street. Large square-riggers and coal barges shared the waterfront wharves with the bustling "mosquito fleet" of small sidewheelers, steam tugs, schooners, and scows that shuttled passengers and freight up and down Puget Sound and adjacent inland waterways. Adding

to the mix were dugout canoes that Indians paddled to Ballast Island near the foot of Washington Street and to points along the shore.

One of the Pioneer Square companies that shipped goods and supplies was Schwabacher Brothers and Company, headquartered in San Francisco, which advertised "everything from needle to anchor." Bailey Gatzert, who married Babette Schwabacher, established a branch of the family retail and wholesale business on the southwest corner of Front Street and Mill Street in 1869, then brought in other family members for local and regional expansion. Schwabacher Brothers was the first of several commercial businesses in the district south of Mill Street established by German immigrants who were Jewish. In the 1870s, Gatzert was elected mayor of Seattle.

During the 1880s, Seattle's major exports were

Dugout canoes beached at the foot of Washington Street in the early 1890s. They remained a part of the waterfront scene well into the twentieth century and were a favored mode of transportation for Indians who traded and shopped in the city. Courtesy of Paul Dorpat

lumber, wheat, and coal, followed by meat and manufactured goods. Shipbuilding was a major industry. Local companies produced leather goods, ironware, clothing, shoes, beer, cigars, candy, coffee, ice cream, canned fish, and more. The city's primary markets were California and British Columbia, and it was establishing strong commercial ties with Alaska. In addition, it had become the major supply and distribution center for the Puget Sound region.

Seattle remained predominantly a blue-collar town, with a growing labor force that kept pace with industrial expansion. Most unskilled workers lived and spent their free time near the wharves, shipyards, railroads, and packing plants. The transient population was made up primarily of people on the move rather than drifters. It and "the bachelor problem" intensified with waves of men coming from regional lumber camps and mines on their days off and

during winter storms. Mill Street was becoming a dividing line between two distinctly different neighborhoods.

The prominent Territorial University building, crowned with a cupola, was an apt symbol for the high-mindedness that characterized the neighborhood to the north. This was the home of all of the city's public schools, its hospital, its imposing new opera house, and all but one of its churches. The city's only Roman Catholic church was at Third Avenue South and Washington; built by Father Francis Xavier Prefontaine in 1870, Our Lady of Good Help counted nearby City Hall, brothels, and saloons as its neighbors and their patrons among its parishioners.

Oblivious to the dividing line, the two blocks on Commercial Street between Mill and Main held forth as the city's premier commercial strip for most of the 1880s. There were hotels, restaurants, bars, banks, hardware stores,

Looking north from Commercial and Main in 1884 at downtown's busiest commercial strip. Squire's Opera House is the large building on the right. It included the Hotel Brunswick, which promoted itself as the "only first-class hotel in the city on the European plan" with rates of 50 cents to $1.50 per day. Museum of History and Industry, Webster & Stevens, 83.10.6,343

an opera house, a combination toy and gun store, tobacco shops, a ship chandler, barbershops, clothing stores, a tailor, jewelry stores, a grocery store, a fish merchant, a bakery, a variety store, a newspaper office, a real estate office, law offices, a bill collector, and more.

In October 1880 some two thousand citizens turned out for a gala reception at Governor Watson C. Squire's new Opera House to shake hands with President Rutherford B. Hayes, the first U.S. president to visit the West Coast. The building was the first in the city to have a stage and seating area necessary for hosting large touring road shows, many of which originated in New York City. Grand opera made its Seattle debut in this building in 1881, when the Inez

Fabbri Opera Company presented Gounod's *Faust.*

The population explosion meant booming business, but at a price. The city's original commercial strip was quickly becoming a social and economic island, confined to much the same physical space as the geographic island where Doc Maynard had founded his store and the city's original downtown. In the 1880s, the industrial waterfront and railroad tracks flanked its west side. To the north was the civic center. South and east was the burgeoning district that was home to blue-collar workers and transients. It included cheap workingmen's hotels and boardinghouses, a variety of small businesses, and a proliferation of establishments that catered

John Leary built the Post Building at Post Alley and Mill Street in 1881 for the daily Seattle Post, *forerunner of today's* Post-Intelligencer. *Other tenants included a real estate office, a brokerage house, Lowman and Hanford Stationers, and the post office. Historian Paul Dorpat says, "The men here are awaiting the arrival of the mail, often a frustrating experience since the Northern Pacific contrived to delay Seattle-bound mail in Tacoma for as much as twenty-two hours." Courtesy Seattle Public Library*

to the baser instincts of its largely male residents. As this population swelled, it had an ever-increasing presence on the commercial strip.

Commercial Street had yet another parallel to the former island (called Denny's Island by the first settlers), which at its north end had been separated from the mainland at low tide. Now there was a new physical barrier, reminis-

Frank Osgood launches Seattle's first streetcar on its inaugural run in 1884 with Mayor John Leary and other dignitaries on board. George Washington, an African American, is the driver. In the foreground, two Chinese men look on. The Occidental Hotel is on the right and the Yesler-Leary Building is in the background. Photo by Asahel Curtis, 1884. Museum of History and Industry, 898

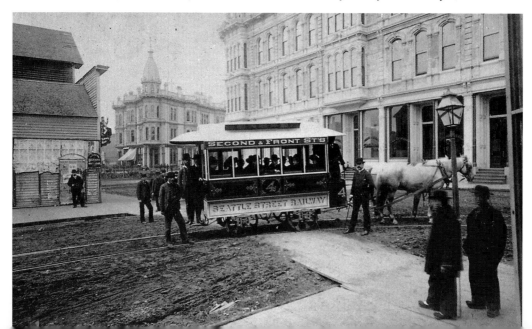

cent of the tidal inlet: the commercial strip ran into a wall of wood-frame buildings at Mill Street. Drivers had to jog right, then left, making two sharp turns through what was known as "the throat" to continue north on Front Street. Southbound traffic followed the reverse procedure through the narrow street. As volume swelled, a traffic policeman was always on duty, trying to ease the gridlock of horse-drawn surreys, carriages, wagons, and streetcars.

In the mid-1880s, the flamboyant Victorian Yesler-Leary Building was built in place of the former row of wooden buildings on Mill Street. It was part of an architectural renaissance that included several structures in the vicinity of lower Mill Street. Blocked off from the new development, Commercial Street remained a strip of primarily wood-frame buildings not unlike other frontier western towns in outward appearance. Because of established businesses owned by the likes of Arthur Denny, Dexter Horton, Watson Squire, and Schwabacher Brothers, the street continued to attract customers, but it was no longer a prestigious address for new businesses.

Along with striking new Victorian architecture, Seattle was witnessing technological and engineering advances. Electric lights were replacing gas lamps on city streets. The Spring Hill Water Company pumped freshwater from Lake Washington to reservoirs on Beacon Hill that supplied city residents and industries. The Seattle Street Railway System began operation in 1884 under the direction of newcomer Frank Osgood. It was the city's first horse-drawn streetcar service, with a line that extended from Main Street up Second Avenue to Pike Street. It soon provided service to lower Queen Anne Hill and

Lake Union, sparking residential growth in those areas.

In 1887 the company took a cue from San Francisco and began constructing a cable-car route up Mill Street and down the hill to Lake Washington. To finance the venture, the owners purchased much of the land along the route and sold residential and business lots for a substantial profit by the time the line was completed. From the start, Osgood and his partner envisioned a system powered by electricity. As soon as the technology was available, they installed a steam-powered generator that supplied current to the cars through overhead lines. On March 31, 1889, the city's first electric cable car clanged up and down the hill to Lake Washington, then came back on Jackson Street, where it turned north on Second Avenue South to complete its oval loop. Proud citizens marveled that their public transit was the fourth such system in the world and one of the most technologically advanced of the day. Yet within a few feet of the tracks, people sometimes drowned in potholes in the streets.

Like the cable car, boomtown Seattle rushed headlong toward the future. But the frantic pace of development was proceeding almost without a plan. What everyone knew but tried not to think about was the vulnerable infrastructure from the city's pioneer past, including sewers that flooded at high tide, narrow wooden streets jammed with horse-drawn conveyances, rotting wooden water mains, and the deep bed of sawdust that lay beneath much of downtown. These problems were about to go up in the smoke of the Great Seattle Fire, a catastrophe with a silver lining that made way for a modern city.

3 Rise of the Urban Center

Karin Link

By the end of the 1880s, Seattle looked toward the future with unbridled optimism. The population had increased tenfold within a decade, and the economy was booming. The hub of Seattle's business district consisted of a half-dozen blocks along Front and Commercial Streets (now First Avenue and First Avenue South, respectively). It included banks, retail stores, newspaper offices, bawdy houses, saloons, office buildings, wholesale houses, and water-front piers. It was a fairly primitive outpost, consisting mostly of wooden buildings.

There was also a sense of opulence in some of the newer buildings, such as architect John Nestor's Frye Opera House, which rose to four stories on Front Street. It housed not only a 1,300–seat theater, but also shops on the ground floor of Front Street as well as offices. Entrepreneur John Collins's Occidental Hotel was designed by Donald McKay in the French

The opulent Occidental Hotel during the 1884 snow. MSCUA, *University of Washington Libraries,* UW 5856

A crowd looks south on First Avenue at the ominous beginning of the Great Seattle Fire, 1889. Museum of History and Industry 83.10.6.204

Empire style and constructed in brick and stone. The Yesler-Leary Building, designed by W. E. Boone in brick and wood, rose across the street from the Occidental Hotel in Victorian splendor.

Because nineteenth-century American cities and towns were typically filled with wooden buildings, many suffered dramatic fires. San Francisco had suffered six major fires by 1852. Chicago had a "Great Fire" in 1872. More locally, devastating fires burnt down major portions of the cities of Spokane and Ellensburg in 1889.

In June 1889, the weather in Seattle was unseasonably warm, with day after day of sunshine. There was no rain. On June 6, tinder-dry downtown erupted in flames that engulfed wooden sidewalks, streets, buildings, and even waterfront wharves. The fire started at 2:30 in the afternoon in a cabinet shop in the basement of the Pontius Building at Front Street and Madison. The *Post-Intelligencer* was still giving accounts of the fire in its June 21 edition, based on firsthand, eyewitness testimony. James

McCough, a painter whose workshop was located above the now infamous cabinet shop, reported:

From my best information, the fire broke out in the shop of Clairmont & Co, cabinetmakers, who occupied the ground floor basement. The one who started the conflagration is a Swede named Berg. He threw a bucket of water over a burning glue pot on the stove which spread the flame at once. A heavy draft swept through the room from the two side doors at the rear and the front."

The whole shop then went up in flames. In a contemporary newspaper story, another Clairmont and Company employee described his amazement at Berg's apparent clumsiness and stupidity. Poor Berg, called "Back" in other accounts, was blamed for setting all of downtown on fire. The *Post-Intelligencer*'s account ended with a solemn pronouncement: "Berg, the unconscious incendiary is yet in this city, looking about for work, but his former employ-

Remains of the Occidental Hotel after the Great Fire in 1889. Photo by John P. Soule. Museum of History and Industry, SHS 1, 267

When the fire burst from the doors and windows near the Madison corner, the firefighters tried unsuccessfully to beat it back. It reappeared again with renewed force in one storeroom after another. Further abetting the fire, a strong shifting wind blew from the northwest. The flames and heat became greater and greater. Meanwhile, firefighters were thwarted by the city's low water pressure. Eventually the fire progressed down Front Street, destroying Seattle's most imposing buildings between Mill and Columbia Streets. The Occidental Hotel at Second and Mill exploded into flames. Instantly, buildings on the south side of Mill caught fire.

By sunset, the fire, which had consumed thirty blocks, had been contained, but flames still lit the sky. Coal bunkers at the foot of King Street would continue burning for days. Bagley wrote:

Nothing but broken walls remained of the city's finest mercantile row. . . . West of First Avenue and south of University Street, for a distance of four-fifths of a mile, every wharf, warehouse, mill, factory, machine shop and lumber yard was utterly destroyed, and the waterfront was nothing but blazing timbers and piles.

To quell the damage, a bucket brigade wetted down rooftops; smoke-covered men continued to pile up salvaged merchandise. Along the waterfront, Schwabacher's Dock was the only wharf to survive the fire. On Third Avenue, Henry Yesler's forty-room mansion, the county courthouse, and Father Prefontaine's Catholic church remained. Made of wood, these buildings continued to smoke from the heat. Today, at the corner of Third Avenue and James Street, the wooden Drexel Hotel, since raised on a solid masonry ground floor, is thought to be the only prefire building in Pioneer Square.

ers do not want one who caused their misfortune and that of so many others."

Historian Clarence Bagley later described the speed with which the fire progressed. Responding to the fire alarm, Seattle's first steam fire engine rushed to the scene. The firefighters tried to douse the blaze but "did not prove equal to the occasion." As other firefighters with hoses arrived, dense smoke enveloped the entire row of two-story buildings between Marion and Madison Streets. When they pried up planks from the sidewalk, they found the basement completely ablaze. Because there were no walls of more sturdy or fireproof construction below, the fire had worked its way easily at the basement level from building to building.

The two-story Drexel Hotel—covered with modern-day siding and raised on a ground floor with masonry walls—is the only known remains of prefire Pioneer Square. The King County Courthouse is on the left and the Collins Building is on the right. Photo by Karin Link.

Its original historic exterior is now well camouflaged by deteriorating modern-day siding.

Although final reports indicated that there had been no deaths, the fire had destroyed almost everything from the waterfront up to Third Avenue. The next day, the *Seattle Daily Press* lamented, "Oh, light-hearted industrious Seattle, pushing rapidly to industrial and commercial greatness, with hearts full of cheer and hands so willing to work, to be reduced to ashes in a single afternoon, and to have the sun of prosperity darkened by a cloud of mocking smoke." A distinguished visitor, Rudyard Kipling, wrote in *Coast to Coast*, "In the heart of the business quarters, there was a horrible black smudge, as though a Hand had come down and rubbed the place smooth."

Disaster and Opportunity

On the evening of the fire, as the *Seattle Post-Intelligencer* made the observation that the flat area south of Mill Street could once again become the heart of the city, proclaiming, "Never again need this section be used for despicable purposes," Mayor Robert Moran imposed an 8 P.M. curfew. The Washington National Guard was called in to prevent looting. The business district remained under martial law for about two weeks. At the mayor's request, the townswomen volunteered to prepare meals for the military and the destitute with provisions supplied by the city. In addition to sending firefighters, the city of Tacoma sent a train and three boatloads of food, which their volunteers unloaded at Schwabacher's Dock. Over a period of two weeks, the Tacomans served thousands of meals. San Francisco, Portland, Olympia, and many other cities also made substantial donations.

The morning after the fire, Mayor Moran called a meeting at the armory to solicit opinions on reconstruction. Six hundred businessmen— in Clarence Bagley's words, "representative of the city's best energy, hope and confidence"— participated. As the meeting progressed, the sense of disaster turned to one of opportunity. There was unanimous agreement that wooden buildings would be prohibited in the "burned district." Only buildings with brick and stone exteriors would be allowed. In the interim, businesses could operate out of tents.

This was also seen as a good time to widen and straighten downtown streets. The disaster had provided a further opportunity to stem the northward tide of the business district and return its heart to the flat area south of Mill Street. Banker Jacob Furth spoke for his fellow citizens, saying: "The time is not far distant when we shall look upon the fire as an actual benefit. I say we shall have a finer city than before, not within five years, but in eighteen months."

Tent City

Within a month, Seattle was a tent city. Seattle's inhabitants slept where they could. Thomas Prosch, editor of the *Post-Intelligencer* in 1889, wrote: "The city was a vast encampment where business was carried out under canvas by day and many hundreds slept in the open air on those hot summer nights or occupied cots in hallways, alleys and on roofs."

Marveling at the legendary "Seattle spirit," *Harper's Weekly* reported later in the month, "The people of Seattle are not disposed to look upon the visitation as an unmitigated calamity. . . . Laborers were set to work as soon as practicable to clear away the debris, and in less than a week, the people had recovered from the shock and were laboring with renewed enthusiasm. . . . the work of rebuilding had begun."

During the period of rebuilding, the legendary Seattle spirit attracted thousands of newcomers, including entrepreneurs, construction workers, and building designers. Jobs and investment opportunities were readily available. Seattle's move toward reconstruction was heralded by slogans such as "Rise like a Phoenix" and "Let's all pull together." A wide variety of businesses and services operated successfully from tents. An account, entitled "A Tented City," gave the following description:

Along Second Street between the north to the limits at Union Street and its junction with Yesler Avenue, are 100 business tents, twenty of which are not yet completed. The businesses conducted there are: general merchandise, two; dry goods, six; restaurants, eight; grocers, five; hardware, four; boots and shoes, three; furniture, three; confectionery, three; drugs, two; offices, nine; clothing, three; jewelry, two; barber shops, six; cigar stands, eleven; tailors, two; hatters, two; second hand, two; glassware, one; photographers, one; dentist, one; meat market, one; sewing machine, one; stationers, one; newspapers, one . . .

Beneath the large stairway of the residence on the southeast corner of Second and Main streets are a broker's office, a boot repairer and a candy stand.

Throughout 1889, the local newspapers, including the *Post-Intelligencer,* carried many articles documenting both the tent city and the quick rebuilding of the city. An often repeated pun was: "Our business is intense."

The Building Ordinance: Raising of the Streets

Seattle, its citizens, and its builders, contractors, and architects received advice from other cities that had suffered a similar fate. For instance, according to a June 20, 1889, *Post-Intelligencer* article, Francis Porter, chief of the Underwriters' Inspection Bureau of San Francisco, traveled to Seattle to give advice about "slow burning construction." The expression "slow burning construction" meant building of brick or stone and in such a way as to cut down the spread of any fire. Porter recommended the use of "wire-lattice" with plaster rather than wood lath, very prevalent in this period, and the "stripping of all spaces between studs and floor joists and the extension of upper wall partitions to the underside of the roof." The last practice is still required by building codes today.

The equivalent of Seattle's first building code, Ordinance No. 1147, was enacted on July 1, 1889. It required that exterior walls be of stone or brick and interiors be, at the very least, "slowly-combustible," such as heavy timber joists. It incorporated many of Porter's suggestions. Its requirements, as in the case of more recent building codes, were very specific. This passage refers to the outer masonry bearing walls of a four-story building: "The basement or foundation (walls) shall not be less than twenty one inches in thickness, the first, second and third stories not less than sixteen inches in thickness, and the fourth shall not be less than twelve inches in thickness."

Another ordinance, this time described in the July 10, 1889, *Post-Intelligencer,* created an "Inspector of Buildings." It stipulated that he must be an experienced builder and, during his term of office, not employed or involved with "building or furnishing materials for the State."

To relieve chronic flooding and improve sanitation, the Seattle City Council voted to replat as well as to elevate many of the city streets. The proposed changes to the business district's topography were detailed in an ordinance, described at length in an article in the June 22, 1889, issue of the *Post-Intelligencer* entitled "The Replat Consummated": The city council widened "Front Street [later First Avenue] to 84 feet. Second and Third Streets [now Second and Third Avenues] were widened

by 24 feet to 90 feet. The ordinance also established by how much each street would be raised. James Street, for example, was scheduled to be raised at the east line of Front Street, 18 feet; at Second Street, 32 feet." Mill Street (now Yesler Way) and Washington, Jackson, and Main Streets were all to be raised by similar amounts. What later became the major avenues—for example, West Street (now Western Avenue), Commercial Street (now First Avenue South), and Second, Third, and Fourth Streets (now Occidental, Second, and Third Avenues South)—were also to be raised by anywhere from six and a half feet to about nineteen feet.

From Private to Public Water Supply

In 1888, at the beginning of his term, Mayor Moran had broached the idea of constructing a gravity-fed water system for Seattle that would flow from the Cedar River in the Cascade Range, but as of June 1889 this had not been realized. Water was mainly supplied by the Spring Hill Water Company's pump, located on the shore of Lake Washington.

The Great Fire galvanized support for the plan to construct an improved water system for Seattle. Citizens blamed the inability to fight the fire on low water pressure. Voters concluded that the growing city could no longer rely on a private water supplier. In the July 8, 1889, election, they overwhelmingly authorized a $1 million bond for the construction of the Cedar River Water Supply System. Unfortunately, politics and economics would delay its construction; water from the Cedar River was not distributed to Seattle until 1901.

Opposition or Opportunism?

By July 1889, Seattle's ambitious program to rebuild its business district had begun and the streets were being replatted and raised. Some confusion ensued and a few property owners were mightily irritated. Henry Yesler claimed that the city council had not consulted him on the replatting of the streets. He complained that the council's decisions would have a nefarious effect not only on him but on other property owners and the City of Seattle in general. Yesler was quoted at great length in the July 1, 1889, *Seattle Post Intelligencer.* His eloquence speaks volumes about not only the kind of confusion that must have reigned in the rebuilding of early Seattle, but also the character of one of Seattle's most prominent pioneers:

I shall resist the ordinance by every lawful means. Even if I am paid for the property, I will not get near what it is worth, as the income from the buildings I should erect there is very large and would enable me in a short time to repay the heavy debt that is now hanging over me. If the council had not replatted the city, I would have rebuilt the Yesler-Leary Building and completed the Pioneer Building, as fast as men and money should accomplish the work. I would have built a fine new brick building on my property extending from the Pioneer Building north to the southeast corner of Front and Cherry streets. . . .

I can tell you one thing, sure, and that is, the city council will have one of the biggest lawsuits

First Avenue South, looking north from Main Street in the late 1890s. Most of the buildings still stand today and have been restored, including the Grand Central on the right. Photo by Asahel Curtis. MSCUA, *University of Washington Libraries, A Curtis 00492*

on hand they ever heard of. I think I have done about as much for the city as any man in it, and I would much prefer to go ahead and do all in my power to make it a city celebrated all over the United States for its beautiful buildings and well graded streets. I should like to erect the much talked about Pioneer Building, for it has been a hobby of mine to build the structure on that corner; but I can not build it now. The widening of Front street on both sides is uncalled for. Five feet on each side would be plenty enough, and I do not think that there is a property owner on the street who would not give that much gratis. I would give that much of my property, in fact, I had drawn plans for the Pioneer Building to stand back that far; but I do earnestly object to giving four feet more, as I have all the iron and terra cotta to be used in the building to be ordered now and it will be entirely worthless and will cost me from $15,000 to $20,000 to replace it, if the building is cut off four feet. I think seventy six feet is wide enough for any thoroughfare, and I shall not put up with this needless change without considerable trouble to the city.

Moses Korn, another property owner, showed less vehemence than Henry Yesler in his reaction to the replatting of the streets but felt that he should be reimbursed by the city for the "damage inflicted on his property." The outcome of Korn's objections is not known. The second Korn Building (there was one before the fire), designed by Elmer Fisher, still stands today on Yesler Way at 101 Occidental Avenue South. At the time, its design was hailed as superior to that of the previous Korn Block: "A glance at the plans in Architect Fisher's office show that the building will present a much handsomer appearance than the old structure. There will be more ornamentation, terra cotta, stone and galvanized iron being literally distributed over the front elevations."

Despite the protestations of Henry Yesler

and others, the city streets were significantly widened and raised. To facilitate its plans, the city paid the then-exorbitant price of $125,000 for "Yesler Corner," now Pioneer Place, at First Avenue and Yesler Way so that it could clear the triangular obstruction and create a direct route from First Avenue to First Avenue South. In the end, Henry Yesler did build his Pioneer Building.

Seattle Rises from the Ashes

A new Seattle, built of brick, stone, cast stone, and terra-cotta, rose very quickly from the ashes of the devastating fire. Within a month, eighty-eight buildings were either under way or projected. The Seattle newspapers of 1889 took real delight in recounting the rebuilding of Seattle. Not only was "Rise like a Phoenix" a popular slogan, but journalists discussing Seattle's rebuilding made references to the "wings of the Phoenix." There were very frequent, sometimes daily, articles on building in the 1889 *Post-Intelligencer* from the day of the fire all through 1889. These are often elegantly phrased descriptions of future buildings, complete with the name of the owner, the architect and builder, and the types of materials and decoration that would make these buildings worthy of the newly reborn city. The tone is very positive and congratulatory:

There is a feature of the new life in Seattle which will not grow old and that is the work of building. The scene in the burnt district is gradually changing for the better and excavations and foundations for many new buildings are already under way. . . . New announcements of proposed buildings continue to be made and they are always met with interest and pleasure by the general public.

Construction on some buildings had already begun, and their projected ground floors suddenly became basement levels in anticipation of the raising of the street level. Consequently, buildings were sometimes designed with an entrance at both the new basement level and at the new ground level above. For instance, recent excavations of the Butler Block, at the northwest corner of Second Avenue and James Street, revealed that it had two arched entryways, one on top of the other.

The raising of the street level created Pioneer Square's subterranean catacombs and areaways, first popularized in the late 1960s by Bill Speidel's "Underground Tours." The basement levels were daylit at the new street level, thanks to square glass prism blocks set into the sidewalks. These glass blocks, which have turned a purplish color over time, can still be seen in the sidewalks of Pioneer Square.

Seattle's Early Architectural Style

Several architects, many of them trained originally in the building trades, contributed to Seattle's sudden growth after the Great Fire. Their individual work sheds interesting light on early life in Seattle after the fire. The architect Elmer Fisher, by the sheer number of buildings his office produced, played a significant role in defining the Pioneer Square Historic District as we know it today. Credit also belongs to architects such as W. E. Boone, John Parkinson, Charles Saunders, and E. W. Houghton for their work in the wake of the fire. Because only a handful of architects contributed to the rebuilding, the historic district has a distinctive architectural harmony.

The style of these early buildings, especially Elmer Fisher's designs, veered from the fussiness of the Late Victorian style, more suited to wood, to a stately Romanesque Revival style based on the work of H. H. Richardson and contemporary Chicago architects such as Burnham and Root. Typical of the Victorian facade composition was the tendency to divide the facade into marked vertical bays, with additional horizontal and vertical elements. The architecture of the Chicago School was characterized by the use of heavy masonry, Romanesque arches, often low and wide, and facades with a recognizable base, middle, and top.

The early Seattle architects mostly were not formally trained as architects. They tended to reinvent, often in a naive way, their version of the Late Victorian style and especially the Richardsonian Romanesque and Chicago School styles, based on what was available in architectural journals of the time. A small selection of the early buildings, which marked Seattle's "rise from the ashes" and also contribute to the flavor of present-day Pioneer Square, illustrate this distinctive architecture.

Pioneer Place Buildings

As the city was rebuilt, Pioneer Place was set off by a number of notable buildings. Henry Yesler's Pioneer Building (in Pioneer Place at 602–610 First Avenue at Yesler Way), designed by Elmer Fisher, is one of the most prominent. Fisher, in an October 1889 *Post-Intelligencer* article, described the building as "Romanesque, after the great architect of America, Mr. Richardson." In fact, the composition is more Victorian in fashion, dividing the facade into almost discrete vertical bays set off by pilasters, with horizontal masonry bands dividing up these areas at various floor levels. The main and side entrances are marked by heavy masonry arches and accentuated by projecting bay windows above them. The main entrance is further accentuated by pilasters of rough-hewn stone that originally rose several stories to a tower destroyed as a

Architect Elmer Fisher designed Henry Yesler's Pioneer Building. In 1892 the American Institute of Architects proclaimed it "the finest building west of Chicago." On the right, the Seattle Hotel was built ca. 1905 as the Occidental Hotel to replace the former Victorian building of the same name, after the Great Fire in 1889. Museum of History and Industry 83.10.10, 242, Webster & Stevens, 47,822

result of the 1949 earthquake. The entire building is also marked by a very spirited use of window openings of several sizes, some arched and some rectangular. The interior is especially wonderful because of its Italian red marble and skylit atrium. The building won an 1892 American Institute of Architects award for being the "finest building West of Chicago."

Across First Avenue, on the southwest corner of First and Yesler, the Yesler Building, formerly the Bank of Commerce (1890–91), also designed by Fisher, has arched openings in heavily rusticated granite stone. Another story in brick was added later.

A good example of the Chicago School's version of Romanesque Revival, particularly its upper floors, is the Mutual Life Building on the northwest corner of First and Yesler (the site of Yesler's cookhouse, Seattle's first public gathering place). Also designed by Fisher in the 1890s,

The Merchant's Cafe Building, center, and the Korn Building, left, shown here in the 1930s, were erected during the postfire building boom. Washington State Archives, Puget Sound Regional Branch

it has a ground floor with a low, wide arched entryway. The remaining floors were finished by Emil DeNeuf in 1893, in a contrasting light brick, with a later western addition by Robertson and Blackwell.

Elmer Fisher, who was responsible for these buildings, gave an account that he was born in Scotland in 1840, arrived in Massachusetts at age seventeen, and served an architectural apprenticeship—an account that now appears to be untrue. It is known that he came to the Northwest in 1886 and designed buildings in Vancouver and Victoria, British Columbia, and Port Townsend, Washington, before coming to Seattle. As an architect, he was very prolific over a short period of time. By 1891, despite the accolades the Pioneer Building received, he abandoned his career as an architect to run

the Abbott Hotel in Seattle, which he had also built.

The Merchant's Café Building

Across the street from the Pioneer Building stands the Merchant's Café Building, at 109 Yesler Way. Formerly known as the Sanderson Block, it was designed by W. E. Boone in 1889. Its exterior represents the transition between the Late Victorian fussiness of Seattle's early prefire buildings, such as Boone's own Yesler-Leary Building, and a calmer style inspired by the Chicago School's version of Romanesque Revival.

The Merchant's Café itself has a colorful history, dating even before its association with the Klondike gold rush. It is thought to be the oldest existing restaurant in Pioneer Square. From 1889 to 1910, its basement served as a "Sunday bank" for those trading gold dust. The upper floors of the building were originally designed as office space, although in the 1900s and 1910s, these floors are said to have housed a brothel. A photo from 1910 shows a sign advertising "masquerade costumes" below the third floor. By the 1930s, the upper floors were occupied by a hotel. Photos of the period show an incredible amount of activity in front of the building: many signs and large crowds of people.

Born in Pennsylvania in 1830, W. E. Boone, the architect of the Merchant's Café Building, was described in his 1921 obituary in the *Post-Intelligencer* as a direct descendant of Daniel Boone. He worked in railroad construction in Chicago, then in building construction in Minneapolis and the Bay Area. There he began to enjoy some prominence as the designer of the Institution for the Deaf, Dumb and Blind in Berkeley and a Masonic Temple and a City Hall in Oakland, California. He arrived in Seattle around 1882, where he remained until his death.

His architectural career in Seattle is interesting, because he had a known practice before Seattle's Great Fire and was a partner in several successful offices well after the fire, a rarity among the architects who contributed to the rebuilding of Seattle in 1889. He was responsible for many buildings in what is now the Pioneer Square Historic District, including the prefire Yesler-Leary Building, which stood at the intersection of Yesler Way and First Avenue; the Globe Building (see below); and the Seattle Quilt Building, at 316–318 First Avenue South, between Main and Jackson Streets. In partnership with William H. Willcox, he completed the now demolished but spectacular New York Building (1889–1892), at the northeast corner of Second Avenue and Cherry Street, and

designed the J. M. Frink Building, now known as the Washington Shoe Building (1891–1892), at the southeast corner of Occidental Avenue South and South Jackson Street. In 1893, in *A History of Washington, the Evergreen State, From Early Dawn to Daylight,* Julian Hawthorne wrote of Boone:

"This well-known citizen, though not among those who came to Seattle at the earliest day of the city's history to lay here the foundations of municipal and commercial greatness, is a prominent and representative man of the re-enforcement [sic] that came when the place was beginning her larger growth; and to this re-enforcement much of the credit of the city's remarkable advancement is due."

The Interurban Building

Also previously known as the Puget Sound Interurban Railway Building, the Interurban Building, located on the corner of Yesler and Occidental across the street from the Korn Building, was originally built as the Seattle National Bank Building in 1890–92. In 1902 it housed the ticket office and waiting room of the new Puget Sound Interurban Railway, which took passengers to Tacoma and stops in between. Architect John Parkinson designed the Romanesque Revival–style building in brick and red sandstone hauled in from Colorado. There is a real harmony in the use of repeated arched bays and in the detailing such as the carved lion's head above the building's main entrance. Parkinson's early work in Seattle typically reflected this type of harmony and attention to detail.

Born in England in 1861, Parkinson was trained there in the building trades and in design. He immigrated to Napa, California, in 1885 and moved to Seattle in 1889. After a stint in Seattle, in 1894 he went on to found the very successful Parkinson and Associates,

The Seattle Hotel

Before the Great Fire, John Collins's Occidental Hotel had stood in the triangle of land between First and Second Avenues and James Street and Yesler Way. Built between 1882 and 1884, the four-story, stucco-faced, brick structure was trapezoidal in plan. It was distinguished by its Victorian composition and detailing, including belt courses, brackets, dentils, and engaged ornamental pilasters, as well as repeated bays, divided into elongated and arched window openings. This was topped by a mansard roof, on which were set repeated dormers, particularly along James Street and Yesler Way.

On the day of the fire in 1889, while watching his hotel burn and topple, a soot-covered Collins hired crews to clean up the building debris as soon as the embers cooled. Defiantly,

John Parkinson designed the Seattle National Bank Building in 1890. It was renamed the Interurban Building after the turn of the twentieth century, when it housed the electric railway's ticket office and passenger depot. Photo by Frank La Roche. MSCUA, University of Washington Libraries, LaRoche 1082

Architect John Parkinson. Museum of History and Industry, 88.33.147

responsible for some of Los Angeles's great landmark buildings.

Parkinson's other significant contribution in the Pioneer Square area was the Butler Building, on the northwest corner of Second Avenue and James Street, originally known as the Phinney and Jones Building. Converted from an office building to an elegant hotel in 1894, it lost most of its upper floors in later years and was then turned into the Butler Garage Building, with retail on the ground level. Still called the Butler Building, it was redeveloped by the Samis Foundation in 2003. The shell of its first-floor exterior was the only portion of the original building that was retained and incorporated into a new garage structure.

he vowed to "show Seattle a bigger and finer building than they ever saw before." He commissioned Stephen Meany, nephew of Edmond Meany (historian and once president of the University of Washington), to design a new hotel. Stephen Meany had worked for W. E. Boone as well as Donald McKay. Now, judging by contemporary newspaper accounts, he was in great demand as a hotel designer.

News concerning the rebuilding of John Collins's Occidental Hotel, later known as the Hotel Seattle and then as the Seattle Hotel, appeared regularly in the *Post-Intelligencer* of 1889. Also trapezoidal in plan, this stately building was notable for its well-proportioned bays with repeated arched windows and its entrance, dramatically set at the intersection of James Street and Yesler Way.

The hotel stood until 1961. The destruction of this once-beautiful building and its replacement by the infamous "sinking ship" garage spurred the creation of the Pioneer Square Historic District in 1970.

The Squire-Latimer Building

South of Pioneer Place is the Squire-Latimer Building, at the northeast corner of First Avenue South and South Main Street, now famous as Grand Central Mercantile. It was designed by San Diego architects Nelson Comstock and Carl Troetsche in 1889.

The southern half of the building stands on the site of Watson C. Squire's Opera House, which opened in 1879 as Seattle's first real theater and was destroyed in the Great Fire. Squire, a former Territorial governor and senator, and his business partner, Norval Latimer of the Dexter Horton Company, helped set the pace for the city's rebirth as their stately new building rose from the ashes. The press, watching

with eager anticipation, described the future building in glowing terms:

The structure will stand four stories high above the basement and cover an area 60 x 111 feet in dimensions, and when completed will be one of the largest and handsomest business blocks in the city. The front and side elevations will be beautiful and attractive with walls of pressed brick trimmed with stone and iron, and handsomely surmounted by an imposing and elaborate cornice.

The exterior appearance of the structure will be most beautiful in design and a gem in architectural appearance.

The Squire-Latimer Building contained the Grand Central Hotel during the Klondike gold rush. Its rehabilitation by Richard White, Alan Black, and architect Ralph Anderson in 1971 was one of the earlier examples of this kind of work in Pioneer Square.

The Globe Building

Across from the Squire-Latimer Building is W. E. Boone's Globe Building, on the southeast corner of South Main Street and First Avenue South, originally known as the Marshall-Walker Block. It was built in 1890–91 on the site of Seattle's first hospital, which was run by Doc and Catherine Maynard.

The Globe Building's exterior is an interesting interpretation of the Chicago School style. It uses rusticated stonework to create a base for the building, in addition to low-slung arched window openings, especially above the entryways. The overall composition shows the tendency to divide facades along a grid pattern. In its original state in 1890, it had an ornamented parapet as well as higher parapets accentuating the various entryways, which created strong vertical bays and a towerlike element at the corner. The horizontal elements include belt courses

The Marshall-Walker Block, now known as the Globe Building. Photo by Asahel Curtis.
MSCUA, *University of Washington Libraries, A Curtis 00492*

and brick corbelling. Like many buildings in this area, its cornice and parapet were damaged in the 1949 earthquake and subsequently removed as a safety precaution ordered by the city.

The building was jointly developed by two owners, Marshall and Walker, who separated their respective portions of the building by a brick wall. On its upper floors, the north half of the building, corresponding to the Marshall wing, was originally designed for fifty offices. In the 1890s, this portion was converted to the Windsor Hotel, in 1898 renamed the Globe Hotel, which operated until the late 1960s. A major fire broke out in the building in 1901. All of Seattle's fire engines and a five-inch stream of water from the fireboat *Snoqualmie* were needed to put out the blaze. In 1924, the premises of the Northwestern Drug Company, a front for illegal liquor production located on the second floor, exploded and showered glass and debris on the street below. At the ground level, from

1891 to 1970, the building also housed a saloon. It now houses the Elliott Bay Book Company. Jones and Jones Architects is a long-term occupant of the top two floors.

The Cadillac Hotel

Prior to the turn of the twentieth century, South Jackson Street was built up on pilings above the high-water mark, and a hodgepodge of run-down wooden buildings, housing mostly work-ingmen's hotels, sprang up here. In 1889 the Cadillac Hotel, on the northwest corner of Second Avenue South and South Jackson Street, originally the Wittler Block, was one of only two brick buildings on the street. It was designed by Hetherington, Clements, and Company. James W. Hetherington, like many of his con-temporaries, is thought to have begun his career as a skilled carpenter before opening an archi-tecture firm in 1889.

The Cadillac Hotel in the late 1920s, with rooms available for 25, 35, and 50 cents a night. The restaurant advertises soft drinks and ice cream. Museum of History and Industry, 83.10,1603

The building is distinctive because of its arched window openings and simple decorative brickwork, which even echoes the curves of the arched openings. Engaged brick pilasters mark off vertical bays, while horizontal courses show the separation of floors—another gridlike pattern. When the building opened in 1889, its main tenant was the fifty-eight-room Derig Hotel on the upper two floors. Early main-floor businesses included a bar, a cigar store, a drugstore, and cheap restaurants. Cable cars rumbled down Jackson Street, then turned north on Second Avenue beside the hotel. Jackson Street changed dramatically from 1900 to 1902, when brick factories, warehouses, and railroad buildings replaced former wooden hovels.

In February 2001, this building was badly damaged by the Nisqually Earthquake. Between then and early 2002, its fate was hotly contested. Local citizenry and Historic Seattle, an organization committed to the preservation of Seattle's built heritage, waged a successful fight against its demolition.

Hard Times

In 1890, several major American financial institutions failed, signaling the seeds of recession. The economic Panic of 1893 that swept the nation hit hard in Seattle. For a time, the pace of local development continued, fueled by the momentum of the postfire building boom. But by 1893, many local corporations and streetcar lines were forced into bankruptcy. Unemployment swelled. The blow was cushioned in part by the arrival of the Great Northern Railroad, the city's first direct transcontinental connection. Other forces were on the horizon as well.

A New Building Wave

In 1897, the Klondike gold rush ushered in a wave of building that lasted until the early 1910s. This period also marked a new sophistication and variety in architectural practice in Seattle. National trends would increasingly influence local development. Newcomers, who often came to stay, had more worldly educational backgrounds and connections with innovative firms throughout the country.

Seattle's international ties were also being strengthened. To celebrate its growing stature and to promote itself, Seattle hosted its first world's fair, the Alaska-Yukon-Pacific Exposition, in 1909. The city built an elegant and massive comfort station beneath the cobblestones of Pioneer Place to accommodate visitors. Crowning it was the ornate Victorian pergola designed by Julian F. Everett. The pergola doubled as a shelter for people waiting for the trolley and later became a symbol of the entire Pioneer Square Historic District.

Several landmark buildings, some by architects of national renown, signaled this new wave of architectural development. From the turn of the twentieth century to 1914, the partnership of Charles Bebb and Louis Mendel brought to the city a direct connection with the Chicago School of architecture. Bebb, as an employee of the acclaimed Chicago firm of Adler and Sullivan, had first come to Seattle to supervise the construction of their design for the Opera House, which was never built. The stylized floral bas-reliefs above the ground floor and at the top of Bebb and Mendel's Corona Building (1903) at Second and James highlight the

People gather under the Victorian pergola in Pioneer Place, 1910. It provided ornate shelter for a massive underground restroom, a popcorn stand, and passengers waiting for the trolley. Seattle Municipal Archives, Engineering Department Photographic Collection, Item 11922

The Corona Building, flanked by the Alaska Building, left, and the art deco Hartford Building, right. Photo by Karin Link

Bebb and Mendel's Frye Hotel, one of the few Beaux Arts buildings in Pioneer Square. Courtesy of Low-Income Housing Institute

Detail of the Sullivanesque ornament on Bebb and Mendel's Corona Building. Photo by Karin Link

The Alaska Building, 1904. Photo by Asahel Curtis. Museum of History and Industry 83.10.7 317.2, Webster & Stevens, 3,021

influence of Louis Sullivan. Similar ornamentation can be seen above the two entrances of the Schwabacher Hardware Company Warehouse (1903–1905) at First and Jackson.

Bebb and Mendel, however, produced buildings in many styles. The Frye Hotel (1906–1911) at Third and Yesler is one of the few Beaux Arts–inspired buildings in Pioneer Square. The main facade consists of a wide central bay flanked by two narrow ones, creating strong edges at each corner, above a strong base consisting of a ground floor and mezzanine. Details also include ornamental shields with fruit at the entrance of the building and an elaborate projecting ornamental cornice at the top. In 1911 the Frye Hotel was one of Seattle's tallest steel-frame buildings, and it housed an elegant hotel.

Adjoining the Corona Hotel is the fourteen-story Alaska Building (1904) at Second and James, considered Seattle's first skyscraper. Eames and Young of St. Louis designed the building with local architects Saunders and Lawton. It features ornate terra-cotta panels on the lower two floors and a penthouse that was originally home to the Alaska Club, a social organization for businessmen and other members with ties to Alaska.

Another landmark, the King Street Station, reigned (along with the Smith Tower, which was completed in 1914) for decades as the most prominent building on Seattle's skyline—and the railroads' gateway to the city.

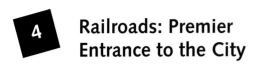

4 Railroads: Premier Entrance to the City

Mildred Andrews

The prominent clock tower of the King Street Station, at Third and Jackson, beckons local residents as well as travelers by land and sea. Built in 1906, it exhibits design sophistication and grandiose scale that were unknown in the Pacific Northwest at that time. But the tower signaled far more than architectural bravura. It was modeled on the campanile at Piazza San Marco in Venice, a city that dominated trade in the Renaissance world. Visionaries with similar hopes for Seattle saw the tower as a fitting monument to a new era of transportation and trade.

In 1911 the neoclassical Oregon and Washington Station—now called Union Station, at Fourth and Jackson—rose a block east of the King Street Station. During the golden age of railroad transportation, the neighboring grand depots formed the premier entrance to Seattle. The legacy of Seattle's railroads began in the 1860s with civic-spirited pioneers' relentless

King Street and Union Stations. Photo by Asahel Curtis. MSCUA, *University of Washington Libraries,* UW 530

quest for a transcontinental connection (see chapter 2) but gathered steam in the 1890s.

Northern Pacific Courts Seattle

The Great Seattle Fire of 1889 sparked more than a construction boom. Between 1888 and 1890, the city's population rocketed from 19,000 to 43,000, then continued to soar. The burgeoning local economy attracted new businesses and industries. Merchants supplied outlying mill towns, shipping goods via rail and the mosquito fleet. Local railroads transported trainloads of coal, lumber, and agricultural produce from the hinterlands to freight yards on waterfront wharves. Seattle was quickly outstripping its rival, Tacoma, a fact that was not lost on Henry Villard, who had owned a controlling interest in the Northern Pacific in the early 1880s.

By the time of the Great Fire, Villard had regained control of the Northern Pacific, and he made good his promise to extend direct transcontinental service to Seattle. Having twice spurned the city in favor of Tacoma, the Northern Pacific now made the official announcement that "all discrimination was removed." The *Seattle Post-Intelligencer* reported that the news prompted "great rejoicing." Southbound travelers no longer had to endure fifteen- to twenty-hour layovers in Tacoma; eastbound trains connected with the main line at Franklin in the foothills of the Cascades, then steamed through the new Stampede Pass tunnel. Villard eventually built a modest passenger depot at Columbia Street and Railroad Avenue (now Alaskan Way). Veteran city booster Judge Orange Jacobs declared, "Seattle was determined to conquer, and she has triumphed most gloriously."

But Villard was keenly aware of aggressive new competitors, including the Union Pacific in Oregon, which rejected his proposal for an alliance. In 1892 the Canadian Pacific Overland sped through Sumas, Sedro-Woolley, and Snohomish on the Seattle, Lake Shore and Eastern's newly completed northern branch. Seattle passengers boarded the red wooden cars at the Columbia Street Station to journey north, then east through Canada.

Villard was determined to checkmate his rivals. He made what the *Post-Intelligencer* called "swift and mysterious movements on Wall Street" to acquire a majority of shares from the ailing Seattle, Lake Shore and Eastern. The move gave the Northern Pacific control of much of bustling Railroad Avenue, the downtown waterfront, and the northern branch, which it would continue to share with the Canadian Pacific until the World War I era. Seattle was, in the words of the *P-I,* a "Northern Pacific Town." But a more formidable competitor than Villard had ever known was en route.

James Jerome Hill's Milwaukee, Minneapolis and St. Paul (soon to be renamed the Great Northern Railway) was carving its way across the northern states toward Puget Sound. Once again, Seattle had hopes of becoming the western terminus of a transcontinental line.

The "Empire Builder" and the Great Northern

Born in Ontario, Canada, in 1838, Hill had dropped out of school at age seventeen and boarded a train for the frontier Minnesota town of St. Paul, located at the head of the Mississippi River. Hill found work as a shipping clerk for a steamboat company. In 1865, following the Civil War, he went into business on his own, contracting with packing companies and local railroads. A man of prodigious energy, he was a ruthless competitor who slashed rates and orchestrated purchases of financially distressed rail lines for a fraction of their value. He recruited prominent American and Canadian

James Jerome Hill. Museum of History and Industry, SHS 18554

investors as business partners, then quickly took charge.

Jim Hill was the consummate man of the steel rails. He saw transportation as the backbone of commerce. He understood engineering, mining, and finance and was a hands-on executive who personally inspected his work sites. The Great Northern cost more to build than the Northern Pacific, but it was 100 miles shorter, had gentler grades, and was made of tempered steel rails instead of iron—which rusts. Ultimately, the Great Northern would be cheaper to operate even with substantially lower rates for both passengers and freight. As he pushed west, Hill built branch lines and amalgamated a number of smaller lines into an integrated system.

Hill's agents in Europe recruited tens of thousands of immigrants, mostly Swedes and Norwegians, whom he found to be reliable as both railroad workers and farmers. He once said, "Give me enough Swedes and whisky, and I'll build a railroad to Hell." He financed the railroad in part by selling land along the route, with generous rebates, to immigrants and others for immediate agricultural and real estate development. In contrast, Villard had built the Northern Pacific trunk line relying on massive government land grants to secure his investments.

Unlike other transcontinental lines, most of Hill's railroad was financed privately. The exception was the Red River Valley in the Dakotas. There he claimed checkerboard sections of land that Congress had offered some thirty years earlier to the first railroad to cross the valley. Farmers in the then-settled area howled in protest at the prospect of a declaration of eminent domain that would force them to sell their land. Politicians rallied to their support. A chagrined Congress happily accepted Hill's proposed solution and granted him the right to choose equal amounts of unsettled government land in other regions; as a result, Red River Valley farmers kept their land. In exchange, Hill selected vast Northwest landscapes, studded with virgin forests and rich in commercial potential. Consequently, when the Great Northern arrived in the Northwest, it was the biggest landholder in the region.

Seattle Wins the Terminus

As the railroad moved toward Puget Sound, Hill kept everyone guessing about his choice of a terminus. Tacoma, Seattle, Bellingham, and Everett all vied for the prize. Local newspapers trumpeted their city's advantages while downgrading the competition. The tide turned in Seattle's favor in 1889. Hill's representative

Railroad Avenue, looking north from south of Yesler Way. MSCUA, *University of Washington Libraries, 1675*

hired one of the city's foremost boosters, Judge Thomas Burke, as the Great Northern's agent.

Burke was an attorney and former Territorial judge. He had not forgotten previous snubs by the Northern Pacific. In addition, as president of the Seattle Lake Shore and Eastern, he was personally galled when Villard bought the majority of shares and took over the line. Burke resolved to make deals and concessions to win the Great Northern terminus and not risk once again losing the prize. But as historian Roger Sale observes, he "forgot how much Hill or any other builder of roads to Puget Sound needed Seattle. . . . [which] was where the people and the facilities were, where everything Hill needed was. . . . If the Great Northern's western terminus were to be anything like what it had been

in Saint Paul on its eastern end, it would have to come to Seattle."

Burke set to work on several fronts at once. Keeping prices in line, he quietly bought up property at Smith Cove and on the still submerged tide flats in south Pioneer Square. He drafted an agreement for a Great Northern subsidiary, the Seattle and Montana, which began laying track northward along the shoreline toward the Canadian border. At Bellingham Bay, he negotiated acquisition of the Fairhaven and Southern line. Back in Seattle, the Seattle, Lake Shore and Eastern still controlled an unused thirty feet of Railroad Avenue, which Burke transferred to the Great Northern.

This was not enough for the audacious Hill, who demanded a larger share of Railroad

Avenue on the central waterfront and threatened to select a different terminus if Seattle turned him down. Burke successfully petitioned the City Council for an additional sixty-foot right-of-way on Railroad Avenue, plus rights for the Great Northern to build sidetracks and sheds on South Jackson Street. Hill agreed to share with the Northern Pacific the old SLS&E passenger depot on Columbia Street. At this juncture, Hill had secured the prime access on the Seattle waterfront, while the Northern Pacific and other lines had to share the rest.

Tunnel Tactics

But not everyone bowed to Hill. Seattle City Engineer Reginald Heber Thomson advised the City Council to rescind the decision. An outraged business community and press voiced fears of losing the terminus. "That man Thomson," as he was called by one frustrated columnist, was branded a traitor, but he refused to budge. He argued forcefully that adding a major railroad to the waterfront would put a stranglehold on the already congested city and stifle commercial development. Acting as intermediary, Judge Burke arranged a meeting between Thomson and Hill.

Thomson proposed that the Great Northern and Northern Pacific join forces to bore a tunnel beneath downtown and construct passenger and freight facilities on the tide flats south of Pioneer Square. Hill agreed to the plan, in part because he already owned considerable tidelands property. He also envisioned Seattle as a major Northwest city whose growth and prosperity would benefit the Great Northern. Because of

The city erected the "Mineral Palace" at Pioneer Place in 1893, a temporary exhibition hall that showcased locally manufactured goods. It heralded the arrival of the Great Northern Railroad and its promise for the local economy. Photo by Frank La Roche. Museum of History and Industry, SHS 12400

financial pressures, Hill made it clear from the outset that it would take some time before he could construct the tunnel. It took ten years.

Downtown was not the only place where a railroad tunnel was needed. In 1892 laborers laid Great Northern tracks across perilous Stevens Pass in the Cascade Range. Hill authorized switchbacks with twelve miles of track to traverse four and one-half miles of actual terrain. Trains had to decouple into segments of four or five cars, so that engines fore and aft could push and pull them over the steep grade. Hundreds of men shoveled winter snow from the tracks of what became known as "death mountain." Hill's solution materialized eight years later with the mammoth 13,000–foot Cascade Tunnel that brought trains through the mountains underneath the switchbacks.

The Great Northern Arrives

In February 1893, the first Great Northern freight trains steamed into Seattle, followed by passenger service in June. Hill, the undisputed hero of the day, lead the Fourth of July parade from Pioneer Square up First Avenue. Citizens lined the sidewalk, cheering and basking in the vision of their city's future.

In addition to making Seattle the terminus, Hill slashed fares well below the Northern Pacific's prevailing rate. For a first-class ticket to the Chicago World's Fair, Great Northern passengers paid only $35, instead of the Northern Pacific's $60. The Great Northern lowered its rate for hauling Puget Sound lumber to an unprecedented 50 cents per 100 pounds. As a result, existing mills significantly increased their output and scores of new mills sprouted throughout the region. Great Northern ads rightfully boasted the lowest freight rates, the lowest passenger fares, and the "shortest route to and from anywhere east of Fargo."

The Panic of 1893

The new transcontinental line sparked a local population and construction boomlet that stagnated later in the year with the worldwide economic Panic of 1893. Banks collapsed, businesses closed, and the ranks of the unemployed swelled. Out-of-work people built driftwood shacks along the shores of Puget Sound, where they dug clams and picked berries to survive. The Northern Pacific and Union Pacific Railroads were among the 25 percent of the nation's railroads that sank into receivership. Tacoma was especially hard hit, dragged down in the wake of the Northern Pacific's hard times and no longer in the running as Seattle's rival.

Seattle weathered the depression better than most cities, thanks to a diversified economy, its regional status as a mercantile center, and the Great Northern Railroad. In addition, lumber mills served by the Great Northern continued to flourish. Hill had foreseen the downturn. By undercutting his competitors, he had manipulated the market, ensuring that his trains would carry full loads to buyers back East. The Great Northern was the only line on the Pacific Coast that continued to pay a shareholder dividend. However, Hill's rate slashing and dividends were by no means altruistic. Hill had never paid top dollar for labor, but as a cost-cutting measure he announced a 35 percent or more reduction in wages. Great Northern workers were still employed, but the cost for many was too high.

Typically, railroad laborers worked seven days a week, twelve hours a day, and often in a hazardous work environment. Great Northern coach cleaners in Seattle had subsisted on wages of $2 a week but now saw their paychecks slashed in half. Labor's response to management was to organize as Railroad Brotherhoods. In addition to protesting wage cuts, they documented and publicized shocking statistics.

When Jacob Coxey called for recruits, six hundred jobless men enlisted in his Seattle Army during the first week. Here in south Pioneer Square, a contingent passes muster before moving out to deliver its message to the nation's capital. Photo by C. L. Andrews. Museum of History and Industry, 16535

According to historian Carlos Schwantes, in 1893 "2,727 railroad workers were killed and another 31,729 injured in the line of duty. One of every 320 employees was killed that year, with the greatest number of injuries while coupling or uncoupling cars."

Local members of the American Railway Union participated in its nationwide strike to shut down railroads west of Chicago. They joined forces with jobless men, who rallied around Jacob Coxey, a disgruntled scrap dealer from Massilon, Ohio. "Coxey's Army" planned to march on the nation's capitol to deliver a "petition with boots on" to Congress. Schwantes writes, "The spectacle of unemployed workers making their way east via empty boxcars and an occasional stolen train was one of the most enduring images left by the depression of the 1890s."

At first Hill refused to budge and hired scabs. But the specter of armed confrontation on the Great Northern tracks was enough to make him yield to what was widely considered a union victory. While strikes paralyzed most of the railroads west of Chicago, the Great Northern continued its runs.

Nonetheless, Hill was no friend of the unions and clearly aligned himself with capitalists. In subsequent years, he undercut the solidarity of mainstream "white" unions by hiring crews that included ethnicities and races ineligible for union membership—notably Japanese and eastern European immigrants. Responding to pressure from the Railroad Brotherhoods, Hill gradually increased salaries to midscale among American railroad workers.

Taming a Tangle of Tracks

When the Great Northern began doing business in Seattle, a tangle of trestles, tracks, and freight facilities crisscrossed the saltwater tide flats that sprawled west from Beacon Hill and south from Pioneer Square. Perched atop bluffs in between were thriving industries, including Moran Brothers Shipyard and Stetson and Post Mill,

This turn-of-the-twentieth-century view from Beacon Hill shows the bustling maze of tracks and trains that was stifling commercial development. The tip of the tall smokestack on the right pinpoints the end of the block-long Great Northern freight shed on South Jackson Street. Museum of History and Industry, 83.10.6049.3

which were linked to the tracks by spur lines. A trestle extended west across the mouth of the Duwamish River to huge grain elevators in West Seattle. Tracks ran from Beacon Hill to coal bunkers on King Street Wharf and neighboring piers. From King and Jackson Streets, lines curved northward to congested Railroad Avenue. There, eight sets of tracks formed a danger zone between the business district and the commercial waterfront. Trainloads of lumber, agricultural produce, and coal steamed from the hinterlands to wharves and docks, where laborers coupled and uncoupled cars and transferred cargo to waiting ships or outbound trains.

In 1895 Hill exercised his right to erect freight facilities on South Jackson Street. Workers began filling in tide flats and dismantling ramshackle structures built on pilings. Many breathed a sigh of relief when Great Northern crews tore down the Never Touch Me Saloon and a bleak array of crib houses in Whitechapel and Blackchapel, the most notorious part of the Tenderloin District. A new blocklong freight terminal took their place. In addition to enhancing efficiency for the Great Northern, it provided a safer work environment for laborers.

Gateway to Asia

During the 1890s, Hill maintained a low public profile with only occasional visits to Seattle.

He negotiated an exclusive trade agreement between the Great Northern and the Nippon Yusen Kaisha (Japanese Steamship Line), fulfilling a long-sought dream. In August 1896 fireworks, brass bands, cheering crowds, and a flotilla of boats of all kinds welcomed to Seattle the *Miike Maru,* the first steamship to maintain a regular schedule between Seattle, Japan, and Hong Kong.

Other trade agreements followed with China. Silk soon became the Far East's most lucrative export. Longshoremen hastened to move perishable bales of the precious stuff onto the Great Northern's Silk Express, which sped to Hoboken on the eastern seaboard within an astonishing three days. The innovative collaboration between rail and ship put Atlanta cotton in Shanghai 197 days faster than any previous trade arrangement.

Chin Gee Hee was an importer and labor contractor whose business was at Second and Washington. He enjoyed respect from leading Seattleites, as did Asian diplomatic and trade delegations. But Japanese and Chinese laborers who worked for him continued to encounter racial prejudice, especially in stressful economic times. Photo by Asahel Curtis. MSCUA, *University of Washington Libraries, A Curtis 01281*

Ad in The Seattle Times, *August 1896, for the arrival of the Japanese Steamship Line.*

Hill's transcontinental lines consistently made the best time. He built two massive freighters and founded the Great Northern Steamship Line to bolster Asian trade. The "Empire Builder" predicted that Asian markets would take all the wheat Washington could raise and that timber sales would generate far more wealth for the state than any gold rush.

Portal to the Klondike

In 1897 the Great Northern was primed to benefit from the Klondike gold rush. Its trains and ships brought legions of prospectors, get-rich-quick entrepreneurs, and supplies to Seattle. Historians Lisa Mighetto and Marcia Babcock Montgomery note that at the end of the nineteenth century, Washington state's rail transports increased by as much as 50 percent per year.

Long before the gold rush, the Alaska Steamship Company and the North American Transportation and Trading Company had borne passengers and freight from Seattle to the far north. Between 1897 and 1898, the city's oceangoing fleet tripled in size. Seattle established itself as the West Coast's premier portal to Alaska and the Yukon. Locally, the economic depression came to an end, and Seattle's business community catapulted back to financial health.

Monopolistic Moves

The significance of Hill's enterprises did not go unnoticed in the local press. Alden Blethen, whose two Minneapolis newspapers had gone broke, had promoted Hill's empire in the Midwest. Knowing Blethen as a charismatic and outspoken ally, Hill loaned him $23,000 in 1896 to purchase *The Seattle Times*. Even after he repaid the loan, Blethen supported Hill's ventures and proclaimed him "the greatest railroad man of the age." Hill also bankrolled John L. Wilson's purchase of the *Seattle Post-Intelligencer*. While Seattle's morning and evening dailies disagreed on almost everything else, both gave unwavering support to the Great Northern. In 1897 *The Argus,* a Seattle weekly edited by Harry Chadwick, proclaimed "the Great Northern owns . . . *The Seattle Times.*"

In the mid-1890s, Hill made his move toward a railroad monopoly. With Henry Villard's encouragement, he laid plans to acquire the bankrupt Northern Pacific and bring it back to financial health. He arranged a meeting with financial titan J. P. Morgan, who agreed to back what was termed a merger. According to historian Kurt E. Armbruster, it bound the Great Northern and the Northern Pacific in "permanent alliance, defensive and in case of need offensive, with a view of avoiding competition."

By 1901 Hill was in control of both railroads. His giant Northern Securities Company effectively eliminated railroad competition in the state of Washington. He went so far as to enter into a short-lived agreement with Edward Henry Harriman, stipulating that Harriman's Union Pacific would not enter Washington and that Hill's railroads would stay out of Oregon. Historian Richard Berner notes that the agreement ensured high freight rates in the Northwest; at the same time, support of the dominant Republican Party effectively squelched would-be opponents.

Hill now turned his attention to the Northern Pacific's colossal land grants. His understanding of the politics and potential of lumber was no doubt influenced by lumber baron Frederick Weyerhaeuser, his neighbor on Summit Avenue in St. Paul and a member of the Great Northern's board of directors. At the time, Midwest forests were a diminishing resource, and clearcuts scarred the region. Hill arranged for Weyerhaeuser to purchase 900,000 acres of Northern Pacific timberland in Washington state at the phenomenal bargain price of $6 per acre. Within a decade, Weyerhaeuser's waterfront sawmill in Everett mushroomed to the largest in the world. Soon other Great Lakes investors came west to establish their own lumber companies that shipped wood and wood products via Hill's railroads.

Locating the Premier Entrance

Thanks to the Great Northern, the Klondike gold rush, and Seattle's diversified economic base, the city's population almost doubled during the 1890s. At the turn of the twentieth century, there were 80,671 residents. Newcomers continued to arrive at a steadily increasing rate, and there was no end in sight for the population boom. Thus, visionaries were reconfiguring

The Northern Pacific's depot at the foot of Columbia Street served passengers from 1892 to 1906. The towering smokestack behind it marks the Seattle Steam Plant, which is still in operation. Most of the other large buildings in the area are commission houses that bought and sold meat, dairy products, and produce from regional farms. Museum of History and Industry, PEMCO, 83.10.6939

the city to accommodate growth and foster economic development.

Seattle's maze of railroad tracks and inadequate passenger facilities was no longer adequate. For more than a decade, the Great Northern and the Northern Pacific had shared the dilapidated wooden depot at the foot of Columbia Street. Historian Welford Beaton recalled: "It was perhaps the worst excuse for a depot operated by any railway in the world in a city as large as Seattle had become. It was a sore spot with the citizens, who had to apologize for it." Whenever anyone complained, Hill responded with his oft-quoted maxim: "He is a wise farmer who develops his farm before he builds a palace on it." With his own agenda in mind, he explained, "It is more important to Seattle to have goods delivered to it cheaply than to have a fancy depot." Nonetheless,

Seattle's patience was wearing thin. Ever the pragmatist, Hill weathered the recessionary 1890s, quietly accumulating property on the tide flats south of Pioneer Square.

Shortly before the end of the nineteenth century, the Northern Pacific's president, Charles S. Mellon, proposed his own grand scheme for Seattle's railroads. He wanted to transform the downtown waterfront into a giant freight yard and erect an imposing $500,000 passenger station in the heart of the city. Years earlier, city engineer R. H. Thomson had persuaded Hill to change his original plans for this area, which would have worsened congestion on the waterfront and in Pioneer Square. This time, the Hill forces used the same arguments to convince the Seattle City Council to reject Mellon's proposal.

When Hill gained control of the Northern

Pacific, he unveiled plans to build a passenger depot on his property at King Street. At the time, buildings and streets in the vicinity stood on pilings above the high-tide mark. Hill planned to fill in the tide flats south and west of the depot for a unified system of tracks, sheds, and freight yards.

But Henry H. Dearborn, a realtor and investment broker, argued tenaciously for placing the station farther south. He explained to the January 6, 1901, *Daily Bulletin:* "We think railways terminating at Seattle should not be allowed to monopolize nearly all tide land south of King Street, as much of this property will soon be indispensable for business. Unless it is decided now to place the depot as far south as Atlantic Street and freightyards at least two miles out, everyone, including railroad officials will regret it." Nobody listened when he said, "A depot on King Street would more effectually cut the town in two than coal bunkers, freight yards and railroad warehouses now do."

Dearborn peered into the ooze at the mouth of the Duwamish and envisioned huge values buried in the mud and under acres of salt water that extended east to the foot of Beacon Hill and south. Streets on the tidelands had been platted some twenty-five years earlier, but boundaries were still marked by buoys instead of stakes. In July 1912, *Sunset Magazine* reported that at businessmen's clubs, chairs reportedly became vacant and groups dispersed when Dearborn approached to begin his inevitable refrain: "Waal, friends, tidelands has riz. Better come over to the office and let me fix up a deed to a piece of it. It'll only cost you ten a month, and it'll make you a fortune." Few took him seriously when he explained that, once filled, the tidelands would connect the city with lowlands extending south for more than twenty miles. He explained that "business always seeks a level, yet strangers say our city is all hills."

Dearborn watched, waited, and continued giving his spiel while city engineers hatched schemes to lower Seattle's steep hills and level downtown streets.

From Tunnel to Terminal

In 1903 the Great Northern and the Northern Pacific began work on the downtown tunnel beneath Fourth Avenue that Hill had promised to construct a decade earlier. With picks and shovels in hand, a crew that eventually numbered 1,000 men started digging at both ends. When they met in the middle a year and a half later, the hole was off by only one-eighth inch at the ceiling and one-fourth inch at the walls. The tunnel was almost a mile long, with ample room for two parallel tracks. As of this writing, it remains in service, and passenger trains continue to roll through it underneath the downtown core. A still-told joke is that it is "the longest tunnel in the world, running all the way from Virginia to Washington" (Streets).

Before work could begin on Hill's depot, crews moved earth from the tunnel to fill in the marshy site south of it, where tracks and terminal yards would be located. The Pacific Coast Coal Company tore up its tracks on King Street, along with its massive coal bunkers. Pile drivers drove a forest of underpinnings into the ground to form a foundation for the new "Union Depot," so-called because it would serve more than one railroad (now King Street Station).

Hill commissioned esteemed architects Charles A. Reed and Allen H. Stem of St. Paul, who had designed more than a hundred railroad stations throughout the nation, including New York City's Grand Central. They modeled the signature clock tower of King Street Station after the campanile of Piazza San Marco in Venice, Italy. The base structure typifies popular depot design of the era: large passenger waiting

The Great Northern tunnel under construction. Museum of History and Industry, 8903

rooms, lunch counters, ticket counter, and baggage handling facilities on the main floor, with offices upstairs. The public areas featured neoclassical design elements, including coffered ceilings, intricate plaster panels, and high marble wainscoting, topped with a belt of glass and gilded mosaic.

A crew of craftspeople, decorators, and painters labored to complete the interior finishes by June 1906 for the targeted grand opening. But Hill changed his plans and sent word that the first trains would arrive on May 10. Because the interior was still unfinished, the station opened without celebratory speeches or ceremonies. According to the *Post-Intelligencer,* "Crowds thronged the depot all day long . . . and the workmen finishing the interior of the magnificent passenger structure had difficulty to continue work at times during the day." The article heralded the opening as "the passage of the old and the beginning of the new in this city."

The contrast between the former shabby passenger shed and the new depot extended beyond the architecture to a new sense of decorum. King Street Station doubled as a civic center. The eclectic mix of tourists, Alaska-bound miners, businessmen, passengers both rich and poor, and immigrants from all over the world remained, but the depot was no longer home to large numbers of drunks and "unwashed men." One of the features was the elegantly furnished Ladies Waiting Room, staffed by a depot matron, as in other cities. Sue Stine was hired and supervised by the Young Women's Christian Association, but the railroads paid her salary. An important part of her job was "to guard and guide young women traveling alone." If they were without resources, she referred them to the YWCA to keep them out of reach of pimps and ne'er-do-wells who lurked about on streets near the depots. The program was the forerunner of the Travelers Aid Society.

The July 10, 1906, *Post-Intelligencer* covered Hill's speech at the prestigious Rainier Club, at Fourth and Columbia, in which he paid tribute to Seattle and underscored the Great Northern's impact on the city's fortunes. Reminiscing about

Stationmaster J. A. McBean presides at King Street Station. Photo by James Patrick Lee. MSCUA, University of Washington Libraries, Lee 20011

his choice of the terminus years earlier, he said: "There were other harbors certainly as good as this to the north of you. [But] the crowd of people in Seattle even in those days impressed me, and I thought that it would be cruel not to give them a chance to work out their own salvation. . . . We have received loyal support here . . . but we have put more money into Seattle than we ever took out in profits. . . . Today there is no city of your size anywhere that has the terminal facilities you will have within the next six months. It is only your hope and inflexible pluck that has saved your lives."

Leveling Seattle

Within a short time, King Street Station stood in stark contrast to chaotic surroundings. City Engineer R. H. Thomson was obsessed with the idea that business seeks level ground. On completion of the railroad tunnel, he came up with a master plan to reconfigure Seattle's topography to what today's residents accept as nature's design. Beginning with the Jackson Street Regrade (1907–1908), workers borrowed techniques used by hydraulic miners in the goldfields. They pumped water under high pressure to flush tons of earth from the steep hill into the tide flats. The regrade cut away the hill by as much as eighty-five feet, lowering the steepest grades from 15 to 5 percent. Almost every building was razed or moved. Chinatown and Japantown (now the International District) took root on the leveled ground.

Former state governor Eugene Semple headed another large-scale project, to dig a south canal waterway from Elliott Bay through Beacon Hill to Lake Washington. His project included filling in tide flats in what is now the South Downtown (SoDo) neighborhood and selling reclaimed land. Representing the Great Northern, Judge Burke outmaneuvered Semple. He successfully pushed through a plan to build the canal north of downtown from Salmon Bay to Lake Union and on to Lake Washington. In the meantime, Semple's landfill contributed

Telephone operators at King Street Station, 1907. Photo by James Patrick Lee. MSCUA, University of Washington Libraries, 20109

Jackson Street regrade, looking west. King Street Station is right from the center. The men could be workers taking a break or curious bystanders. Museum of History and Industry, 83.10.8131

substantially to Seattle's industrial heartland, extending from south Pioneer Square to Georgetown.

Public Versus Railroad Interests

For years, the Seattle City Council had wooed the railroads with franchises and gifts of public tidelands. The situation had parallels across the nation, where rapidly expanding frontiers created unprecedented opportunities for growth and industrial development. Men of genius and cunning made fortunes. A ruthless competitor, Hill strove to control commerce by monopolizing transportation. He and J. P. Morgan headed the board of the giant Northern Securities Company, an umbrella for the Great Northern, Northern Pacific, and Burlington Northern Railroads. In 1902 the U.S. Attorney General successfully brought suit against Northern Securities, making it the first major target of the Sherman Anti-Trust Act. President Theodore

Roosevelt subsequently earned his reputation as a trustbuster. Hill nonetheless found ways to continue to exert a controlling influence on both the Northern Pacific and the Great Northern.

In Seattle, trains ran back and forth through Hill's tunnel beneath downtown, but Railroad Avenue remained chaotic. Squabbles for rights-of-way continued. Congestion worsened, reflecting the city's explosive population and economic boom. A danger zone of railroad tracks, spur lines, and freight yards continued to separate downtown from waterfront wharves. Private ownership had resulted in a lack of railroad traffic laws. As a result, teamsters could block traffic with their wagons; junk dealers could leave scrap on the tracks; and railcars frequently had to be switched from track to track. Gridlock traffic, accidents, and speeds of five miles per hour were commonplace.

Citizens fought back, organizing a campaign against the decades-long corporate dominance

*Union Station's Great Hall and the magnificent semicircular window that spans its entire
south facade. Photo by Asahel Curtis. Washington State Historical Society, Tacoma*

of Railroad Avenue. In 1911 a majority of voters
created the municipally owned Port of Seattle,
which put the city's harbor under public ownership and management. Hill and other railroad
interests attempted to squelch the move through
the courts, but public sentiment prevailed. The
victory was a high point for the local Progressive
Movement.

Hill Keynotes Opening of World's Fair

On June 2, 1909, Governor Marion E. Hay welcomed James J. Hill on behalf of Washington
State to keynote the opening ceremony of the
Alaska-Yukon-Pacific Exposition, Seattle's first
world's fair. Hill used the occasion to recap the
enormous impact of the railroads on the development of the Pacific Northwest. He made a
case for the potential of regional private enterprise unimpeded by government constraints. At
the same time, he urged the Northwest not to
make the mistakes of older parts of the country
and to protect its remaining natural resources,

notably lumber, soil, and fisheries. The "Empire
Builder" saw no contradiction between his
appeals for unfettered private enterprise and
protection of the environment. His speech,
which was reprinted in the *Post-Intelligencer,*
is excerpted here:

"Men of our day move toward their material
advances largely through the struggle for wealth. . . .

"The occasion [AYPE] marks a change in conscious attitude of the Pacific Coast toward the rest
of the country. . . . There was once a certain aloof-
ness, a certain supremacy of separate and independent interest . . . a kind of indifference about what
might be happening beyond the mountain barrier
to the East. . . . The coming of the transcontinental railroad first shattered this isolation. . . .

"In 1866 people of Washington asked Congress
to secure fishing rights in Alaskan waters. Gold
no longer constitutes her chief promise. . . . All
the precious metals, coal in abundance, fisheries
of great value; timber that may possibly become
the last resource of a wasteful nation . . . Alaska has
modified profoundly and accelerated the progress

and increase of wealth on the Pacific Coast. This great city [Seattle] reckons her resources and her trade as its most valuable asset.

"When capital can be enticed back into railroad investment by assurance of proper protection and a reasonable return, the progress of construction will do more for the Pacific Northwest than for any other part of the country.

"The Pacific Coast completes our national heritage. [Here] first rose a vision of Oriental trade which if left to develop without legislative interference might by this time have realized all anticipations."

The Union Pacific Comes to Seattle

While government chipped away at their power, the Northwest's two railroad titans, Hill and his rival, Edward Henry Harriman, were finding new strength in collaboration. The Great Northern extended service into Oregon, while Harriman's Oregon-Washington Railway, a subsidiary of his Union Pacific, reached across the border into Washington. The lines agreed to share tracks between Portland and Seattle.

Shortly after the opening of King Street Station in 1906, Harriman began purchasing underwater acreage in south Pioneer Square for his own future station and freight yard. The move set off the boom that the aging realtor Henry H. Dearborn had predicted years before. He posted his slogan "Tidelands has riz!" on his building in south Pioneer Square, and speculators lined up at his door. Dearborn became a "tide-flat millionaire."

Harriman entered Seattle as a fierce competitor, building his depot a block east of King Street Station. Designed by architect Daniel J. Patterson, the neoclassical Oregon and Washington Station (now Union Station) opened in 1911, heralded as the "handsomest on Harriman's lines." Notable architectural features include the barrel-vaulted Great Hall

and the magnificent semicircular window that spans its south facade. Promotional literature touted the station's "sanitary elegance," noting for example that there were no spittoons in the Great Hall. Within a week, Harriman's depot began providing service to a second line, the Milwaukee, the nation's last transcontinental railroad. Sometime later, the depot's name was changed to Union Station.

Interurban Railways

At the turn of the twentieth century, newly available electric trolleys sparked nationwide interest. Under management of Boston-based Stone and Webster, the Seattle Electric Company laid tracks through the White River valley to Tacoma for the Puget Sound Interurban Railway, which commenced service in 1902.

The electric train to Tacoma picks up passengers at Seattle's Interurban depot in 1903. The photographer, Asahel Curtis, was looking north on Occidental Avenue toward the Seattle Hotel on Yesler Way. MSCUA, *University of Washington Archives, A Curtis 05611*

Passengers waited at the Interurban depot at Occidental Avenue South and Yesler Way to board the wooden cars that made the seventy-minute run each way every hour.

The system gave rural residents easy access to city shopping and provided city dwellers with inexpensive outings through scenic valley farmlands. Daily freight runs brought fresh produce, dairy products, and meat to urban markets. Branch lines provided connections for Renton and Puyallup, while other companies served Everett and Bellingham. The electric trains supplanted the steam rails as the favored mode of local transit. In the 1920s, public preference changed again; the interurban lines closed down, giving way to the automobile and the bus.

Porters serve passengers at a Seattle station in 1934. African American railroad workers, most of whom were porters, cooks, and waiters, were members of the Sleeping Car Porters Club. Founded in 1892, it was an employment and recreation center located at Second and Jackson. Museum of History and Industry, PEMCO 139,954

Then and Now

The history of railroading in Seattle parallels the city's development and vision of its future prosperity. Like today's communications networks, railroading in the nineteenth century represented more than steel tracks and trade. The romantic and practical potential of the rails wooed communities, especially in the West, much as Web commerce entices contemporary generations. In a 1902 magazine article, a fictional teacher asks a student, "Who made the world?" The student replies, "God made the world in 4004 B.C. But it was reorganized in 1901 by James J. Hill, J. Pierpont Morgan, John D. Rockefeller, and Edward H. Harriman." Today the student might credit Paul Allen and Bill Gates for the world's reorganization in the late twentieth century.

When they were new, King Street and Union Stations served as transportation and civic centers that gave definition and stature to a proud city and that fueled the regional economy. In the 1990s, Paul Allen's Vulcan Northwest and Nitze-Stagen formed Union Station Associates, a partnership to develop adjacent office, parking, and retail projects. Lead partners Kevin Daniels and Frank Stagen saw the potential of the historic station as a natural "front door" to their projects, with the potential of reclaiming its original role. In 1996 they met with Sound Transit, following the endorsement by voters in King, Pierce, and Snohomish Counties of a seamless system of regional "Sounder" commuter trains, "Link" light rail, and "ST Express" bus service. Sound Transit's board gladly accepted Daniels' and Stagen's offer to restore the historic station as the agency's headquarters and return it to public ownership and use. Today Union Station is meticulously restored as the hub of the regional transportation system, while King Street Station serves as the passenger depot for Amtrak. The century-old tunnel underneath Fourth Avenue remains part of the rail corridor for Amtrak and Sounder passenger trains.

Other public transportation and related projects are contributing to the historic transportation center. Thanks to former City Councilor and Municipality of Metropolitan Seattle (Metro) Chairman George Benson, Seattle once again has vintage streetcars that run from the central waterfront through Pioneer Square to their final stop near the historic depots. And Metro buses carry passengers through the Downtown Transit Tunnel, constructed beneath Third Avenue in 1990, to its southern terminus, the International District station and plaza, adjacent to Union Station. The new Weller Street pedestrian bridge crosses lines of track,

providing easy access from Fourth Avenue South to Seahawks Stadium and Safeco Field.

Today the historic red brick depots form a dramatic hub for regional transit and an anchor for the contemporary office buildings, parking garages, and sports stadiums that loom behind them. Significantly, the architectural complex preserves Pioneer Square's legacy as a premier entrance to the city.

But Seattle's role as a regional transportation center predates its historic stations. By the mid-1890s, the Great Northern had established efficient transcontinental connections that made it possible for enterprising city boosters to take full advantage of the Klondike gold rush and the Spanish American War, two seminal events that helped further shape the city's identity.

Sound Transit's vision of the regional transportation center. Rendering by J. Craig Thorpe. Courtesy of Sound Transit

5 Prospectors and Patriots

Marc Blackburn

Between 1890 and 1910, Seattle's population nearly quadrupled, from 43,000 to a staggering 200,000 people. The railroads contributed to the growth while creating a national transportation network that enabled the city to capitalize on two vastly different events: the discovery of gold in the Klondike and the Spanish-American War. The synergy of transcontinental rail lines, gold fever, and well-connected entrepreneurs rocketed Seattle out of the depression of the 1890s. The Klondike gold rush and the war in the Philippines brought a unique blend of characters to the already colorful city.

The Stampede of '97

In the summer of 1896, a tall, wiry man with small, intense eyes and a mustache that drooped across his lips like walrus whiskers walked into Bill McPhee's saloon at the Fortymile mining camp, located below the mouth of the Klondike River in the Canadian Yukon. Boasting to anyone who would listen, the man exclaimed that he had found gold on Rabbit Creek, a tributary of the Klondike River. George Washington Carmack's boasts fell on deaf ears until he dumped the contents of a rifle cartridge onto the bar. As the gold dust and nuggets spilled across the liquor-stained surface, the spectators knew that Carmack was telling the truth: gold had been found in the Klondike.

Would-be millionaires rushed out to stake their claims. They toiled through the bitterly cold winter of 1896–97, mining the permanently frozen, gold-bearing gravel. With the arrival of the spring thaw and a supply of running water, the great piles of gravel were sifted and the gold removed. The richest claims produced thousands of dollars' worth of gold nuggets and dust in just one season, forever changing the lives of the claim holders. Many of these newly minted millionaires then ventured south by ship to such cities as San Francisco and Seattle.

In the late spring of 1897, two ships—the *SS Excelsior* and *SS Portland*—departed from St. Michael, Alaska, an old Russian trading post close to the mouth of the Yukon on the Bering Sea. The *Excelsior* arrived in San Francisco on July 15, 1897; the *Portland* arrived in Seattle two days later. In anticipation of the *Portland*'s arrival, an enterprising reporter for the *Seattle Post-Intelligencer,* Beriah Brown, chartered a tugboat that intercepted the *Portland* in the Strait of Juan de Fuca. After quickly interviewing some of the miners, he returned to the tug and filed his story from a telegraph office in Port Townsend. On July 17, Brown's story dominated the front page as headlines screamed, "Gold! Gold! Gold! Gold!—Sixty-Eight Rich Men on the Steamer Portland."

Newsboys spread through the streets of Seattle, selling papers as fast as they could be purchased. Spurred on by the news of Klondike gold, thousands of people came to the waterfront to greet the treasure ship. As the *Portland* tied up, its passengers saw thousands of cheering people welcoming them to Seattle and the Northwest.

The *Portland*'s cargo of gold captured the nation's imagination, triggering a stampede north to the Klondike that had far-reaching effects on Seattle. The coming of the gold rush accelerated the explosive growth that had begun a decade earlier with the arrival of the Northern Pacific and Great Northern Railroads. It immediately ended the lingering effects in Seattle of the Panic of 1893. It also forged a link between Seattle, Alaska, and Canada that is evident to this day.

Gateway to the Klondike

While many cities on the western seaboard, from San Francisco to Vancouver, British Columbia, took advantage of the Klondike excitement, Seattle offered several unique advantages. The first was geographic proximity; the second, transportation.

In 1897 the most direct path to the goldfields was by boat through the Inside Passage, the route that threads through the islands of the panhandle of southeast Alaska. A thousand miles from Seattle, in the far northeastern corner of the passage, is Skagway. It was the hub for the two primary routes that crossed the coastal moun-

Stampeders compete for passage on Alaska-bound ships. Here, a throng jams the dock to give the Queen *a rousing sendoff. Photo by Anders B. Wilse. Museum of History and Industry, 88.33.116*

tains to the headwaters of the Yukon River. From Skagway, the stampeder could cross the mountains into Canada from either the Chilkoot or White Pass Trail. Once across the mountains, the miners continued north 500 miles on the Yukon River to Dawson City and the Klondike goldfields—a 1,500-mile journey from Seattle. Despite the rigors of travel across the mountains, the trails from Skagway offered the most direct and affordable route to the goldfields.

An alternative route to the Klondike was entirely by water. It was also, not surprisingly, a more expensive route. A ship took the miners from Seattle to St. Michael, Alaska, via the Aleutian Islands. From St. Michael, riverboats took passengers from the delta of the Yukon through central Alaska to the goldfields, a total distance of more than 3,700 miles.

Whether a stampeder chose to ascend the heights of Chilkoot Pass or brave the rough waters of the Gulf of Alaska and Bering Sea, Seattle was the largest and closest American city to the Klondike goldfields. This geographic advantage was further strengthened by the presence of steamship companies that took passengers and freight north. The Pacific Coast Steamship Company, the Alaska Steamship Company, and the North American Transportation and Trading Company had ticket agents in Pioneer Square and ships that left regularly from the wharves that dotted the Seattle waterfront. Seattle was also the western terminus of a number of local and transcontinental rail lines. The Northern Pacific, Great Northern, Canadian Pacific, and Union Pacific Railroads all had direct rail links or spurs to Seattle. This allowed local merchants relatively easy access to goods from the nation's manufacturing and distribution centers and provided rail passengers direct routes to the city.

Mining the Miners

Complementing geographic proximity and transportation to the goldfields were the goods and services offered by Seattle's merchants. The great distances miners had to travel from the states, the lack of a commercial infrastructure in Dawson City in 1897, the Yukon's atrocious winter climate, and Canadian regulations governing travel to the goldfields provided Seattle merchants with a unique opportunity to provide services to the prospectors. A marketing campaign was unleashed across the country to attract business to the city.

Prior to the discovery of gold in 1896, a seasonal Native fishing camp occupied the site of the future Dawson City. Supplies could be procured at the Fortymile mining camp a few miles below the mouth of the Klondike River or in a small trading post at the foot of the Chilkoot Trail, 500 miles to the south. In either case, these small trading posts served only the most immediate needs of their communities. Even Juneau, Alaska, the most substantial settlement along the Inside Passage, 600 miles south of the goldfields, was neither prepared nor able to handle the needs of stampeders who headed north expecting to get a head start by skimping on preparations in the name of expediency.

As the first waves of the stampede hit the Klondike goldfields in the late fall of 1897, many miners were caught unprepared for the long winters typical of the Yukon River basin. Once the river froze, usually by December, travel by boat was impossible. To prevent a famine as well as preserve the health and welfare of the people who were about to embark on the difficult trek, Canadian officials issued a ruling that required everyone crossing its border to have in their possession the necessary provisions and equipment for one year in the goldfields.

To fulfill these obligations, most stampeders

Cooper and Levy Pioneer Outfitters, located on the southeast corner of First and Yesler, piled supplies on the sidewalk. Nearby hotels, saloons, brothels, and banks did a lively business. Photo by Asahel Curtis, ca. 1898. MSCUA, *University of Washington Libraries, A Curtis 26368*

purchased their outfits at their point of departure. With its robust and knowledgeable merchant community, established maritime links to Alaska, a comprehensive regional and intercontinental rail system, and geographic proximity to the goldfields, Seattle stood ready to reap the rewards of the Canadian ruling, which was rigorously enforced by the Royal Canadian Mounted Police.

Retailers in Seattle craved the business that the gold rush would bring. Since the Panic of 1893, the nation had been locked in a deep depression and was in the throes of a political debate that would dominate the decade of the 1890s. The Populists, led by William Jennings Bryan, and the political establishment of the time waged a war of words over the relative merits of silver versus gold currency. Despite the rural roots of this populist revolt, Bryan's pro-silver arguments resonated with small-business owners, who had difficulty securing

investment capital to sustain their businesses. High unemployment and labor unrest kept profits down.

The arrival of the *Portland* and subsequent excitement over Klondike gold transformed struggling businesses virtually overnight. The November 25 *Seattle Daily Times* enthusiastically reported, "Six months ago everyone looked blue, money was scarce and employment hard to secure. . . . Today large business houses are doing a rushing business, almost every week new business blocks are going up to be occupied by moneyed men from the East." Spurred by the demand, outfitters, clothiers, and hardware stores saw their business skyrocket in the opening months of the Klondike gold rush.

A Ton of Goods

Virtually every item, from necessities to extravagances, could be obtained in Seattle. Everything

Some prospectors bought dog teams and sleds in Seattle to carry their supplies through the snow. Any dog that seemed strong enough could be pressed into service. Here, men inspect a team made up of St. Bernards, laborador retrievers, and mixed breeds. Museum of History and Industry 88.33.244

from packhorses to liniment, boots to portable stoves and even sled dogs could be purchased at any number of establishments in the commercial district. Two prominent outfitters in the Klondike trade, Cooper and Levy and Schwabacher Hardware Company, were located in Pioneer Square. Despite being across the street from one another at the corner of First Avenue and Yesler Way, the two stores reaped huge profits, selling goods to the miners going north. Both establishments offered all of the provisions and equipment needed to complete an outfit.

To attract potential customers, many of the outfitters offered standard lists and prices for an outfit—food, clothing, and equipment—available for one price at one retail establishment. The basic list of provisions and equipment did not vary considerably from one store to another, though the prices paid for these goods could range from $150 to $250—a considerable sum in 1897. Outfitting guides such as *The Chicago Record's Book for Gold Seekers* feature a typical outfit of provisions and equipment required of each individual for a year.

FOOD

Bacon	150 Pounds
Flour	400 Pounds
Rolled Oats	25 Pounds
Beans	125 pounds
Tea	10 Pounds
Coffee	10 Pounds
Sugar	25 Pounds
Dried Potatoes	25 Pounds
Salt	15 Pounds
Pepper	1 Pound
Dried Fruit	75 Pounds
Baking Soda	8 Pounds
Evaporated Vinegar	8 Ounces
Compressed Soup	12 Ounces
Soap	9 Cakes
Dried Mustard	1 Can
Matches	1 Tin
	(for four men)

1 Stove

Gold Pan

Set of Steel Enamel Buckets

Large Bucket

Knife, Fork, Spoon, Cup, Plate

Frying Pan

Coffee and Tea Pot

Scythe Stone

Two Picks and One Shovel

One Whipsaw

Pack Strap

Two Axes (for Four Men) and one extra
Handle

Six 8–inch Files and two Taper Files

Draw Knife, Brace and Bits, Jack Plane,
Hammer

200 feet of 3/8–inch Rope

Five pounds each of 6, 8, 10, and 12 Penny
Nails

Shoemaker's Thread

Shoemaker's Awl

Gum (for patching gum boots)

10 x 12 Tent (for four men)

Canvas (for wrapping)

Two Oil Blankets

Five yards of Mosquito Netting (for each man)

CLOTHING

3 Suits of Heavy Underwear

1 Heavy Mackinaw Coat

2 Pairs of Heavy Mackinaw Trousers

6 Pairs of Heavy Wool Socks

6 Pairs of Heavy Wool Mittens

2 Heavy Over Shirts

2 Pairs of Heavy Snagproof Boots

2 Pairs of Shoes

3 Pairs of Blankets (for two men)

4 Towels

2 Pairs of Overalls

Cooper and Levy advertisement from the
Seattle Times.

1 Suit of Oil Clothing

2 Rubber Blankets

While these outfitting merchandisers aggressively advertised their services in the local newspapers, their success could be attributed to a citywide marketing machine that sold Seattle to the world.

Seattle Markets Itself

To help cement in the mind of the public the city's reputation as an outfitting center, an alliance of city boosters and merchants inaugurated a marketing campaign. At the end of August 1897, the Seattle Chamber of Commerce called an all-city meeting to discuss possible strategies for bringing business into Seattle. Hundreds of people attended the meeting and proposed the creation of a Klondike Information Bureau to market Seattle's goods and services across the country. Six respected business leaders were chosen to staff the committee,

Sales skyrocketed at M. and K. Gottstein Wholesale Liquors and Cigar, located at First and Cherry. Courtesy of Meyer Gottstein's great-grandson, Kenny Alhadeff

and Erastus Brainerd, the seventh member, was chosen as the group's secretary.

Brainerd became the prime mover behind the committee, working nearly single-handedly to make the city the epicenter of the Klondike gold-rush outfitting trade. He had moved to Seattle in 1890 from Philadelphia, Pennsylvania, where he had worked in the newspaper business. With his background in journalism, Brainerd became the editor of *The Press-Times* and ingratiated himself with the Seattle social scene. He joined the Rainier Club, the city's posh gentleman's club, and made the necessary connections to the local political, cultural, and economic elite. As secretary of the Klondike Information Bureau, Brainerd mobilized the business community to leverage Seattle's advantages as *the* outfitting center for the Klondike gold rush.

Rather than depend on the Chamber of Commerce for funding, the Klondike Information Bureau solicited pledges of monetary support directly from the business community. From October 1897 to the following March, the committee was able to collect nearly $10,000 from a wide variety of businesses across the city.

Using his connections with the elite, along with his journalistic instincts, Brainerd concluded an agreement with the *Seattle Post-Intelligencer* to print 200,000 copies of a special advertising supplement for distribution to post offices and public libraries around the country. Great Northern and Northern Pacific Railroad employees also aggressively distributed Brainerd's materials in stations and on passenger trains along the lines headed into Seattle.

Brainerd closely supervised the advertising campaign to insure its success. With the aid of a news clipping service, he kept track of how major newspapers throughout the country were reporting on Seattle and the services it provided for the stampeders. If he found an omission of fact or a fabrication, he would pen a letter to the editor with the necessary corrections. His letters appeared in the editorial sections of several prominent newspapers, including the *Boston Globe, New York Mail, Salt Lake Herald, Denver Times,* and *St. Louis Post Dispatch.*

Brainerd also arranged to have Seattle publicized through several national magazines such as *Harpers Weekly, Scribner's,* and *Cosmopolitan.* He received help from outfitting guides published by individual merchants and trade associations. Publications entitled *The Alaskan Intelligence Bureau, Klondike Grubstakes,* and *Facts for Klondykers* all unabashedly declared that "Seattle stands unrivaled" as the gateway to the Klondike.

Seattle offered every service a prospective miner needed: a bed for the night, outfitters, grocery stores, hardware stores, clothiers, steamship ticket agents, and entertainment. After a hectic day of preparations, a fatigued stampeder could find plenty of diversion; there were saloons, dance halls, theaters, and houses of prostitution on the fringes of the commercial district, including much of Pioneer Square. The crowds of people wandering the streets also attracted pickpockets and petty thieves from across the region, ready to prey on unsuspecting victims.

Brainerd's enthusiasm and dedication helped spark the commercial revival of Pioneer Square, revitalizing a community that had grown stagnant during the recession of the 1890s. While the merchants welcomed the new business, not everyone was happy about the mobs of expectant miners descending on the heart of old Seattle. Chapter 6 explores the effects of the rougher side of the miner trade on what was commonly known as the Tenderloin or Skid Road District.

Bankers at the Scandinavian National Bank on the southwest corner of First and Yesler stand behind a counter loaded with gold. Seattle boosters successfully persuaded the federal government to establish an assay office in the city. Photo by Asahel Curtis. Museum of History and Industry, SHS 404

Prosperity in the Shipyards

Outfitters and purveyors of vice were the most visible beneficiaries of the Klondike gold rush, but the great stampede north also stimulated other industries, in particular shipbuilding. In the late nineteenth century, the area south of King Street was dominated by a great tidal mudflat, a prime location for shipyards—and a very successful location at that.

In 1889 Robert Moran and his two brothers purchased a twenty-three-acre site on those tide flats (on the current site of the Seahawks Stadium) to expand their successful machine shop into a full-blown shipyard. They incorporated as Moran Brothers Shipyard and had the capacity to build machinery as well as wooden and steeled-hulled ships. They quickly garnered a number of government contracts and orders from the private sector.

With the Klondike gold rush, a mad scramble ensued to provide ocean and river transportation for miners. The Seattle-based Yukon Company secured a contract with the Moran Brothers Shipyard to build twelve river steamers and five barges to work the length of the Yukon River, carrying supplies and passengers from Dawson City to the Alaskan coast.

By the early spring of 1898 the boats were finished, and Robert Moran accompanied the small fleet on the perilous journey from Seattle to St. Michael for delivery. The makeshift flotilla departed Seattle in May 1898 and reached St. Michael, via the Aleutian Islands, nearly two months later. In the course of this harrowing voyage, one of the ships was lost in a storm and another damaged. But the shipyard continued to prosper after the gold rush.

The Spanish-American War Rallies Seattle

While the nation's attention was focused on the Klondike, another drama was unfolding on the other side of the continent, and it would quickly push the story of the gold rush off the front page of newspapers across the country. On February 15, 1898, as the battleship USS *Maine* swung lazily at its anchor in the harbor of Havana, Cuba, a tremendous explosion suddenly shattered the quiet night and sent her quickly to the bottom. Two hundred sixty-six sailors did not survive the blast. Newspaper headlines screamed for revenge as "Remember the Maine" became the public's rallying cry. Despite his reluctance to enter the fray, President William McKinley demanded that Spain end its occupation of Cuba. Undeterred, Spain declared war on the United States on April 23, 1898; the United States reciprocated two days later.

In a wave of patriotic jubilation, young men across Seattle volunteered for service to fight Spanish forces in the Caribbean, and Governor John R. Rogers mobilized the Washington

National Guard. More than twelve hundred men filled out the ranks of the First Washington Infantry Regiment, including two companies of infantry from Seattle and ten others from both sides of the Cascade divide. As they impatiently trained at Camp Lewis in Pierce County, the campaign in Cuba came to a close, opening up the possibility that these men would be shipped instead to the Philippine Islands.

In May 1898, Admiral George Dewey took his squadron of warships to the Philippines, smashing the Spanish naval flotilla in Manila Bay. His presence gave revolutionary Emilio Aguinaldo hope of securing American support in the fight for Philippino independence. Dewey, uncertain of the situation, requested that the War Department send soldiers to the Philippines. The First Washington Infantry Regiment boarded ships in Seattle that steamed south to San Francisco, then the Philippines, arriving on Thanksgiving Day 1898.

Rather than granting the Philippines independence, Spain ceded the archipelago to the United States as part of the peace settlement, the December 1898 Treaty of Paris, that ended the Spanish-American War. Tensions between the Americans and Aguinaldo's troops increased as scattered skirmishes escalated into a full-fledged conflict by February 1899. As the war unfolded, the First Washington Infantry Regiment was involved in the siege of Manila and the subsequent campaigns in the area surrounding the city.

On the home front, supportive citizens formed a variety of patriotic organizations. In June 1898, 100 women met at the Elks Hall in the Colman Building (at First Avenue and Columbia Street) to organize civilian support for American troops going overseas. The women responded enthusiastically when Mary B. Brainerd, Erastus's wife, who was a close friend of Clara Barton, suggested forming a local Red Cross Society. Members sewed comfort bags, knit bandages, and collected wagonloads of food to ship to soldiers stationed in Cuba and the Philippines. According to Mary Brainerd's report in the Red Cross archives, "There was much to do as the nine transports which sailed from Puget Sound received their last American cheers from us."

Exhausted after eighteen months of fighting, the Washingtonians were sent home, where they received a magnificent welcome. The celebration, held at the beginning of November 1899, lasted three days, attracting thousands of people from all over the region. The main event was a grand regimental parade through Pioneer Place and down First Avenue. A *Seattle Daily Times* reporter noted, "There was not a foot of the avenue that was not jammed with human beings. . . . It was a great day." The celebrations ended with a spectacular pyrotechnic display.

Over the course of the campaign, the First Washington Infantry Regiment had lost 129 men, including Captain George Fortson, a popular company commander who had served as Seattle city attorney before the war. The city memorialized his loss with Fortson Square, located at Second Avenue and Yesler Way just west of the Louisa C. Frye Hotel (Captain Fortson's widow was a member of the George Frye family). The lives of the officers and men of Washington were memorialized with the dedication of Volunteer Park atop Capitol Hill to honor the veterans of the Spanish-American War.

Enduring Legacies of the Gold Rush-Era

Despite the Klondike gold rush fading from the headlines, those years left an indelible mark on Pioneer Square and the city of Seattle. Miners

The victory parade down First Avenue ends at Pioneer Place with a celebration to honor returning volunteers from the Spanish-American War. On the left, the Mutual Life Building is now a treasured Seattle landmark, but buildings adjacent to it have been replaced by parking garages. Photo by William Hester, 1900. MSCUA, University of Washington Libraries, Hes 318

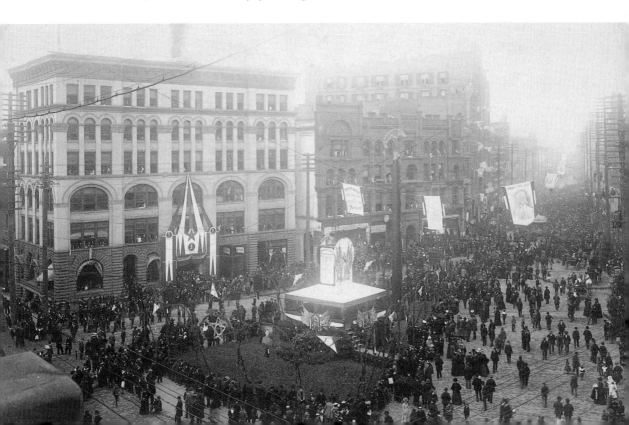

On October 18, 1899, a crowd gathers at Pioneer Place for the official dedication of Seattle's stolen totem. Looking south down First Avenue South, the Olympic Block is on the left and the Maynard and Terry-Denny Buildings are on the right. Seattle Municipal Archives, Don Sherwood Parks History Collection, Item 29981

and entrepreneurs who returned from the hustle and bustle of the Klondike cashed their raw gold in the new federal assay office (located in Seattle, thanks to Erastus Brainerd), and many made Seattle their home.

John Nordstrom, who had lived in Seattle prior to joining the stampede, returned from the goldfields with more than $10,000. He invested it in a shoe store that eventually was transformed into the upscale department-store chain that still bears the family name.

In June 1900, George Washington Carmack, whose discovery had triggered the Klondike gold rush, met Marguerite Saftig, a cigar shop owner in Dawson City, and began a whirlwind romance that culminated with their wedding in October. Carmack abandoned his Tagish Indian wife, Kate, who had worked shoulder to shoulder with him in the goldfields, and sold his interests in the Klondike discovery claim to her brother, Skookum Jim Mason. After returning to Seattle from the Klondike, Carmack purchased a number of properties in Pioneer Square, including the Maud Building on First Avenue South, and mining properties along one of the forks of the Snoqualmie River east of town. Carmack's destiny, like the city of Seattle, had been shaped by Klondike gold.

Gold and the mystique of the Canadian Klondike and Alaska cemented Seattle's relationship with the far north. In 1899 a group of city boosters stole a Tlingit Indian totem pole from a village on the island of Tongass in southeast Alaska and erected it at Pioneer Place. Despite attempts by the tribe to have the pole returned as well as be remunerated for their loss, it remained in Seattle. In 1938 an arsonist torched the historic pole; the U.S. Forest Service then commissioned and paid Tlingit craftspeople to use the remains as a model and carve a duplicate. The pole remains in Pioneer Place today as a powerful reminder of the city's links to southeast Alaska.

The Spanish-American War also had a major impact on the regional economy, forging early and enduring links with the Philippines and

Parents and their children gather around the totem pole at Pioneer Place to welcome Santa and his reindeer. A local department store imported Donner and Blitzen from the far north for a gold rush–era Christmas promotion. Museum of History and Industry, SHS, 15,307

Moran Brothers Shipyards launches the USS Nebraska, *the first steel ship and the first naval battleship to be built in the Pacific Northwest. At the launching, dignitaries made speeches, bands played, and a huge crowd turned out to cheer. Photo by Asahel Curtis, October 7, 1904. Museum of History and Industry, SHS 2,042*

Pacific Rim. A brisk trade ensued, which helped establish Seattle as San Francisco's rival in the Far East. In concert with the growth of Far Eastern commercial ventures, the U.S. Navy rapidly expanded.

As contracts were advertised for battleships, the Moran Brothers Shipyard responded. Buoyed by their previous success in the Klondike gold rush and the successful completion of other government contracts, they submitted a bid for the battleship *Nebraska.* The Moran Brothers Shipyard's bid, though the lowest, was higher than the amount Congress had appropriated for the project. Navy officials told the Morans that if they could trim $200,000 off their bid, the project was theirs. They wanted the work but were hesitant to absorb the loss.

To offset the Moran Brothers Shipyard's loss, the Seattle Chamber of Commerce led a communitywide subscription drive to raise $100,000. The people of Seattle enthusiastically responded, raising $135,000 and helping the

Moran Brothers Shipyard to win the contract. The keel was laid on July 4, 1902, and the ship was launched on October 7, 1904. The *Nebraska* went on to serve a distinguished career with the U.S. Navy, sailing around the world in the company of the Great White Fleet and protecting American convoys to France in the First World War.

In the aftermath of the Spanish-American War and the Klondike gold rush, Seattle emerged as the commercial nexus for the far north and the Pacific Rim. The impact of these events provided the city's boosters a stage on which to celebrate Seattle's newly gained affluence. In June 1909, the city hosted the Alaska-Yukon-Pacific Exposition. Over the course of that summer, thousands of people from around the region and across the country descended on the fairgrounds on the campus of the University of Washington to experience the gaudy excitement of the world's fair. The exposition celebrated Seattle's commercial and cultural ties, real as well as imagined, to Alaska, the Canadian Yukon, and the Pacific Rim. At Pioneer Place, the city erected its ornate, filigreed Victorian pergola to welcome visitors to the fair and the downtown business core.

In the 1970s, as Pioneer Square was saved from the wrecking ball, the arrival of the National Park Service there aided in the rediscovery of the story of Seattle at the turn of the twentieth century. In 1976 President Gerald R. Ford signed a bill into law creating Klondike Gold Rush National Historical Park, with a unit in Skagway, Alaska, and one in Seattle. The park commemorated the Klondike gold rush and allowed the National Park Service to restore and protect the historic buildings and trails associated with the gold rush. In the years since the Seattle unit first opened its doors, it has become an integral part of the cultural scene in Pioneer Square.

At the dawning of the twenty-first century, the adventuresome spirit of the gold rush lives on in Pioneer Square, where visionaries rehabilitate derelict buildings and infuse them with new life, where established and cutting-edge artists find an audience, where entrepreneurs pursue their dreams in one-of-a-kind small businesses, and where government and business leaders launch state-of-the-art sports stadiums and exhibition space for major events. The cast of characters in the gold-rush era covered a broad social and economic spectrum from the elite to the destitute, and issues such as vice versus virtue, management versus labor, the immigrant experience, and the decline of the Skid Road followed in their wake.

6 Skid Road

Mildred Andrews

For Seattle boosters, the slogan "Rise like a Phoenix" had a broader connotation than just the building boom of the 1890s following the Great Fire. Civic leaders envisioned the flat area south of Yesler Way as the revitalized heart of downtown. Property owners in Pioneer Square, however, spanned the social spectrum from bankers to saloon keepers, and most of them hastened to rebuild where they had been before. What idealistic visionaries overlooked were hard-headed economic realities: questions of profit, loss, and competition.

Roll call of the Seattle Police Department at City Hall, 1905. A survivor of the Great Fire in 1889, the wooden building was nicknamed "Katzenjammer Kastle" because of a hodgepodge of additions. ColorOne Photographic and Digital Imaging

As stately brick and stone buildings rose, the district became the city's center of banking and commerce. There were grand opening celebrations during which developers and civic leaders took their bows. Men in top hats and tails escorted wasp-waisted ladies to admire fanciful terra-cotta, intricate ironwork, and luminous marble halls. The *Seattle Post-Intelligencer* proclaimed, "Never again need this section be used for despicable purposes."

Anyone who looked beyond the splendor, however, could see that the district south of Yesler Way remained steeped in contradictions. Banks and luxury hotels were but a stone's throw away from establishments that catered to the poor or the disreputable. During the construction boom of the 1890s, laborers flocked to the city, eager for paying jobs. They resided in boardinghouses and cheap workingmen's hotels located on the fringes of the business district. There, building and civility codes were not enforced, and shoddy wood-frame construction was commonplace. Absentee landlords, saloon keepers, madams, gamblers, and police officers on the take had something in common: each of them was after a buck and meant business. Here too, economic reality prevailed.

Seattle's oldest and most socially and economically diverse neighborhood felt the impacts of moral reform crusades, labor organizations, and community constituents. Nonetheless, rich and poor, men and women, and members of different social and cultural groups all contributed to the district's unique and complex fabric.

City's Commercial Center

Pioneer Place remained the city's premier gathering place well into the twentieth century. A patriotic, rain-drenched throng gathered there in 1891 to welcome U.S. President Benjamin Harrison, who gave a brief address from the balcony of the Yesler Building. This was where the city erected temporary arches, gazebos, or review stands for welcomes that included the Great Northern's James J. Hill in 1893, the return of troops from the Philippines in 1899, and Santa Claus in a sleigh pulled by Alaskan reindeer during the Klondike gold rush. Buildings around Pioneer Place housed banks, law offices, insurance companies, retail establishments, the *Seattle Post-Intelligencer,* and the *Seattle Daily Journal of Commerce.*

Thanks to new streetcar lines, residential communities sprouted in outlying areas such as East Madison Street, where Bill Grose purchased acreage from Henry Yesler to establish an upwardly mobile African-American neighborhood. Most white and African-American people who owned businesses or had offices in Pioneer Square no longer lived there but commuted to work. A few maintained residences at posh hotels in the area, including the elegant Butler and Seattle Hotels (both of which have been demolished and converted to parking garages). Here, they mingled with out-of-town visitors and the city's elite to enjoy fine dining and entertainment. Gentlemen joined the nearby fashionable City Club on First Avenue South.

A Wide-Open City

During the heady days of postfire construction, unskilled workers could find cheap lodging, food, and entertainment on the rough and seedy fringes of the city's Victorian showplace. The newly arrived immigrant poor included large numbers of Scandinavians, many of whom came on days off to the city from logging or farmwork. Almost all of the city's Chinese and Japanese gathered in enclaves south of Yesler Way and east of Second Avenue South. Historian Quintard Taylor notes that working-class and transient black males gravitated to

The east side of First Avenue South, south of King Street, in 1905. Signs advertise numerous saloons with furnished rooms upstairs "beds 15 cents, day or night," a public bath, a barbershop. and a laundry. Museum of History and Industry, Webster & Stevens, 83.10.6,937

cheap boardinghouses and hotels south and east of Chinatown.

In the 1890s a worldwide economic depression, the arrival of transcontinental railroads, and the Klondike gold rush combined to draw new waves of men in search of "lady luck." Missions and other charitable organizations served increasing numbers whose luck had turned sour.

Turn-of-the-twentieth-century census statistics show that Seattle men still outnumbered women by a ratio of 1.7 to 1. According to some estimates, the ratio was 15 to 1 in the district south of Yesler Way. The demographic imbalance intensified the "bachelor problem" and accounted for one of the nation's most notorious vice districts. At different times in its history, the neighborhood has been called, variously, the Great Restricted District, the Lava Beds, Below the Deadline, Down on the Sawdust, the Tenderloin, and the Skid Road.

The district's topographical and moral low point was along Jackson Street, where rows of cheap wood-frame buildings stood on pilings above the tide flats. Sounds of lascivious laughter and honky-tonk piano rose above the rumble of trains, heard across the nearby maze of tracks and trestles. Numerous saloons, brothels, and gambling houses encouraged drunkenness. Dealers and neighborhood drugstores sold morphine and opium. Pickpockets and pimps roamed the muddy streets, and there were frequent acts of violence.

In his memoirs, J. T. Ronald recounts how he shut down the notorious Whitechapel and Blackchapel enclaves during his 1892–93 term as mayor of Seattle. They were located on the sites of today's Union and King Street Stations, respectively. In Ronald's words, they were a "stench in the nostrils of decency and a disgrace upon the good name of Seattle." Each of the "chapels" comprised one and a half to two blocks housing one hundred or two hundred cribs—tiny, sparsely furnished rooms where the most dissipated prostitutes lived and worked. Ronald wrote:

They constituted a part of that human wreckage found in seaport cities. . . . To keep body and soul together, they must live in cheap tenements and minister to any comer, and in any form, in any way, after any mode or custom, and at any price. So long as they could pay to the owners the rental— exorbitant considering the crib—they were permitted to occupy the place. . . . Whitechapel was peopled by women of all nations who were white, while the denizens of Blackchapel consisted of black or brown or yellow from whatever part of the earth, including Siwash Indians.

Local newspapers often reported bodies of infants found at low tide in the garbage underneath the shacks.

From the chapels, the vice district spread north. There were white-only and black-only brothels and so-called "pink" brothels that featured Asian prostitutes. The latter sometimes served an all-Asian clientele and sometimes only Caucasian men. The House of All Nations flaunted variety, advertising six hundred women from seventy-five nations.

Procurers of different races lured young women to the city under false pretenses. According to government reports, Seattle was one of the nation's three major centers for "white slavery" (a gold rush–era euphemism for prostitution trafficking). Some women chose the illicit trade rather than working for rock-bottom wages as a maid or laundress. Abbie Widner, who sometimes worked in brothels in the Puget Sound area, was a prostitute by choice. She described her degradation and dreams in a letter to her sweetheart, Johnie: "I have made this week $39.50, so I am not doing bad if I dont have it stolen from me but ever time a man

tuches me if I had a dager in my hand I would stab him in the heart, but I won't always bee a sport, no so help me God." In another letter, she wrote, "Johnie how would you like me to go up into the gold fields for a while untill I mak a stake and then come to my boy. dont you think that a wise plan?"

While most women in the trade struggled to survive, an occasional madam made a fortune. One was Mary Thompson, the African-American owner of Blackchapel's Minnehaha Saloon, which had a brothel on the upper floor. Another might have been Dorothea Georgine Emile Ohben, who adopted her showgirl stage name, Lou Graham. Public records show that she was fined more than once for selling liquor without a license and that she acquired substantial wealth. According to author Bill Speidel, her three-story brick building at Third and Washington was an upscale "palace of sin." If so, it provided dramatic contrast to Our Lady of Good Help Catholic Church, which was located across the intersection. If anyone in the Tenderloin District or at nearby City Hall feared for his or her soul, Father Prefontaine was on hand to hear confessions.

One of the mainstays of the Tenderloin was the "box-house," a type of saloon and gambling establishment that featured burlesque theater. Real estate magnate Henry Broderick explained, "Overlooking the stage at the rear of the balcony were a series of loggias, each equipped with chaise lounge and opaque curtains where waitresses offered shenanigans at market prices." Main-floor seating included the bar and card tables. Actresses entertained an all-male clientele with song, dance, and comedy routines. When they were offstage, they hustled drinks or dealt cards with games ranging from penny ante to high stakes. The price of admission was low; profits came from liquor sales and gambling.

High-minded city administrations occasionally clamped down on vice. In 1892 during his first week in office, Mayor Ronald made the chapels "absolutely tenantless." He later wrote, "I well recall how numerous people criticized me for closing these vicious and criminal resorts, declaring that I was ruining the city by driving loggers and visitors to Tacoma or to other places where they could spend their money enjoying themselves."

But through much of its history, Seattle was known as a wide-open city that prospered from licensing fees for prostitutes and gambling tables. In addition, there was a flourishing pay-off system. Box-house owner John Considine, called "the Boss Sport" by local newspapers, prospered in this milieu, investing in real estate and expanding his empire both south and north of Yesler Way. His People's Theater was in the basement of the Considine Building, which still stands on the northwest corner of Second Avenue South and South Washington Street. Considine exerted a strong influence in the Fourth Ward; it included the district south of Yesler Way, which had more potential voters than any other section of the city.

Vice Trial and Acquittal

In 1900 the Seattle City Council assuaged the powerful Law and Order League by conducting a hearing on vice in Seattle. It erupted into vicious sparring between Considine and the young chief of police, William Meredith. On leaving the courthouse, Meredith commenced enforcing a law that prohibited women in box-house theaters from serving liquor. He targeted Considine's establishments on Washington Street but no place else. Considine fought back, using his considerable influence to portray Meredith as a "bunko" artist. When the mayor asked him to resign, the chief of police unhappily complied, then blustered for a few days,

The Considine trial was fodder for the press, beginning with this sensational front-page news in the June 21, 1901, Seattle Post-Intelligencer. *University of Washington Libraries, Periodicals*

telling anyone who would listen that he was out for revenge.

On the morning of June 25, 1901, he followed the Considine brothers, John and Tom, into G. O. Guy's Drugstore at Second Avenue South and Yesler Way, pulled out a sawed-off shotgun, and fired at John from close range but missed. Meredith fired again, wounding John slightly, shattering the arm of a hapless drugstore clerk, and nearly hitting G. O. Guy, who ducked behind the counter. In self-defense, John tackled his smaller assailant. Tom wrestled the shotgun away, then used it as a club to savagely beat Meredith over the head and fracture his skull. Incoherent and bleeding, the ex-chief of police staggered to his feet, whereupon John pulled out his own revolver and shot him dead. Newsboys hawked the next morning's *Post-*

Intelligencer with the headline "Ex-Chief of Police W. L. Meredith Shot and Killed by John W. Considine."

Five months later, the state of Washington put Considine on trial for premeditated murder and sought a sentence of death by hanging. Reform-minded groups had made Meredith their martyr and Considine the symbol of all of the evils of the vice district. In effect, the trial pitted wide-open-city advocates against law-and-order coalitions. The outcome was touch and go until the jury rendered its verdict: "not guilty."

Following his acquittal, Considine moved most of his operations north of Yesler Way to liquor-free, family-oriented venues. Other proprietors were ready to fill the shoes of "the Boss Sport." A new neighbor of the People's Theater was the legendary Wyatt Earp, who opened a saloon near the corner of Second Avenue South and Yesler Way in the building now occupied by ColorOne Photographic and Digital Imaging. Earp and his showgirl wife spent their winters in Seattle but during the summers they returned to Dawson City in the Canadian Yukon to rake in gold-rush profits in a similar business. The Clancy brothers operated a saloon at Second Avenue South and South Jackson Street, where they controlled much of the neighboring property along with protection rackets. They built cheaply, exploited corrupt interests, paid off police and city officials to look the other way, and maximized gutter profits.

Rescue and Redemption

Not all of proper Seattle turned its back on the Tenderloin District. In 1883 Olive "Ollie" Ryther joined her husband, Noble, to work at the City Mission on Commercial Street (now First Avenue South) that served destitute men. At first the Rythers and their three daughters took their meals with the men. While there, Ollie turned her attention to "fallen women" and began raising funds from the city and businessmen to rescue them from the trade, help unwed pregnant women, and care for unwanted children. When the city appointed her as women's jail matron, she locked the prisoners in upstairs rooms in her own home, since there was no separate jail for women.

Ollie gained support from other women, notably Emma Ray, an African American who worked with her husband, Lloyd, in another of the district's missions. Ray played a leadership role in the Women's Christian Temperance Union (WCTU) and organized the Frances Harper Unit, made up of women from the African Methodist Episcopal Church. Its members visited people in jail and sought out the sick in squalid rooming houses. They cleaned and cooked for them, invited them to come to church, and exhorted them to mend their ways. In Buddhist and Japanese-Protestant churches, *fujin kai* (women's organizations) rescued and provided shelter for Japanese prostitutes, many of whom had been forced into the trade against their will.

Other women joined units of the WCTU and the Florence Crittendon Rescue Circle, which offered prostitutes shelter, job training, and a way to a decent life in return for leaving the trade. In the meantime, Ollie Ryther turned her attention to orphans and established the Ryther Child Home. During the next fifty years, the legendary "Mother Ryther" took in more than three thousand children.

In 1899 the Seattle Benevolent Society arranged to dry-dock the hull of the old side-wheeler *Idaho* at the foot of Jackson Street. Dr. Alexander de Soto, a Spanish Jesuit turned Protestant, converted it into the Wayside Mission Hospital, which was staffed by missionaries and served predominantly Skid Road patients.

Even though it lacked running water and plumbing, in its wheelhouse physicians performed surgery. The small room behind the wheelhouse served as an isolation ward, and the main and upper decks were general wards. The structure remained in service as a charity hospital until 1909, when the city instituted services for indigent patients in the new Public Safety Building at Yesler Way and Terrace Street.

During the early twentieth century, social reform crusades were a way of life. Seattle's most zealous advocate was the Reverend Mark Matthews, pastor of the huge First Presbyterian Church at Seventh and Spring. In a booming baritone, he delivered stinging diatribes, using his pulpit to expose and fight corruption. He blustered, "It's time for the decent people of Seattle to stop ignoring the cesspool in our midst and set about to have it removed. Yesler Way was once a skid road down which logs were pushed to Henry Yesler's sawmill on the waterfront. Today it is a skid road down which human souls go sliding to hell!" So powerful was his metaphor that it spread throughout the national vernacular as "skid row," a synonym for the urban slum.

The lanky six-foot-five evangelist prowled the Skid Road, clad in black suit and wide-brimmed hat. On an April evening in 1905, he and other religious leaders organized an ecumenical march of 15,000 church-going protestors, including a high percentage of "white-haired grandmothers and middle-aged matrons with their children." Accompanied by the Salvation Army Band and singing hymns, they descended into the Tenderloin to bring a message of salvation to those who frequented the city's "bottomless cauldron of sin."

Historian Kathryn S. Brandenfels notes that "although many who participated probably had good intentions, the majority seemed to come out of a condescending curiosity to view 'for the first time in their lives the haunts of the low and the depraved.'" A *Seattle Times* reporter observed that the marchers "halted in their walk to stare with wide open eyes and mouths" at the "fallen creature" of which they had read so much but whom they had never before seen. When "the soiled doves in their gilded trappings" laughed and chattered, and when one of them shouted, "Hypocrites!" the reformers responded with the hymn appropriately

Frances Harper Unit of the Women's Christian Temperance Union. Emma Ray is fourth from left in the back row. Her story is recorded in her autobiography, Twice Ransomed, Twice Sold. *Courtesy of Esther Hall Mumford*

entitled "Glory Enough for Me." In this case, the reformers may have widened the gulf between propriety and sin. All they achieved was confirmation of their own moral superiority and the chance to show their children the consequences of a misstep.

Gillism and Graft

From its early history, Seattle had experienced occasional "moral spasms," with clampdowns on the vice district. But corrupt interests financed their candidates' campaigns for elective office. For the most part, successive city councils and mayors turned their backs on a pro-respectability agenda in favor of an air of boom-town swagger.

In his book *Skid Road,* historian Murray Morgan describes how Charles W. Wappenstein (known as "Wappy") took graft to new depths following his appointment as chief of police in 1902. Wappy encouraged proprietors to open brothels in return for paying him $10 per month per prostitute. Police on the beat honored the protection racket and came down hard on any establishment that shortchanged their chief. When moralists gained control of city government, Wappy followed orders to clean up the Skid Road. Unwilling to put up with the restrictions, purveyors of vice moved uptown and into residential areas, opening saloons and brothels throughout the city.

Hiram Gill, a scrawny lawyer and member of the City Council, frequently excused himself from meetings so that he could arrange bail for his brothel-owner clients. When Gill ran for mayor, he argued that an open town was "healthy" for a seaport with a frontier heritage. He maintained further that morality could not be legislated and that a movement to stamp out vice would only drive it underground. He won the 1910 election with a promised compromise to keep the town open but to return the vice district to the area south of Yesler Way.

Mayor Gill quickly forgot the second part of his promise. With Wappy at his side, he put gambling on the same basis as the sex trade and encouraged his friends to go into the business. The city levied "fines" of $30 per month per poker table and $100 per month for blackjack games. Brothels and gambling joints operated openly in Pioneer Square but also in residential districts and uptown.

The national press took note, with feature stories that gave Seattle widespread publicity as a den of vice. Morgan quotes *McClure's Magazine,* which was investigating corruption in city governments across the country:

The city seemed to have been transformed almost magically into one great gambling hell. All kinds of games simultaneously started up, in full view of the public. Cigar stores and barbershops did a lively business in crap-shooting and race-track gambling, drawing their patronage largely from schoolboys and department-store girls. . . . At one time it looked as if the whole of Seattle were going mad over faro, roulette, blackjack, and numerous other forms of entertainment provided in thirty or forty gambling places opened up under the administration of Hi Gill.

In another article, *McClure's* focused on the giant Northern Club on First Avenue South:

No American city has ever seen anything comparable with it. . . . In order not to lose any possible patronage, the Northern Club ran twenty-four hours a day, including Sunday. . . . A few days after the club opened, a self-appointed committee of Seattle lawyers, curious to learn how Gill was redeeming his open-town pledge, made the rounds. They found the Northern Club filled to suffocation with two or three hundred of their fellow citizens, and from sixty to eighty attendants were solitously providing for their needs. Everywhere the wheels were clicking and the bones were rolling. A particularly impressive sight was a heavily gold-braided police captain who benignantly elbowed his way in and out of the throng.

Recall and Reform

But antivice coalitions had recourse in the form of the newly ratified recall amendment to the Seattle City Charter. Within a few weeks of the election, law-and-order proponents drew up a petition. Labor unions and Protestant churches began gathering signatures. Gill fought back with substantial support, including the *Seattle Times*. He might have prevailed had there not been a significant change in the electorate.

In 1910 Washington state's male citizens voted to ratify the woman suffrage amendment, making the state the fifth in the nation where women could vote. The Washington Woman Suffrage Association, the Mothers' Congress, the Women's Christian Temperance Union, and the Seattle Federation of Women's Clubs joined in the recall campaign. With the rallying cry "Ladies,

get out and hustle!" more than 22,000 of Seattle's newly enfranchised voters tipped the balance for law and order and hustled Gill out of office. Reform candidate George Cotterill defeated him in his bid for reelection. A staunch temperance advocate, Cotterill was a leading member of the Prohibition Party who had served in the International Order of Good Templars as Grand Templar of the United States.

The Cotterill administration made a concerted effort to put a stop to protection rackets and close down the town. Within a month, police estimated that the number of prostitutes on the Skid Road had decreased by more than half. According to Murray Morgan, an observer described the departure of some two hundred "soiled doves" who boarded a train at King Street Station: "A few of the girls were weeping but many were in their gaudiest finery. Some were accompanied by their pink-cuffed fancy men. A crowd of spectators had assembled to see them off and the girls took their pleasure in calling old customers by name and waving at respected men whose names they did not know."

Housed in the Mutual Life Building, Seattle First National Bank was only a half block north of the notorious Northern Club. MSCUA, University of Washington Libraries, 2084

Waitresses, seamstresses, and lady barbers organized unions at the turn of the twentieth century. Many of the charter members worked in the district south of Yesler Way. Here, members of the International Ladies Garment Workers Union Local 17 participate in the 1903 Labor Day parade. Courtesy of Ross Rieder

Shortly after his election, Gill had granted sanction to his cronies to lease city property on Beacon Hill so that they could build the world's largest brothel—500 rooms. The partners incorporated as the Hillside Improvement Company, openly touting their plan to create a model red-light district. Under Cotterill's administration, the intended brothel was converted to a legitimate rooming house.

Bolstered by the women's vote, coalitions in the city and throughout the state ushered in a host of reforms. Washington state made national news when the Legislature enacted a landmark minimum wage of $10 per week for working women (excluding agricultural and domestic workers), followed by a law that limited their workday to eight hours. The suffrage crusade had brought the attention of middle-class

women to the plight of their working-class sisters.

Until the early twentieth century, Seattle waitresses had worked twelve-hour days, seven days a week, for as little as $3 per week in wages. In 1900 the all-male Seattle Central Labor Council and the American Federation of Labor agreed to admit the new Waitresses Union, followed by the Lady Barbers (who were barred from membership in the male barbers' union) and a local chapter of the International Ladies Garment Workers Union. While advocating for their rights as workers, women's unions joined forces with middle-class women's organizations in the suffrage crusade. In Pioneer Square, the new wage and hour laws elevated the status of women in legitimate jobs and dealt another blow to prostitution.

Union members at the Black Bear factory, now the Seattle Quilt Building, on First Avenue South wore Miss Black Bear overalls at work. At a time when women wore dresses in public, the company promoted its overalls for outdoor recreation. Mildred Andrews's collection

Potlatch Summer Festival

The Gill episode had not distracted city boosters, who were eager to showcase Seattle's attributes and fuel the economic momentum generated by the 1909 Alaska-Yukon-Pacific Exposition. In the summer of 1911, the city hosted its first Potlatch celebration, with plans to make it an annual event. Its brazen exploitation of the heritage of Puget Sound Indians

was meant to attract visitors from far and wide.

The weeklong festivities began with the arrival of the Hyas Tyee, the "great chief" of a tribe in the far north, who arrived in his giant war canoe. The organizing committee called itself the Tilikums of Elttaes ("friends of Seattle," the last word spelled backward). Its subcommittees were "tribes" who vied in spirited competition to produce the best events, attract the most people, and get the public involved. The Chamber of Commerce, the Rainier and Arctic Clubs, and real estate developers used the festival to market the city and encourage outside investment.

The *Seattle Times* estimated that 150,000 visitors attended the second "Golden Potlatch" in 1912, which was deemed an unqualified advertising success. A reporter wrote:

Seattle always decorates in gayest attire for the Potlatch; these are great days for the children, brilliantly illuminated night parades, naval and military displays, automobile and floral parades, daring feats of aviation by world-famous birdmen, and music everywhere. The streets are

Drill team wearing totem pole costumes in the 1912 Potlatch parade.
MSCUA, *University of Washington Libraries,* UW 313

An angry mob trashed IWW headquarters in Pioneer Square after the 1913 Golden Potlatch parade. Museum of History and Industry, PEMCO, Webster & Stevens 7068.

thronged by day and by night and everyone is happy.

But the next and final Potlatch celebration was a marketing disaster. An inflammatory article in the *Times* drew attention to "red flag worshippers and anarchists" who participated in the parade, along with military marching bands and troops.

The radical Industrial Workers of the World (IWW, also known as "Wobblies") employed nonviolent tactics to promote workers' rights and to oppose capitalism and the draft. In July 1913, following the grand parade, a rioting anti-Red mob wrecked IWW headquarters on South Washington Street in Pioneer Square and demolished socialist halls in other parts

of the city. The story made front-page news in the national press. Chagrined Seattle leaders decided to end the summer Potlatch tradition.

Regrades and Population Shifts

The summer Potlatch celebrations and the Gill recall took place during an unprecedented population boom. Whereas previous booms had doubled the city's population, between 1900 and 1920, the population tripled from 80,000 to almost a quarter million people. City Engineer R. H. Thomson forged ahead with grandiose schemes to recontour downtown, while politicians grappled with soaring budgets and citizen complaints. Along with the Jackson Street Regrade (see chapter 4), work crews tackled streets that climbed north from Pioneer Square toward precipitous Denny Hill. By 1910 Second, Third, and Fourth Avenues were lowered to a maximum grade of 5 percent and transformed from mud to concrete and macadam. Historians have likened the amount of dirt shifted from Seattle hills to the tide flats to another technological marvel of the era—the digging of the Panama Canal.

Like the topography, the town's population also shifted dramatically because of the newly available land. Nowhere was the city's transformation from boomtown to metropolis more vivid than in the district south of Yesler Way. It swelled, then burst like a giant cocoon. Chinatown and Japantown gravitated east onto the Jackson Street Regrade and what is now the International District. A rapidly expanding industrial district spread south onto former tide flats. The city's commercial center surged north.

As described in chapter 4, James J. Hill and Edward Henry Harriman erected landmark depots that fronted on the tide flats. Landfill from the regrades led to the "tidelands boom" of the early twentieth century. Buoyed by gold rush–era profits, industries expanded and moved south onto reclaimed land. Stately brick warehouse and factory buildings rose west of the train stations along Jackson and King Streets. They replaced rows of cheap, wood-frame structures that had been home to some of the city's most disreputable establishments.

Chinatown and Japantown Spread East

Following the Great Fire, Chin Gee Hee had erected one of the city's first new brick buildings. It anchored Chinatown along South Washington Street between Second and Third Avenues

In 1911 men continued to gather at comfortable, all-male bastions in Pioneer Square, which often featured a free lunch of pickles, cheese, and bread to boost beer sales. Courtesy of Rod Slemmons

Chinese butchers in their Pioneer Square shop. Courtesy of Rod Slemmons

South, where Chinese merchants operated general stores that included living quarters for their families, bed and board for laborers, and gambling facilities. In Seattle, the largely bachelor population of Chinese immigrants found jobs in laundries and on railroad and agricultural crews.

During late-nineteenth-century salmon runs, Seattle's fish canneries had hired skilled Chinese butchers, who deftly manipulated long knives to gut and behead the day's catch. Since there were never enough butchers to meet the demand, this group of Chinese workers had commanded a degree of respect from white employers. In about 1900, Edmund Smith, whose factory was just south of Pioneer Square, invented a fish-processing machine that cannery owners and managers quickly dubbed the "Iron Chink"— a racist name that stuck. With Smith's machine, two Chinese butchers could do the work of ten. The machine put skilled butchers out of work and at the same time eliminated the annual labor shortage. Its efficiency made canned salmon a major regional commercial industry.

As Chinese laborers continued to gravitate to the city, Chinatown became increasingly crowded. Its population rose to a bursting point of almost a thousand residents. In 1907 Chinese merchants began moving east to King Street, which had been leveled, vacated, and resurfaced as part of the Jackson Street Regrade. Most of the community soon followed, to what is now the Chinatown–International Historic District. A few businesses and residents remained behind in what became known as Old Chinatown.

Labor contractors began recruiting Japanese, following the federal Chinese Exclusion Act of 1883 that prohibited immigration of working-class Chinese. When labor shortages slowed, the Japanese government negotiated the 1907 "Gentlemen's Agreement" with the United States to voluntarily curtail further immigration of contract laborers. In return, Japanese laborers were able to save money and send home for a bride. Seattle's Japanese population exploded from 125 in 1890 to 2,990 in 1900, to 6,127 in 1910—the city's fifth-largest immigrant population after Canadians, Swedes, Norwegians, and Germans.

Seattle's Nihonmachi ("Japantown") took root on South Main and Jackson Streets, adjacent to the new Chinatown. In 1911 the Japanese Community Center moved from its home in Masajiro Furuya's Bank Building on Second Avenue South and Main (now Masin's Furniture) to the Nippon Kan Theater Building at Sixth Avenue South and Main. A significant number of Japanese continued to live and work in what is now Pioneer Square. Some ran small businesses and managed bachelor hotels for their kinsmen or for a "western" (non-Japanese) clientele.

Refugees from Eastern Europe

By this time, another immigrant group was establishing a presence south of Yesler Way.

Jewish families who had fled pogroms in czarist Russia had moved into wood-frame buildings on Railroad Avenue between South Main and Washington Streets. They opened second-hand shops and loan businesses, described in a 1905 article in the *Post-Intelligencer* as "picturesque to the extreme." One shopkeeper explained to a reporter that the Russians had forced them to leave because of jealousy. "Why? Because we can trade better than they can, because we educate our children to become good business people; because we make money and they can't." Russian and Polish Jews purchased property and continued to establish small businesses that became an important part of the Skid Road culture.

Harry Buttnick was born shortly after his parents immigrated from Byelorusse. He worked

Harry Buttnick, left, and his brother, Sam, managed family businesses at the O.K. Hotel. Courtesy of Morrie and Meta Buttnick

in the family businesses and purchased a lot between Main and Washington on Railroad Avenue South in 1909. For a time he kept the lot vacant, wrongly speculating that the commercial district would reestablish itself south of Yesler Way. In 1915 he began building the O.K. Hotel, which at first housed World War I industrial workers. The five-story hotel had 192 small rooms, a lobby, and storefronts for other family businesses. Unlike most of the district's bachelor hotels, the O.K. was constructed with light wells, so that even inside rooms had a window that opened. In addition, each room had a sink with running water and a small radiator. Sam Okuba was the manager for many years. When Harry married Meta Bloom, the Okubas gave them an exquisite lacquered sake set as a wedding present. Today it remains one of Meta Buttnick's most treasured possessions, reminding her of the shared immigrant heritage that often formed a bond between Japanese and Jewish families in the district south of Yesler Way.

Downtown Surges Northward

The most devastating blow to the city's original downtown was the northward thrust of the commercial district. By the early twentieth century, all of the city's banks had moved north of Yesler Way, which became a dividing line between proper downtown and its antithesis. Efforts to stem the tide were generally ineffective.

One of the prime movers in the effort to revitalize the Skid Road district was Lyman Cornelius Smith of Syracuse, New York, who had made a fortune manufacturing Smith Corona typewriters. In the early 1890s, he bought out the real estate interests of former Washington state governor Watson Squire, including the Squire-Latimer Building (now Grand Central Arcade) and several other properties in Pioneer Square.

When Smith visited his deteriorating empire in 1909, he devised a plan to reverse the tide of northward development. He hired Gaggin and Gaggin, an architectural firm from Syracuse, to design a building for his lot at Second Avenue and Yesler Way. The lot was the southern anchor of a street of stately office buildings, popularly called the "Second Avenue canyon." Before breaking ground for what would become the Smith Tower, the tallest building west of New York City, Smith gained assurances from the City Council that City Hall would remain at Third and Jefferson Street, a half block east of his building site.

A 1910 article in the *Seattle Times* proclaimed euphorically that the $1.5 million building "will make Seattle remarkable all over the country in the matter of commercial buildings and furnish the city with a landmark that will fix itself upon the memory of visitors from all over the United States."

The next year, Smith began construction of the forty-two-story steel framework. His audacious structure features a gleaming white, terra-cotta facade with liberal use of Alaskan marble and Mexican Pedara onyx in the interior. Handsome carved and gilded Indian heads appear to hold up the lobby's ceiling. The thirty-fifth-floor observation hall is graced with exotic Chinese carvings and furnishings, including the wishing chair, a gift from the empress of China. Smith's only daughter was one of the first to sit in the chair, and true to its legend and her wish, she returned a year later to celebrate her wedding.

On the Fourth of July in 1914, the grand opening celebration drew more than four thousand visitors, who entered hand-operated, brass and copper elevator cages for rides to the observation deck. The visitors reveled in spectacular bird's-eye views of the city and Puget Sound, views unprecedented in an era predating com-

Smith Tower under construction, February 1913. Seattle Municipal Archives, Engineering Department Collection, Item 11930

This view from City Hall Park shows, left to right, the Frye Hotel, the Smith Tower, the Hotel Seward (now Morrison Hotel), and the County-City Building. Photo by Asahel Curtis. MSCUA, *University of Washington Libraries, A Curtis 33395*

mercial airplanes. On the first anniversary of the grand opening, spectators might have spotted the small Curtiss floatplane in which the passenger, William E. Boeing, was taking his first flight and beginning to hatch plans for an airplane factory. Smith, who did not live to see the opening of his tower, was succeeded by his son Burns. Sharing his father's vision of revitalizing the district south of Yesler Way, Burns Lyman Smith purchased the Interurban Building at Occidental and Yesler, which he renamed the Smith Tower Annex.

Some prominent local property owners, along with eastern capitalists, joined in the effort to revitalize Pioneer Square. In 1911 the resplendent, Italianate-style Louisa C. Frye Hotel opened at Third and Yesler. Designed

by Bebb and Mendel, it was the largest hotel north of San Francisco and one of Seattle's finest. George F. Frye named it for his wife and business partner, Louisa Catherine Denny Frye. One of Seattle's founders, seven-year-old Louisa had come ashore at Alki Beach with her parents, Arthur and Mary Denny, and the rest of the Denny Party in 1851. George Frye was a German immigrant who had made the westward journey in 1852, driving an ox team. Henry Yesler had hired the nineteen-year-old as a sawyer in the mill with partial pay in the form of stump-strewn, hillside land, now the site of the hotel. George Frye had bootstrapped his way up to become a prominent developer.

Following George's death in 1912, Louisa and their four daughters incorporated as an all-female board to supervise the family's real estate holdings. Family members worked in the business, including two of the daughters' husbands, who managed the hotel. Across Yesler Way from the Frye was the Hotel Seward (now the Morrison), at Third and Yesler, where men with gold-rush fortunes joined the prestigious Arctic Club. In 1917, the club moved into its new Arctic Building at Third and Cherry.

True to its bargain with L. C. Smith, the city kept its headquarters on Yesler Way. It tore down the old City Hall at Third and Yesler—nicknamed "Katzenjammer Kastle" because of its hodgepodge of additions—and replaced it with a park. The city and King County partnered to erect the County-City Building (now the King County Courthouse) on the north side of the park. Architect A. Warren Gould designed a massive twenty-two-story, H-shaped skyscraper in the Renaissance Revival tradition. Initially only the first six floors were constructed, followed by five additional floors in 1930. Eventually the original grand entrance that faced south and opened into the park was sealed shut, giving way to side entrances on Third and Fourth Avenues.

In the end, the dynamic buildings along Yesler Way failed to draw downtown development into the Skid Road area. Instead, they created a defining southern anchor for the downtown core.

Washington State Goes Dry

In 1914, the Prohibition Amendment was proposed to the state constitution. While rural areas overwhelmingly favored the measure, Seattle was the scene of heated debate. The Reverend Matthews held daily revival meetings to galvanize support among evangelical Christians. Prohibitionists staged a fervent antibooze rally and two-mile-long parade that snaked its

way through Pioneer Square and down First Avenue. Rebuttals came from formidable opponents, including the city's major newspapers and the Chamber of Commerce. Judge Thomas Burke maintained that prohibition would cost 8,300 men their jobs during an economic cycle that was already termed a depression. Brewers waged their own advertising campaign, urging voluntary moderation of drinking habits as an alternative. On Election Day, November 3, 1914, a record 96.4 percent of Washington's electorate marched to the polls to ratify the amendment; Seattle voters approved the referendum by a narrower margin of 61 percent.

To the dismay of many, Hi Gill once again took the helm as the city's mayor. Campaigning on a reform ticket, he explained to voters that they had elected him to run an open town in 1910 and that he had kept his promise. But then voters had changed their minds and "diselected" him. Now he too had changed his mind and believed in a closed town. He argued persuasively that because of his previous dealings with vice, he was the most qualified candidate to run a closed town.

Statewide prohibition became the law on January 1, 1916. Saloon keepers either closed or converted their establishments to soda fountains or cafes. The Rainier and Olympia Breweries stayed open, bottling and distributing nonalcoholic sodas. From the start, bootleggers were in business. A zealous reformer, Mayor Gill led raids on suspect businesses and personally oversaw the destruction of slot machines and whiskey barrels in the vice district. The "Purity Squad" of the Seattle Police Department took matters to extremes in its efforts to stamp out prostitution, sometimes arresting married couples caught downtown after dark or raiding hotel rooms to roust out single women, including the innocent.

But Gill's integrity was short lived. As his

Looking west from First and Yesler in 1929. The photo documents the laying of new sewer lines and pavement on Yesler Way. Notice the Skid Road signage during the prohibition era. Seattle Municipal Archives, Engineering Department Collection

administration flip-flopped, payoffs and illicit operations in Pioneer Square once again ran full tilt. Bootleg liquor was readily available. Some establishments, including the old Seattle Hotel, escorted guests through intricate escape routes during raids. During World War I, Camp Lewis and Fort Lawton placed the Skid Road off-limits to curb skyrocketing venereal disease among troops.

The Iron March of Labor

At the same time, the "war to end all wars" and "make the world safe for democracy" sparked a local population and economic boom. It was a time of high employment, patriotic parades, and voluntary commitments to support wartime industries and "keep the home fires burning."

During World War I, workers swelled the ranks of Seattle's shipyard and metal trade unions. Owners and the federal government met union demands for high wages in return for guarantees that there would be no interruptions in production schedules during the wartime emergency. Laborers crowded into rooming houses and hotels in Pioneer Square, where they had easy access to the industrial district south of King Street. Seattle shipyards set wartime records, building more ships than any other U.S. city. By the end of the war, the shipyards employed nearly 40,000 workers in a total city population of about 300,000.

The 1918 armistice prompted spontaneous celebrations that drew jubilant crowds to Pioneer Place and First Avenue. The cheering had barely died down when shipyard unions demanded that there be no layoffs or cuts in wages. The Federal Emergency Trades Council threatened to cancel future shipments of steel if local employers complied. On January 21, 1919, workers at Skinner and Eddy Shipyard (southwest of today's Safeco Field) walked off the job, followed by 35,000 workers from other yards. One by one, smaller unions voted to lend their support.

A date was set for workers throughout the city to go on strike. On February 4, two days before the walkout, the most famous editorial in the city's history appeared in the *Union Record,* Seattle's largest newspaper and the only daily labor journal in the country. Its author, Anna Louise Strong, had been elected to the Seattle School Board in 1916, only to be narrowly defeated in a recall election two years later. Her fellow board members had instigated the recall in condemnation of her overt pacifism and opposition to the draft. When Strong championed the working class in the nation's first general strike, she effectively ended the possibility of a negotiated settlement between management and labor. Her editorial concluded: "We are undertaking the most tremendous move ever made by labor in this country, a move that will lead—No one Knows Where! We do not need hysteria! We need the iron march of labor!"

On February 6, 1919, 60,000 workers put down their tools and went home. In the next days, there were no disorderly demonstrations. Business was at a standstill, but the unions made sure that essential services continued without interruption. There was milk for babies, clean linen for hospitals, and food for the needy. Police, doctors, and firefighters remained on the job, while the national press had a field day. Perhaps because of reporters' attention, Mayor "Holy Ole" Hanson charged publicly that the revolutionaries were motivated by the "Hell inspired doctrines of Lenin and Trotsky." But as Strong had aptly stated, no one knew where the strike would lead. Labor did not have a destination.

All that the 1919 Seattle General Strike proved was that unions could shut down the city. On the fifth day, workers went back to their jobs and the nonviolent strike ended, with its goals still undefined. Drastic cuts in employment and wages followed; labor candidates lost in the next election; class consciousness intensified; and Strong emigrated to Russia. Hanson resigned as mayor and went on a national lecture tour, telling anyone who would listen about his victory over the Bolsheviks. However, like the General Strike, his bid for the 1920 Republican presidential nomination fizzled without impacting national politics.

Bootleggers Meet Their Match

The year 1919 marked ratification of the "bone dry" prohibition amendment to the U.S. Constitution, making the manufacture, sale, and possession of alcoholic beverages illegal throughout the nation, except for druggists. Both bootleggers and vice squads escalated their activities. Rather than eliminate corruption, as was intended, the law fomented a black market that many considered semirespectable. Putting aside vestiges of Victorianism, respectable young women shortened their skirts, doffed their corsets, bobbed their hair, and smoked in public. Speakeasies proliferated. At "bottle clubs," waiters looked the other way when customers added a shot of something to their beverage. Dance halls gyrated with the Charleston, and the seemingly carefree "flapper" became a symbol of the "roaring twenties."

Stills proliferated in rural areas and in Skid Road back rooms. Seattle's proximity to Canada resulted in a pipeline with a steady flow of name-brand liquor. Rumrunners sneaked across the border in trucks and cars or loaded their boats in British Columbia to smuggle contraband cargoes into Puget Sound's coves and inlets. The most notorious rumrunner was Roy Olmstead, whose capers made him a local folk hero. After his dismissal from the Seattle police force, he

Passengers board the electric streetcar on Second Avenue in front of the Butler Hotel, left, and the Bailey Building later renamed the Broderick Building. The cable car on the right is about to go past the Oriental Building and up James Street, ca. 1890. MSCUA, *University of Washington Libraries, Boyd and Braas 140*

paid a fine, then resumed smuggling in earnest. He dumped his wife and married young Elsie Campbell, with whom he established a radio station. When Elsie told children's stories, her broadcasts were a front for coded messages that helped Olmstead and his men dodge police and pirates to become King County's largest boot-legging operation.

In 1924 Bertha Knight Landes was president of the City Council. When Mayor Edmund "Doc" Brown was out of town, she took over as acting mayor and made national headlines by firing the chief of police, a man who had boasted publicly about corruption in his depart-ment. Temporarily taking on his duties herself, she instructed officers to enforce regulations "to stamp out the potential for evil in dancehalls"

and called on good citizens to blow the whistle on suspected bootleggers.

A leading clubwoman, Landes ran for mayor in 1926 on a platform of "municipal housekeep-ing." She defeated Brown by six thousand votes to become the first woman mayor of any major American city. During her administration, Roy Olmstead's arrest and subsequent five-week-long trial were a media sensation. By the time it was over, former Mayor Brown and many of Seattle's social elite were linked to the under-world via the formerly corrupt police force. The prosecution exposed a double standard, showing that police had ignored the flow of good liquor to elite social clubs, while raiding vulnerable Skid Road establishments without mercy.

At first police, business proprietors, and

"proper" patrons openly resisted the municipal housekeeping. The popular Rose Room at the Butler Hotel at First and James was the scene of several raids, where police arrested waiters and bartenders, then quickly released them. On November 14, 1927, a mellow crowd was sipping drinks and dancing to the tune "How Dry I Am," played by Vic Meyers's orchestra. Federal agents busted in and put eighteen customers under arrest, along with staff. *The Seattle Times* reported that when patrons realized what was happening, "hundreds of glasses were shattered and their contents spilled." The Rose Room was closed and its furnishings sold at auction.

Landes ran an administration that was honest and scandal free, turning the tide against widespread corruption in city government. She supported public ownership of key utilities, such as City Light and street railways. For the first time in years, the city's financial house was in order. In her bid for reelection in 1928, Landes had endorsements from all of Seattle's major newspapers, the Seattle Central Labor Council, the Prohibition Party, and women's organizations.

Despite her high ratings, she lost the election to Frank Edwards, a political unknown, whose support came from interests that favored private ownership of utilities. Landes attributed her

Fortson Square was an immigrant's haven, with a polyglot of small businesses run by Chinese, Japanese, Greeks, Scandinavians, and Italians. The neighborhood was permanently disrupted in 1929, when the city sliced through the buildings on the right to extend Second Avenue, shown here crossing Yesler Way, and create a direct route from downtown to the railroad stations. The corner of the Smith Tower is on the left; the Frye Hotel dominates the background; and on the right, the sign "Guy's Cut Rate Drugs" marks the entrance of the drugstore in the Metropole Building. Photo by Asahel Curtis, 1919. Seattle Public Library 22635

defeat to her opponent's lavish campaign budget and to "sex prejudice." Frequent references to Seattle's "petticoat mayor" in the national press had fueled a popular sentiment that a city of stature should have a man at the helm. Two years later, Edwards was defeated in a recall election. In the meantime, speakeasies and graft had made a comeback. But the municipal housekeeping program continued to run its course on the Skid Road.

Access for Autos

In 1926 Louisa C. Frye Associates erected a parking garage directly behind the Frye Hotel, making it the city's first hotel with facilities for the increasingly popular automobile. Travelers had easy access from the new Pacific Coast Highway that followed Fourth Avenue through downtown Seattle. As before, overnight guests also came from the nearby railroad stations, but in steadily decreasing numbers.

Seattle leaders, who still placed a high value on King Street and Union Stations, came up with a plan to revitalize railroad travel to and from the city. They reasoned that the squalid area between Yesler Way and the stations was a deterrent to passengers. The street scene included hucksters and gambling joints. As home to a multicultural community and the struggling poor, this part of the Skid Road was rife with cheap hotels, flophouses, small ethnic businesses, warehouses, and sweatshops. Unmindful of any virtues in the neighborhood, city leaders saw an opportunity for municipal housekeeping with the economic potential of increasing railroad travel in and out of Seattle. At the end of the decade, city engineers sliced through blocks of buildings to extend downtown's Second Avenue from Yesler Way directly to the train depots.

Contrary to planners' expectations, the project did not lure bus and auto travelers back to trains. Instead, the Second Avenue Extension claimed its toll. One of the casualties was the headquarters of the Seattle Fire Department, which rebuilt at its current location on South Main Street. Another was almost all of Seattle's original Chinatown. One of the few survivors was the Chin Gee Hee building, which housed the Hop Sing Tong (a *tong* is a family association). The family ran a gambling operation that attracted both Chinese and non-Chinese customers until after World War II. Today, the building with its characteristic second-story balcony is the sole vestige of Old Chinatown. The former multicultural, working-class neighborhood had been permanently uprooted. The Great Depression followed on the heels of the demolition, propelling the area adjacent to the Second Avenue Extension into a decadeslong downward spiral.

7 The Era of Booms and Busts

Mildred Andrews

Heedless of the gathering political storm clouds in Asia and Europe, upscale Seattleites neared the end of the roaring twenties in style, reveling in the jazz and ritz of trendy downtown. Political reformers continued to hurl rhetoric against bootleggers and speakeasies. Business leaders took their bows for the decade of prosperity, which had increased American production by some 200 percent. In 1928 Herbert Hoover ran on the Republican ticket and won the presidential election by a landslide. Most voters were unaware of high tariffs that were already putting a choke hold on world trade or of growing numbers of laid-off workers from farming, steel mills, and the building trades.

Carefree complacency culminated in a crash. Wall Street collapsed on now legendary "Black Tuesday," October 29, 1929. Within two years, American bank failures numbered more than five thousand, while world trade sank a staggering 70 percent. Like the cold, damp fog of winter, the Great Depression enveloped the nation, leaving thousands out of work and homeless.

Locally, the trade-dependent economy was hit hard. As exports dropped, railroad and maritime workers joined the ranks of the unemployed. Lumber mills made severe cuts in production, and coal mining came to a virtual standstill. The 1920s construction boom went bust. Manufacturers slowed production, laying off workers or cutting back on their hours and paychecks. Decreased consumer dollars forced many a retailer to close up shop.

In Pioneer Square, a few long-standing businesses survived and prospered. But the district's strongest Depression-era legacies came from the influx of unemployed and underemployed people for whom the Skid Road was the last resort. The need was beyond the capacity of missions and charities that had served the down-and-out for decades.

Pioneer Square became the nexus of the local self-help movement and soon joined forces with organized labor to become an influential voice in regional and national politics. A new liberal political alliance formed the backbone of the Democratic Party, electing Franklin D. Roosevelt as president in 1932. Washington state—especially the Puget Sound region—moved from its Republican tradition to become a Democratic stronghold. Roosevelt implemented his New Deal, which expanded the role of the federal government to provide economic and social assistance at the state and local level. Americans began to demand, expect, and accept a larger governmental role in their lives.

Federally funded relief programs took root in Pioneer Square, which today has more social services than any other Seattle neighborhood. As early historic preservationists worked to revitalize the district, they were determined to retain housing and services for its elderly and low-income residents. According to the 1998 Neighborhood Plan, Pioneer Square's unique social and economic diversity has become one of its "most beloved attributes."

Brother, Can You Spare a Dime?

By the 1930s, hundreds of unemployed men roamed about the Skid Road, looking for food or a night's lodging. Several small restaurants offered full meals for twenty cents, and a nickel would buy a bowl of soup or a sandwich, but many still went hungry. As the Depression worsened, missions and other charities did what they could to help.

Martin Johanson, sweeping the steps to the Millionair Club in 1926. He is listed as its secretary/manager in city directories. Museum of History and Industry, Seattle Post-Intelligencer, *22382*

Since early pioneer days, faith-based missions have served the homeless in the district south of Yesler Way. The Salvation Army worked to redeem souls and help the poor during the Klondike gold rush era; its Harbor Light Center at 416 Second Avenue was a mainstay in the district's social service programs until 1992, when it moved to the International District. Another ongoing mission is the Lutheran Compass Center at 77 South Washington, whose original driving force was Pastor Otto Karlstrom. Martin Johanson, a fellow Swede and Seattle businessman, founded the Millionair Club in 1921 to serve the city's unemployed. He personally managed the organization, which provides nourishing meals and acts as a clearinghouse for temporary jobs. Johanson chose the name, dropping the final *e,* because he said helping others made him feel like a millionaire. (Today, the Millionair Club is located in Belltown, north of the downtown commercial core.)

During the Depression, some of today's missions purchased substantial buildings in the Skid Road neighborhood at rock-bottom prices, so that they could provide free beds, meals, coun-

seling, employment programs, medical clinics, spiritual guidance, and hope for the destitute. In 1932, the Union Gospel Mission opened its doors in the former Ace Hotel building at 318 Second Avenue Extension, and in 1939, the Bread of Life Mission took over the Matilda Winehill Block, a gold rush–era hotel at First and Main.

Numerous other missions that no longer exist did what they could to help. Faye Chapman, a former dance-hall girl turned missionary, opened the Glad Tydings Temple and later Sister Faye's Mission at 211 Yesler Way. Wearing stylish high heels and fur coats, "Sister Faye" played the banjo and preached on Skid Road corners to recruit one of the largest mission followings in the district. In related efforts, volunteers opened soup kitchens and bread lines to feed the needy. Ivar Haglund, later famed for his Acres of Clams restaurant, operated a soup kitchen in a storefront at Washington and Occidental.

As relief dollars became available, government-funded facilities opened. One of them was the Blue Ox Lodge on Yesler Way

"Hooverville," south of Pioneer Square, was one of many impromptu shantytowns that sprang up in the Puget Sound area. The Seattle Health Department declared it unfit and ordered it burned down on two occasions before 1932, when the new municipal administration relented. Local businesses contributed surplus materials and food, and Hooverville residents elected their own mayor and commissioners. Photo by James Patrick Lee. MSCUA, University of Washington Libraries, Lee 20102

just west of First Avenue in the Schwabacher Hardware Company building, with steel bunks for 130 men on each of the three upper floors. Noted for hygiene, the Blue Ox had strict rules. An applicant went to the main-floor clinic for a medical exam; when approved, he took a bath and all of his clothes were washed. As required by law, each man received clean towels and bedding, and all of the floors were scrubbed daily.

As Skid Road missions and flophouses overflowed, some of the homeless moved into abandoned basements (some of which are now accessible via the Underground Tour). Others scavenged materials to build makeshift shacks in "Hooverville," a shantytown that sprawled across the former Skinner and Eddy Shipyards southwest of today's Safeco Field. Like similar communities across the nation, it was named for President Hoover, whom many blamed for the economic crisis. An unofficial 1934 census conducted by a University of Washington graduate student found 632 men and 7 women living in the self-organized community. The population was racially mixed, with more than half foreign born.

Self-Help and Relief Efforts

Between 1931 and 1932, Seattle's relief rolls doubled to 30,000 people—10 percent of the population, a ratio that would increase to 26.5 percent within three years. Local charities and voluntary organizations were stretched to the limit. At the beginning of the Depression, county and state programs provided meager assistance and facilities for the deaf, blind, insane, and indigent poor. However, there was no provision for the problem of mass unemployment.

The city acted quickly to expand its public works program, but efforts on the part of the city and county governments to create jobs and provide relief were insufficient. The unemployed began taking matters into their own hands.

In the wake of the stock market crash, local Communists demonstrated against the capitalistic system, and Mayor Frank Edwards had several of them arrested. He blamed the economic downturn on the foes of capitalism, stating publicly that "Communism is the root of the present trouble." Party members from eastern Europe quickly toned down their revolutionary stance in the United States, turning their attention to organizing self-help, neighborhood-

In the early 1930s, the city put men to work tearing down the dilapidated streetcar trestle that turned from Washington Street onto Railroad Avenue, now Alaskan Way. It was designed during World War I to whisk workers to and from the shipyards but was constructed after the armistice. Following the demolition, several buildings, from left to right, the O.K., Old Boston, and Our House Hotels and Schwabachers Hardware Company Warehouse, had unobstructed waterfront views. Museum of History and Industry, 8801

based programs for the unemployed, who in turn would agitate for economic and political reform. The local headquarters of the Workers' Alliance was in the New England Hotel building at First Avenue South and Main. In Pioneer Square, streetside orators aimed their recruiting efforts at hungry unemployed men, including laid-off seasonal workers. Hazel Wolf, a single parent and an unemployed secretary, was one of the first of many local white- and blue-collar workers to become a card-carrying Communist. She explained, "I was in a bad way. I had sense enough to know that you can't do anything much alone in the way of struggle against the establishment."

In 1931 Mayor Edwards fired the popular City Light Superintendent, James D. Ross, who promoted municipal ownership of utilities—a move that many thought would provide low-cost, plentiful electricity to citizens while creating jobs. Conservatives held that the idea was socialistic. Ross's supporters launched a recall campaign against Edwards that ousted him from office. Some of the leaders in the campaign were staunch anti-Communists with socialist and labor union backgrounds. Shortly after the recall, they organized the Unemployed Citizens League, whose major goal was work relief for members. But at first, supplemental relief took precedence.

The UCL was a self-help organization that operated on a barter basis without dues or paid staff. Members did the work they knew, such as sewing garments, cutting hair, or repairing each other's shoes, roofs, or cars. They gathered firewood from vacant lots, caught fish, and harvested unsold crops. The UCL demanded and received county and city relief funds to purchase additional food for distribution. At its peak, the local league had 50,000 members. It formed a state federation in which the unemployed in farming communities exchanged produce for goods manufactured in cooperative urban workshops. A national UCL followed, as the idea caught fire in other states.

The Seattle league backed John Dore, a public power advocate, for mayor. During the economic collapse, Mayor Dore kept Seattle in the black and supported the business community by lowering taxes. He also laid off scores of city employees—a move that angered the UCL and led to his defeat in the next election. When Republican Governor Roland Hartley refused Dore's and other mayors' requests for state relief, Washington's UCLs planned a Fourth of July protest march on Olympia "to call the attention of the representatives of the owner class to the need for drastic action." Historian Murray Morgan writes, "Wobblies and Communists and Socialists all struggled to dominate the League and to control the protest march." The nonviolent demonstration ended without response from the Legislature or the governor, in part because the marchers could not agree on what benefits to request. But they concurred that there was a need for change.

In the 1932 election, change meant throwing Republicans out of office, and Washington's voters made some unorthodox choices. Vic Meyers was a popular Seattle danceband leader who drew crowds to the Butler Hotel in Pioneer Square. He staged a gag campaign for lieutenant governor, saying that if elected, he hoped someone would tell him what he was supposed to do in office. His win prompted commentary from editorial writers across the nation about the fate of Washington state, but Meyers's antics continued to entertain voters, who supported his subsequent reelections.

Marion Zioncheck won his bid for Congress in 1932 and again in 1934. The son of Polish immigrants, he grew up among the struggling poor on the Skid Road, where he caught rats (at ten cents a head), peddled fish, and found sea-

A Skid Road flophouse, ca. 1920s. As required by law, beds were made daily with clean sheets and pillowcases. Museum of History and Industry, Seattle Post-Intelligencer, 865.11829.1

sonal jobs in logging camps. He worked his way through the University of Washington, passed the bar exam, then became a political power by organizing the recall campaign against Edwards. In campaigns for the Seattle Congressional seat, Zioncheck often began his speeches with "I am a radical." In his second term, he drew national attention with his alcoholism and bizarre acts that culminated in a suicidal dive from the fifth floor of the Arctic Building at Third and Cherry.

Along with the sensational choices, Washington's voters made sound ones as they shifted from a long-standing Republican tradition to Democrat. In 1932, they elected Governor Clarence Martin, a conservative Democrat from Cheney, and supported Franklin D. Roosevelt for president. For cash-strapped Seattle, Roosevelt's election was none too soon. He launched his New Deal with sweeping programs to put

people back to work and feed the hungry. Under Governor Martin's leadership, federal dollars were matched in part by state dollars, which in turn were collected from counties and cities. As relief funds became available, the line of unemployed wound its way around the block to the King County welfare office at Second Avenue South and Jackson, where qualified applicants were paid $1.10 per week. The Works Progress Administration (WPA) created temporary subsidized jobs in construction, theater, art, writing, gardening in public parks, and more. Another innovation was the Social Security Act of 1935.

As federal relief measures took hold, the UCL moved on to form the Washington Commonwealth Federation—a coalition of the unemployed, organized labor, and Democrats. Politicians courted their vote. At the state Democratic convention in 1936, the WCF emerged as the powerful left wing of the party, which endorsed progressive candidates for office and adopted a platform that favored nationalization of all banks and public ownership of all utilities and natural resources. One of the successful candidates, Warren G. Magnuson, was a handsome, first-term member of the state Legislature and a card-carrying member of Seattle's UCL. Seattle voters elected him to the congressional seat that had been vacated by Marion Zioncheck. ("Maggie" served in the House and later the Senate for forty-four years and was regarded by many as Seattle's most influential citizen.)

At the Communist Workers' Alliance, Bill Pennock took up the banner for senior citizens and organized a legislative initiative to establish the Washington Old Age Pension Union, the first such state-guaranteed program in the nation. Pennock promoted the plan through the WCF, which in turn gained the support of progressive Democrats.

As in the past, trade unions often disagreed on priorities, and so did organizations of the unemployed. Nonetheless, the radical left wing of the state's Democratic Party became an effective voice for social reform. Because of its influence and some of the above-noted events, Jim Farley, who served as U.S. Postmaster General in the Roosevelt administration, later referred to "the forty-seven states and the Soviet of Washington."

Dave Beck and the Establishment

By the mid-1930s, Dave Beck had risen from the job of truck driver for a Pioneer Square laundry to head of the local Teamsters Union. Beck sought control of everything on wheels and of unions in shops that his truckers served. With a talent for organizing, he gained dominance by cooperating with big business to support price stability. He said, "We recognize that labor cannot receive a fair wage unless business receives a just profit on its investment." Seattle newspapers at first lambasted Beck, labeling him a dangerous radical who sought control of the movement of goods and services between warehouses and retail outlets.

Beck's strongest adversary was Harry Bridges, leader of the International Longshoremen's and Warehousemen's Union (ILWU), who organized strikes that pitted workers against the moneyed establishment in what he deemed to be a class struggle. As teamsters and longshoremen struggled against each other for control of warehouse workers, the establishment came out on the side of Beck. In 1934 longshore workers from Bellingham to San Diego shut down waterfronts on the West Coast in a strike that lasted eighty-three days. There were violent confrontations at Smith Cove and near the Smith Tower, where strikers tussled with police. The ILWU ended the strike, accepting a ninety-five-cent-per-hour increase in wages. It was a rare victory for Bridges over Beck.

Seattle Mayor John Dore blamed the business community for letting him down and costing him the 1934 election. He did a political about-face to become the champion of labor and win the support of Dave Beck and the Teamsters. In 1936, as newly elected mayor, he addressed the state American Federation of Labor (AFL) convention, saying, "Brother Beck was the greatest factor in my election, and I say again that I am going to pay back my debt to Dave Beck and the Teamsters, regardless of what happens." In *Skid Road,* published in 1951, historian Murray Morgan chronicles Beck's rise to power during the years between the two world wars and his emergence as the city's most dominant figure. Beck was subsequently elected international president of the Teamsters. On that occasion, the Seattle Chamber of Commerce sent him flowers. He was also elected president of the University of Washington Board of Regents. Beck's reign ended in 1959, when he was sentenced for income tax evasion and did time at the federal penitentiary on McNeil Island.

Filipinos Form a Union

Since the Philippines were an American territory, Filipinos could immigrate to the United States as "nationals" without restrictions or passports. A large influx of bachelors and a few women came to the West Coast in the 1920s, seeking employment and educational opportunities. But like others of Asian descent, they found themselves excluded from the mainstream job market. Because of the ban on Chinese and Japanese immigration, labor contractors recruited Filipinos as railroad, farm, and cannery workers. Many became migrant laborers, following agricultural harvests and salmon runs to canneries in Alaska, where more than four thousand of them worked in 1930.

Filipinos stuck together and provided their own entertainment, including boxing competitions. Here, the Moonlight Serenaders join fans to celebrate with bantam-weight champ Speedy Dado. Filipino American National Historical Society

For the most part, the Alaska contractors were a ruthless lot that exploited Filipino laborers, forcing them to do the most menial jobs and housing them in segregated, substandard

Members of the Filipino Cannery Workers' and Farm Workers Union wait near their union hall to cast ballots in a 1938 National Labor Relations Board election. Filipino American National Historical Society

quarters, while foremen ran gambling games and brothels to fleece them of their meager pay. There were a few Filipino contractors, including Peo DeCano and Pedro Santos, who were known for treating their brothers fairly and with respect. As the dispatch city from the states to the far north, Seattle was the *Alaskeros*'s port of departure and return. Those passing through gathered with local residents in Filipino-owned restaurants and pool halls, some of which were located in southeast Pioneer Square.

In 1933 Filipinos leased space in the old Longshore Union Hall at Second Avenue South and Main and organized the Cannery Workers and Farm Laborers Union Local 18257, which was accepted into the AFL. Within three years, the ethnically diverse union had 3,000 members, most of whom were Filipino or Japanese. The CWFLU battled flagrant and rampant abuses against Asian workers, especially the *Alaskeros,* and challenged dishonest contractors.

Resentful contractors and unemployed whites fought back. They pressured Congress, which in 1934 enacted a law that reclassified Filipinos as aliens and imposed an annual immigration quota of fifty per year. Historian Fred Cordova writes:

Contractors hired hoodlums to harass union organizers. On a cold night on December 1, 1936, inside a Japanese restaurant in Seattle, two of the Cannery Workers and Farm Laborers Union officers were shot to death. [Virgil] Duyungan, the president, was gunned down. Also murdered was the union secretary, Aurelio Simon. A third Filipino lay dead on the restaurant stairs; he was the assailant, killed by the dying Duyungan. Duyungan left behind a widow and five children; Simon, a widow and three children.

A funeral procession of more than thirty-five hundred, including cannery workers and other labor figures, marched from the union hall through downtown in honor of the victims.

Turbulence continued to swirl around the union in ensuing decades, as it battled ongoing corruption in the contract labor system. But the union persevered and helped build a Filipino community with pride in itself and an eye on the future. In the 1930s, members socialized at a club near the union hall, where the Moonlight Serenaders played Broadway tunes and Filipino folk songs in American-style arrangements. Since few women had immigrated from the Philippines, there were "taxi dancers"—women of different ethnicities who would dance with anyone for a few cents. During the Great Depression, Filipinos stuck together. Years later they could boast, "We never joined the breadlines."

Repeal of Prohibition

In 1933 liquor interests welcomed the repeal of federal prohibition. Competition was keen among former speakeasies and restaurants, which scrambled for a liquor license and an anticipated surge in profits. To attract a drinking clientele, the Merchant's Cafe across from Pioneer Place sold beer for a nickel, with free sandwiches and hard-boiled eggs. Signage on the Skid Road once again showed a preponderance of saloons. Houses of prostitution and gambling joints operated openly. In response, the state imposed "blue laws" that established state-owned liquor stores, prohibited the sale of hard liquor by the drink, and restricted beer to a very low alcoholic content.

Family Life on the Skid Road

In her book *Nisei Daughter*, Monica Sone (nee Kazuko Itoi) reflects on her childhood in the Carrollton Hotel, which was on the second floor of an old, red brick building (now demolished) at Main and Occidental. Her father bought the hotel in 1918, when it "fairly burst with war workers and servicemen." It was typical of workingmen's accommodations on the Skid Road, featuring twenty rooms with windows to both the outside and a hallway, plus forty interior rooms with skylights for ventilation and light. Each small room had a washbowl, a water pitcher, and a chamber pot. There was only one bathroom with a tub "to keep sixty people clean" and a separate "Gent's Restroom." The Itoi family lived in four small outside rooms that they converted into a comfortable apartment.

Sone describes how her parents cleaned up the "battered, flea-ridden Carrollton." Her father declared, "If I have to manage a flophouse, it'll be the cleanest and quietest place around here." The Itois scrubbed and painted tobacco-stained stairways, varnished the floor, laid out new green runners in the hallways, and repapered each of the rooms. Mr. Itoi was equally careful about accepting tenants. He knew that "among the flotsam of seedy, rough-looking characters . . . were men who still retained their dignity and self-respect." If a man smelled of "plain, honest-to-goodness perspiration, he was in. But if he reeked of wood alcohol or bayrum, the office window came crashing down in front of his nose." Mr. and Mrs. Itoi went from room to room each morning to clean and make the beds. Describing a happy childhood, Sone said, "I thought the whole world consisted of two or three old hotels on every block. And that its population consisted of families like mine . . . and fading, balding, watery-eyed men, rough-tough bearded men, and good men like Sam, Joe, Peter and Montana who worked for Father [and] lived in these hotels."

Along with other Nisei children, Sone and her brother and sister walked from Pioneer Square up the hill through the heart of Nihon-machi ("Japantown") to Bailey Gatzert Elementary School on Twelfth Avenue. After public school, they went to the nearby Japanese school, where they studied the language and cultural traditions. The family had close ties with other Japanese families and was involved in community organizations.

Sone gives a vivid childhood impression of the Pioneer Square neighborhood, beginning with the secondhand clothing store on the ground floor of the Carrollton. Next door was a tavern "around which we were not supposed to loiter," and next to it was a mission hall "filled with hollow-eyed, graying old men. . . ." Other businesses on the block were Mr. Wakamatsu's Ace Café, a Japanese-run barbershop, a hot dog stand, the forbidden burlesque house, a cigar shop, and a Teamsters Union office around the corner. She talks about the Salvation Army Band that was "always there" and about radical orators who exhorted their apathetic audiences at Free Speech Corner (described in chapter 8).

The Tide Turns

Some of the most vociferous orators lived and worked nearby. Trotskyites, Communists, and Teamsters carried their soapboxes to the corner of Washington and Occidental, where they tried to snare a few converts among their largely unemployed listeners.

But by the mid-thirties, government social welfare programs had brought relief to many of the destitute. Trade unions were improving working conditions in logging camps, on ships, and elsewhere and were spearheading a strong anti-Communist campaign. Hitler's alliance with Stalin had changed the minds of millions in America and Europe regarding the Communist Party, and many who had joined resigned on ideological grounds. Even Skid Road denizens began to see themselves as tools for Russian foreign policy and not for betterment of the human condition.

There were those who remained affiliated, even though they disagreed with the international party line. Hazel Wolf explained, "I was a member of the Communist Party of the United States of America, working on problems here." She noted that in her unit, "Nobody talked about overthrowing the government. Meanwhile, we did all kinds of good things for people."

In what her biographer, Susan Starbuck, calls the beginning of the witch hunt, Wolf was dismissed from her WPA job with the Federal Theater Project in 1938 on grounds that she was a noncitizen. Born in Canada, she had moved to Seattle fifteen years earlier with her American husband and was the mother of an American child. Her ineligibility for federal relief coincided with the U.S. House of Representatives' establishment of the House Un-American Activities Committee in 1938, and she subsequently fought her way through years of deportation hearings.

Following her dismissal from the WPA job, Wolf chaired the Grievance Committee at the Workers' Alliance office in Pioneer Square. Many of those she tried to help were unemployed and homeless women, some of whom lived with their children in Hooverville shacks.

By 1937, government-subsidized employment programs had put some fifty thousand Washingtonians to work. According to King County's Advisory Committee on Social Security, the average age of King County men on relief had risen to 59.2, and a high percentage of them suffered from physical disabilities. Reports noted that most of them were "quiet and orderly."

When the New Deal began making severe cutbacks, it effectively threw the region into a new recession. There were demonstrations, including one of five hundred Workers' Alliance members at City Hall Park, where a county commissioner promised them relief vouchers of twenty cents per day so that no one "would be permitted to starve." In 1939, when the state closed the Blue Ox Lodge, some three hundred

During a meeting at the Moose Hall, eight hundred hands rose in unison as WPA workers voted to continue their month-long strike. Supported by the Workers' Alliance of Washington, the strikers voted two days later to go back to work after receiving guarantees of a six-hour day, a five-day week, and union-level hourly pay rates. Seattle Post-Intelligencer, *February 23, 1937. Museum of History and Industry, 86.5.16694*

homeless men marched to the seventh floor of the County-City Building, where they were allowed to spend the night. The next day, county officials reopened the shelter and set up a program to feed a thousand men. As the crisis worsened to conditions like those in the depths of 1932, many blamed the liberal left wing and shifted their support to conservative politicians.

In 1940 the Social Security Administration documented the impacts of New Deal cuts on 123 of the nation's largest cities, stating that Seattle was "by far the most seriously affected." But the crisis was short-lived.

World War II on the Home Front

Regional economics went from bust to boom as the federal government turned its attention to the threat of a second world war. The Nazis were storming Europe, and Japan posed a threat to all of Asia. In 1939 the British Royal Air Force placed a large order for Boeing Aircraft Company's recently developed "Flying Fortress," the B-17, to strike back at Hitler's Luftwaffe. In late 1940 Congress authorized national defense funding to bolster military and defense-related industries, including several in the Puget Sound area.

On December 7, 1941, Japan attacked Pearl Harbor in Hawaii, and the United States was at war. By then, Boeing employed 30,000 workers and was seeking more. Revitalized shipyards, lumber mills that provided in-demand wood and paper products, and other industries flew into high gear with round-the-clock shifts and jobs for every able hand. People in search of wartime jobs migrated to the Northwest, including a large number of African Americans. Between 1940 and 1943, Seattle's population exploded from 368,000 to 480,000. The city ranked as one of the top three in the nation for war contracts.

Before the 1940s, most married women did not work for pay if their husbands could support them. The public schools barred married women from teaching, and during the Depression, the government and several labor unions told women to stay home, so that men could have jobs. The wartime crisis ended the long-debated question about woman's proper place in the workforce. As patriotic young men enlisted in the armed services, a labor shortage loomed on the homefront. The government hastened to produce filmstrips showing neatly dressed and coifed women coming out of factories, where their jobs as welders or machinists were—according to the narrators—no more complicated than baking a cake. Former housewives replaced men on production lines, earning $200 to $250 a month and sometimes more as they mastered special skills. In late 1944, when Boeing celebrated the rolling out of its 10,000th wartime B-17, more than half of its workforce was female.

Like other West Coast cities, Seattle lived in fear of attack and imposed nighttime dimouts to decrease its visibility as a target for Japanese bombers. Volunteers kept watch, scanning the skies for enemy aircraft. In Pioneer Square, dilapidated buildings were patched up and converted to dwelling units to help meet the city's housing shortage. Workers boarded the buses and trolleys, which had replaced the old streetcar system in 1940, en route to and from shipyards, Boeing's Duwamish plant, and other factories located south of downtown and in West Seattle. Others commuted by train from King Street and Union Stations to jobs at Boeing's giant Renton plant or industrial sites in the White River valley.

The armed services leased the Frye Hotel to provide comfortable housing for officers and troops. Schwabacher Hardware Company's warehouse at Jackson Street and Railroad

The U.S. Army, followed by the Navy (shown here) commandeered the Frye Hotel during World War II. Courtesy of Robert Roblee

Avenue (now Alaskan Way) was converted to storage for dragnaughts (torpedoes for navy ships). The Civil Aeronautics Authority moved offices into the Interurban Building (also known as the Smith Tower Annex).

In the midst of patriotic activity, Pioneer Square businesses of all sorts extended their hours to serve workers on daytime, swing, and graveyard shifts and did a thriving business. Customers shopped at a variety of retail establishments, such as G. O. Guy's Drugstore in the Metropole Building at Second Avenue South and Yesler and Schwabacher Brothers Grocery in the State Building at Main and Occidental. Taverns and cafes did a lively business, especially on Friday and Saturday nights with servicemen on weekend leave from Fort Lawton, Fort Lewis, and other nearby military

bases. Chinese lotteries drew crowds to Old Chinatown on Washington between Second and Third Avenues South. Brothels proliferated until late in 1942, when the city closed them down in response to demands from the armed services.

Illegal prostitution continued on upper-floor rooms and in parlors, especially in a red-light district located east of Pioneer Square on the hillside along Yesler Way. With assistance from the U.S. Public Health Department, Mayor William Devin organized a venereal disease treatment center to help cope with what had become a major health issue.

The war sparked a temporary boom in railroad travel, due in part to rationing of gasoline and rubber. To meet the demand, King Street Station employed 425 people, more than at any

Because of national security, interior photos of train stations were generally forbidden during World War II. This rare image is a typical wartime scene at King Street Station. Museum of History and Industry, PEMCO 86.5.13,036.1

other time in its history. The sprawling railroad freight yards also sprang to life after years of decline.

Internment of Japanese Americans

Although the war revitalized the railroads, it had a devastating impact on some of their most dedicated employees. Union Station replaced its Japanese-American redcaps (baggage handlers) with African Americans; King Street Station replaced them with Filipinos, who wore large badges reading "Filipino." Immediately after the bombing of Pearl Harbor, the U.S. military began rounding up leaders in Japanese-American communities and incarcerating them for questioning.

On February 14, 1942, President Roosevelt issued Executive Order 9006 to evacuate people of Japanese descent from the West Coast and transport them to inland concentration camps. In all, 110,000 people were targeted, including

7,000 who lived in Seattle. The order led to what has been called the worst violation of constitutional rights in U.S. history. Japanese-born residents (Issei) and their American-born children (Nisei) had committed no crime but were viewed as a possible threat to national security because of their race. They had two months to prepare to leave their homes and businesses and were allowed to take only what they could carry. Some arranged for friends to care for their property, but many had to abandon their belongings or sell them to bargain hunters at rock-bottom prices.

The incalculable economic and psychological costs to the evacuees have been well documented. But the internment was also a serious loss to Pioneer Square, where Japanese-American families made their homes and ran small businesses and bachelor hotels. Unlike the dominant Skid Road population, they had community organizations and children who walked to school. In April 1942, anxious friends waved

Japanese Americans move into temporary quarters on the Puyallup Fairgrounds. From there, they were transported to inland concentration camps. MSCUA, University of Washington Libraries, 526

good-bye as their neighbors filed past armed troops onto buses bound for the temporary assembly center on the Puyallup Fairgrounds.

From there most of the Seattle contingent was transported to the Minidoka Relocation Center in arid south-central Idaho. Surrounded by barbed wire and guarded by military police, it was one of ten inland concentration camps for West Coast Japanese. In mid-1942 when U.S. Army personnel visited the camps to recruit men for a special Nisei combat unit, thousands enlisted to serve their country. Some of the young women also volunteered for military service, while others were given permission to leave the camps for jobs or college in the Midwest and East.

In August 1945, the United States dropped atomic bombs on Hiroshima and Nagasaki, after which Japan surrendered and the world was at peace.

People of Japanese descent were no longer exiled from the West Coast; the inland internment camps were closed and the inmates were set free. Many of them did not return to their former homes. The more fortunate, including the Itois, were able to reclaim property that friends had cared for in their absence. Others had lost everything and had to start over. Without voicing protest, they struggled to get on with their lives and to put the humiliation and injustice of the evacuation behind them. They coped quietly with anti-Japanese sentiment and nativists who sometimes hollered at them, "Jap, go home!" Within a few years, the Seattle Japanese Hotel and Apartment Operators Association was reestablished, with members once again managing most of Pioneer Square's boardinghouses and bachelor hotels. But the district was no longer the center of Japanese family and community life that it had been before the war.

Return to Normalcy

In the postwar period, Americans wanted more than anything to resume a normal way of life. The government issued new propaganda in filmstrips that showed dirty, crying children neglected by mothers who worked outside the home. At Boeing and the shipyards, women workers resigned or were dismissed, so that returning male veterans could have their jobs. Young couples marched to the altar in droves, and new suburbs blossomed. Husbands commuted to work and ideal wives, like June Cleaver in the popular *Leave It to Beaver* television series, devoted themselves to homemaking— or so the myth goes.

In reality, women—both single and married— continued to enter the job market at an unprecedented rate. Contrary to the filmstrip message, wartime mothers had proved that they could successfully balance their homemaking and

Kanjiro Tashiro, shown here in 1929, founded his hardware store in the late teens at 109 Prefontaine Place. In 1942, then in his sixties, he arranged to put the stock in storage prior to the family's internment. After the war, he reopened the store with the help of his Nisei daughter Billee and her husband, Juro Yoshioka, who continued to run the business until the 1980s. The Tashiro Building is a Pioneer Square landmark that has the family name carved in stone above the entrance. MSCUA, *University of Washington Libraries,* UW 551

workplace roles. According to historian William Chafe, some 10 million American women held salaried jobs in the 1950s—2 million more than at the peak of the wartime emergency. In the late 1940s, the Seattle Public Schools instituted new policies to employ married women and African Americans as teachers. But "Rosie the Riveter" was a phenomenon of the past, and production lines, shipyards, and aircraft factories were once again a man's place. Most women worked in female-dominated job categories with low pay and little opportunity for advancement. On the Skid Road they held jobs in family businesses and small factories or as waitresses in taverns and cafes.

Hum of Sewing Machines

In the postwar period, non–English-speaking immigrant women, including many who were refugees, found jobs as seamstresses and sewing-machine operators in factories in and around Pioneer Square. Here, they could eke out a living while speaking their own language and learning rudimentary English from their American-born co-workers. For many, it was their first opportunity to interact with other ethnic groups.

On her return from the Heart Mountain Camp in Wyoming, Teiko Tomita found work as a seamstress in Seattle. Through her *tanka* poetry, translated by Gail Nomura, she described her growing sense of sisterhood with other immigrant women, many of whom were refugees. They shared common experiences of separation from homeland and loved ones, the horrible costs of war, and the resolve to work hard and rebuild their lives. After several years of sewing, Tomita wrote that "such life is enjoyable."

Wing Luke Asian Museum's 2001 exhibition "If Tired Hands Could Talk—Stories of Asian Garment Workers" used translated oral-history interviews, photographs, and artifacts to bring to light the local sweatshop experience. Founded in 1966, the museum is located at Seventh and Jackson in the International District.

The roots of the area's garment manufacturing industry date back to the Klondike gold rush, which transformed Seattle into a major outfitting post for prospectors. Firms such as C. C. Filson Company and Black Manufacturing Company (in the Seattle Quilt Building, on the east side of First Avenue South between Main and Jackson; later the home of the Seattle Quilt Company) set up shop in Pioneer Square. In 1929 Buttnick Manufacturing Company began making sportswear at First and Washington. Other related local companies were founded in other parts of the city, including Eddie Bauer Inc., Recreational Equipment Inc., Skyway Luggage, and Pacific Trail Sportswear. During

World War II, production schedules ran around the clock to meet skyrocketing orders from the U.S. military.

From the 1940s to the 1980s, Seattle was the outerwear manufacturing capital of the United States. By the 1950s, the garment workers were the Pioneer Square district's largest employee group. Passersby on the street were accustomed to the hum of power sewing machines that emanated from the sweatshops. And many a resident or visitor to Pioneer Square noticed groups of predominantly Asian women who gathered on the sidewalk on pleasant days to gossip, get some fresh air, and eat the home-packed sandwiches or rice dishes they brought for lunch. Many of them joined local chapters of the International Ladies Garment Workers Union, which advocated successfully for better pay and working conditions.

In the 1980s and 1990s, most of the large garment manufacturers moved their plants overseas, where cheap labor was readily avail-

In the 1950s, outerwear and outdoor gear factories became the district's major employers. They provided jobs for non–English-speaking immigrants, especially women. Washington State Archives, Puget Sound Branch

able. Today C. C. Filson, located just south of Pioneer Square, is the only major remaining long-term player among a bevy of smaller firms. Known for admirable working conditions, it continues to employ largely Asian women.

Decline of the Skid Road

While the garment industry survived and prospered, the late 1940s spelled the end of Pioneer Square's temporary wartime revitalization. After the armistice, the district's military offices and installations shut down; small factories lost their defense contracts and laid off workers; residents who had worked in defense-related industries moved away from their temporary dwellings. The flood of commuters and military personnel that had enlivened Pioneer Square businesses slowed to a trickle.

The Schwabacher family closed its grocery business in the State Building at Main and Occidental in 1945, following the death of Nathan Eckstein. As the husband of Minna Schwabacher, Eckstein had headed the family's retail and wholesale grocery division for half a century and had gained a citywide following of loyal customers and friends. They would no longer come to Pioneer Square to buy the company's house brands, especially its popular Gold Medal Coffee.

Pioneer Square's economic decline worsened in 1949, when an earthquake measuring 7.1 on the Richter scale shook the region. (In comparison, the 2001 Nisqually Earthquake was 6.8.) City building inspectors condemned several historic structures as unsafe. In many cases, they required owners to dismantle a destabilized decorative cornice or parapet; in others, owners had to remove one or more upper floors or resort to demolition. In the aftermath of the earthquake, Pioneer Square deteriorated into a down-at-the-heels district of boarded-up

The 1949 earthquake claimed lives and scores of injuries. Here, rubble that fell from the Seattle Hotel is strewn across Yesler Way in front of the Interurban Building. Photo by Ken Harris, April 14, 1949. Museum of History and Industry, Seattle Post-Intelligencer, front page

buildings, warehouses and outerwear factories, small businesses, flophouses, and missions.

In 1950 district merchants decided to sponsor the first annual Father's Day picnic for five hundred Skid Road residents. Trucks and taxicabs took the guests to a resort on Steel Lake, where they found cases of beer and soft drinks, buckets of spaghetti, and plenty of shade trees. Waitresses from Skid Road cafes served the food. A reporter from *The Seattle Times* quoted a "grizzled retired logger" who said, "Brother, this is heaven. Twenty-one years I've lived in Skid Road but I've never seen anything like this. This is the nicest thing anybody ever did for me."

In 1952 more than twenty-one hundred Skid Road residents lined up at the Eagles' Auditorium at Seventh and Union in downtown Seattle for a Christmas dinner financed by donations from Seattle residents. The next year, a banjo band and spirited singing by civic leaders contributed to the fun of the Skid Road Christmas party, held at the Blue Banjo night-club in the Pioneer Building. Participants included Wing Luke and Myrtle Edwards of the City Council and County Commissioner John O'Brien.

At the same time, the Skid Road was becom-ing more isolated. In 1953 the Alaskan Way Viaduct rose on its west flank, replacing Fourth Avenue as the "scenic downtown bypass" for the Pacific Coast Highway. Civic leaders and the media hailed it as an engineering master-piece and a significant contribution to the city's future. But by the 1960s, critics were calling the two-tiered concrete band an eyesore that

obstructed downtown views and access to the waterfront. A growing chorus of citizens began the ongoing proposals for its demolition that continue as of this writing. In the 1960s, many compared the viaduct issue to the early days of railroad dominance, when citizens had waged campaigns for waterfront access.

Social Reform and Public Health

While cleaning up the 1949 earthquake debris, the city instituted a controversial program to control highly contagious tuberculosis on the Skid Road. At the time, TB was Seattle's leading cause of death; though newly introduced anti-

Alaskan Way Viaduct under construction, looking north from Washington Street.
Seattle Municipal Archives, Engineering Department Collection, Item 23510

biotic therapy was available, the city's vagrant population was prone to heavy alcohol consumption and commonly failed to follow physicians' advice. Public health professor Barron H. Lerner writes in *Contagion and Confinement* that the problem was particularly severe in Seattle, where men who had ridden the rails in search of work often reached the end of the line.

City health and law enforcement officials began picking up uncooperative patients from the Skid Road and taking them to Firland Sanatorium, a former naval hospital north of the city. Their rehabilitation prescription meant forced detention—often in the special ward that resembled a jail. While many patients went to sanatoriums voluntarily, the Skid Road patients had no choice, and they soon constituted the overwhelming majority at Firland.

Many debated the ethics of the reform agenda that framed tuberculosis as a social disease and that targeted the poor for forced treatment. There was a growing consensus that medical treatment was not enough and that other circumstances such as poor living conditions and undernourishment were equally responsible for the disease. It was not until the 1970s that the controversial program was abandoned.

Beginning in the mid-1950s, newly developed drugs offered an alternative to hospitalization for psychiatric patients. During the next two decades, the manner of treatment underwent dramatic philosophical changes that resulted in closure of psychiatric hospitals across the nation. "Deinstitutionalization" programs aimed to release mentally ill patients and return them to local communities. Theoretically, mental health centers created by the 1963 Community Mental Health Act would provide mentoring and antipsychotic medications that would enable psychiatrically disturbed individuals to adjust. However, as institutions

Shown here in 1927, a public health nurse staffs the drop-in clinic in the Public Safety Building on Yesler Way. Patients were often referred to the City Hospital's TB Division. Seattle Municipal Archives, Item 2719

discharged large numbers of patients, federal funding for community-based facilities proved grossly inadequate.

Along with tuberculosis patients, former psychiatric patients joined the ranks of the homeless on Seattle's Skid Road. Social service agencies and law enforcement officials struggled with the challenge of helping the mentally ill while maintaining civility in the neighborhood. In 1975 the U.S. Supreme Court ruled against involuntary hospitalization of nonviolent psychiatric patients capable of surviving in the community. As a result, many landed in jail for violent or deviant behavior; prosecuting attorneys had to prove that such patients were substantially dangerous to themselves or others before a judge could send them to a hospital.

In the 1990s a resurgence of tuberculosis led to renewed legalization of detention for uncooperative patients, along with debates about their civil liberties. Studies show that the afflicted are likely to be homeless, to test positive for the Human Immunodeficiency Virus (HIV), and/or to be addicted to drugs. In modern times, missions, government social welfare programs, public health workers, police, and community activists continue to provide services and at the same time to promote public safety and civility for people of all social and economic brackets.

Street People

In 1969 Laurie Olin—now a nationally noted landscape architect—was a graduate student in sociology who took a room in Pioneer Square so that he could roam the streets, talk to the residents, and sketch the people and places he observed. His research culminated three years later in a book, *Breath on the Mirror—Seattle's Skid Road Community,* which was self-published with help from art gallery owner Polly Friedlander and other Pioneer Square business owners. Olin wrote, "Sometimes the men would pester me to draw them. . . . These people whose identity has been brutally denied wanted to see that they were still there. My drawing seemed to re-affirm their existence."

He observed that the residents were often "race conscious and prejudiced" with "overt territorial behavior." Indians predominated around Pioneer Place and down First Avenue South almost to Washington Street; black people congregated around Washington and Occidental; largely white areas were the west side of First Avenue South between Washington and Main and the south side of Main. Racially integrated territory included Second Avenue South, the waterfront, and the west end of Yesler Way, along with the missions, the state's hiring hall, and the state liquor store at Second and James.

Olin notes that in the wake of the 1949 earthquake, some structures were demolished for parking lots "but not for lack of tenants. As long as a cheap habitable room was available it was occupied." In 1970 a horrific arson fire swept through the wood-frame, five-story Ozark

Hotel at Westlake and Lenora, claiming the lives of twenty residents and seriously injuring ten more. It was the worst of several fires in dilapidated old buildings, and it prompted the City Council to enact new fire prevention codes with strict enforcement. As a result, almost all of the Skid Road's cheap hotels and boardinghouses were forced to close. This marked the beginning of street people in Pioneer Square. Most of the displaced residents subsisted on income from Social Security, welfare, or jobs as day laborers on nearby berry and vegetable farms and could not afford to pay higher rent. The region was in an economic recession with scant employment prospects for unskilled workers.

Missions and other social services continued to do what they could. Abie Label and Robert Roblee, owners of the Frye Hotel, went to Washington, D.C., to lobby the Department of Housing and Urban Development (HUD) for renovation funds and federal rent subsidies that enabled them to convert the building to low-income housing. Olin says that the reason more of this was not done was lack of money and incentive. He explains, "Business has no incentive since there is no profit, and everyone has other uses for whatever tax money is collected."

Last Privately Run Hotel

In 1974 Ilze Jones and Grant Jones, business partners in Jones & Jones Architects and Landscape Architects, bought the old Traveler's Hotel, on Yesler Way between Post Alley and Western Avenue, which was due to close because of noncompliance with the Ozark Hotel Ordinance. In an interview with *The Seattle Times,* Grant Jones explained, "We bought it to preserve the Pioneer Square housing for low income and elderly people on the Skid Road." The 120–room

Ilze Jones and Grant Jones in the former alley behind the renovated Travelers Hotel, now the Travelers/Post Mews Building. Courtesy of Jones & Jones Architects and Landscape Architects

hotel was upstairs, with the state's Casual Labor Office and the OK Cafe (not to be confused with the O.K. Hotel, which is unrelated) on the ground floor. Jones & Jones brought the building up to code and retained the manager, Yukio Nakamura, who lived there with his wife, their two children, and his parents. The family had run the hotel for thirty years with strict rules prohibiting alcohol, drugs, and women. In 1977 when the Nakamuras retired, it was the end of an era. By that time, many of the older long-term tenants had moved away.

In 1980 Jones & Jones redesigned the building as Pioneer Square's first upscale condominium, with townhouse units and office suites and with retail on the ground floor. Its new name, the Traveler's/Post Mews Building, derives from the former rear alley (now fenced in), which is reminiscent of an English mews, with lush gardens around the condo entrances and on the balconies. Ilze Jones says that they envisioned the neighborhood's future with housing for people of all income brackets.

Pockets of Prosperity

Throughout its history, the Skid Road has been the first home of destitute immigrants and other newcomers. For many, it became what historian Murray Morgan called "the Place of Dead Dreams"; for others, it was a place to make a start, then move on. But for a few, it was a place to build and prosper.

American Messenger Company/ United Parcel Service

At the turn of the twentieth century, eleven-year-old Jim Casey dropped out of school to go to work and help support his family. The Klondike gold rush had cost his father both his money and his health. In 1907, at age nineteen, Jim and his friend Claude Ryan borrowed $100 to open a delivery service that they named the American Messenger Company (AMC).

The youths rented a small room in the basement of a saloon at Second and Main, installed telephones, and tacked up red and white posters near public phones advertising "Best Service and Lowest Rates." They hired messenger boys who agreed to a strict code of behavior, including no whistling. Wearing visored caps that bore the company name, the boys walked or rode bicycles and streetcars to make deliveries throughout the city. AMC was open twenty-four hours a day, including holidays. At first Casey and Ryan slept at the office to avoid missing a phone call and to be on hand to give the boys directions. By 1912 they employed 100

PORTAGE

AMERICAN MESSENGER Co.

The Messenger Company That Became United Parcel Service

The Puget Sound Steamboats

The Lost Treasure of the S.S. Islander

The Magazine of the Historical Society of Seattle and King County
Volume Three Number Three   *Summer 1982* $2.00

Artist's rendering of the first American Messenger Company headquarters, at Second Avenue South and Main, based on recollections of founder James Casey. Museum of History and Industry, Portage Magazine, *summer 1982*

messengers. Seven years later, when they moved to San Francisco, they changed the company's name to United Parcel Service.

Following UPS's later move to New York City, Jim Casey and his siblings established the Annie E. Casey Foundation in honor of their mother. In 1977 the foundation constructed Waterfall Park at Second Avenue South and Main to commemorate AMC's birthplace. The Casey Foundation recently renewed its roots in Seattle by building new headquarters at Twenty-third Avenue and East Union Street.

Duncan & Sons

George Duncan Sr., a Scottish immigrant, founded his Pioneer Square saddlery business in 1899, when liveries abounded. For more

than a century, four generations of Duncans have run the business, moving it to different locations in Pioneer Square. Their landmark horse statue stood stoically above the front doors of their former store on Second Avenue South, and its duplicate above their building on First Avenue South, which became the company home in the late 1970s.

In its World War I heyday, Duncan & Sons employed 300 people to craft cavalry saddles for the U.S. Army. In the latter part of the twentieth century, major customers included the Seattle Police Department's horse patrol and the National Park Service, for which the company made mule bags. Tourists and horse owners came from far and wide to shop for boots, saddles, boot-cut jeans, and bandannas. The store, the skilled leather workers, the landmark horse statue, and the Duncan family all represented the last direct link to the district's original mode of transportation. When the Duncans sold their building in 2000, *The Seattle Times* ran a feature story lamenting the loss.

Henry Broderick/Martin Smith Inc./ Alhadeff Company

In 1868 Leonard P. Smith and his wife came ashore and settled in Seattle after a two-year voyage on a whaling ship. He was the city's first jeweler, later serving two terms as mayor. In 1948 his great-great-grandson H. Martin Smith Jr. went to work for real estate magnate Henry Broderick. During the population boom at the beginning of the twentieth century, Broderick had bootstrapped his way up from salesman to the city's premier realtor. Between the 1930s and 1960s, his elegant office suite in the Broderick Building at Second and Cherry was the scene of 70 percent of Seattle's major real estate transactions.

Having learned the business from the master,

Smith founded his own company, Martin Smith Inc., in 1974. His sons Greg and Mickey and a partner, Jeff Rousch, eventually joined him in the business, which became the largest privately held real estate firm in the Puget Sound region. Recently Greg branched out to found his own company, Gregory Broderick Smith Real Estate. On several occasions, the Smiths' companies have teamed up with other investors and developers, including Kenny Alhadeff, who now owns the Broderick Building.

As head of his family's real estate enterprises and the Alhadeff Charitable Foundation, Kenny Alhadeff conducts business in Henry Broderick's former office suite. The Alhadeff family's roots in Pioneer Square date back to M. and K. Gottstein's Wholesale Liquor and Cigar, a business founded by Kenny's great-grandfather, Meyer Gottstein, and his cousin Kassel in 1889. Like the Smiths, they invested in downtown real estate.

Recently, both the Smiths and the Alhadeffs played significant roles in developing the twenty-story, mixed-use Millenium Tower. Although it is not officially in Pioneer Square, it is on its north flank, one of several projects infusing the neighborhood with new vitality. In addition, the Alhadeffs and Smiths have purchased and undertaken restoration of several historic buildings in Pioneer Square. Kenny Alhadeff sums up their philosophy: "If you walk through the area, you'll see the fabric of Seattle—the hope and the energy, and also some of the despair and discomfort. The key is to make the historic treasures a vibrant and meaningful part of the future."

Masin's Furniture

In 1927 Eman Masin founded the store at Second and Main that became Masin's Furniture. With a tasteful eye, he expanded the business to feature an extraordinary range of fine furnishings and an award-winning staff of accredited interior designers. The store's location did not deter an elite clientele, which came from far and wide even as the surrounding neighborhood fell into decline. Masin's son and grandson joined him in the family business. Today, Ben and Bob Masin remain at the helm, where they maintain the traditions of exquisite selection, design, and service that attract discerning customers to the original store in Pioneer Square and a second store in Bellevue.

From past to present, additional entrepreneurs, artists, and fringe groups have found fertile ground to make their start in the culturally and economically diverse Skid Road district.

8 Left Bank

Mildred Andrews

By the 1960s, Pioneer Square was once again at the vortex of cultural trends. Artists saw the drafty lofts in long-vacant buildings as an opportunity to secure affordable live/work space. It was a well-known occurrence, seen as well in New York City's Greenwich Village, in New Orleans' Vieux Carre historic district, and in the famed Bohemian Left Bank in Paris— a district on the left bank of the Seine River. "Starving artists" moved into undesirable fringe areas of a city with ample space and rock-bottom rents. These urban pioneers invested sweat equity to make dilapidated buildings habitable. They established communities that nurtured creativity with visual, musical, theatrical, literary, architectural, and culinary arts all coming into play. Galleries, restaurants, and theaters opened and buildings were rehabilitated. Visitors to Seattle's Skid Road district began seeing its cultural and economic attributes in a new light.

While serving as a catalyst for revitalization, a successful Bohemian community ironically sets the stage for its own transition. Within a relatively short time, gentrification and rising rents force many of its pioneering artists to look elsewhere for another abandoned district and a new frontier. In Pioneer Square, the artists were challenged not only by development but by the Kingdome and new sports-oriented businesses

that often seemed antithetical to the arts. At the same time, the influx of well-to-do customers created unprecedented opportunities for shopkeepers. Today Pioneer Square houses some of the city's finest galleries, bookstores, and music clubs. The community retains some of its Bohemian character, thanks in part to public/private partnerships that subsidize a small but significant number of live/work spaces for low-income artists.

But the roots of the neighborhood's creative spirit run deeper than the latter decades of the twentieth century. They were nurtured by spirited pioneers, fanciful terra-cotta, gold rush–era swagger, cultural diversity, and the free-speech movement of the early 1900s. Even in its darkest days, Pioneer Square was an incubator for fringe groups and new ideas. The vice-versus-virtue dichotomy helped propel bawdy Skid Road theater into a respectable trendsetter and a leader in American entertainment. During the first two decades of the twentieth century, Seattle was a vaudeville center, outstripped by only New York City.

The Birth of Vaudeville

Gold-rush links with the Canadian Yukon and Alaska put Seattle on the world map. In the first decade of the twentieth century, its population

The Lyric Theatre at Occidental and Washington. Photo by Asahel Curtis.
MSCUA, *University of Washington Libraries, A Curtis 25386*

quadrupled to almost a quarter of a million. Legions of adventurous schemers and fortune hunters swarmed to the city, infusing it with the boomtown swagger and reckless rhythms that gave birth to vaudeville. From notorious Skid Road roots, a unique theater scene evolved, as box-house theaters catered to the waves of lonely men who found women in short supply (see chapter 7).

The undisputed king of Seattle's box-houses was John Considine, a debonair, teetotalling Roman Catholic and a good family man. Having left Seattle during the recession of the mid-1890s, he returned in 1897 to capitalize on the gold-rush boom. His People's Theatre, located on the northwest corner of Second and Washington, and a neighboring establishment competed openly for customers. Every evening their musicians emerged onto the street and took turns, each trying to outperform the other

with lusty tunes. The July 30, 1899, *Seattle Post-Intelligencer* gave the following colorful description of the antiphonal battle, which included a third regular competitor:

Suddenly around the block is heard the discordant blare of an untutored brass band and the voices of men and women upraised in a popular street ditty. But the words are strangely out of joint. They seem to have been adapted from a hymnbook and misfitted to the tune. It is the Salvation Army! Fifty strong, the uniformed Soldiers of the Lord swing into the street in front of the theater and march up toward their Yesler Way barracks, flags flying, torches smoking and sputtering, musicians playing like mad.

Trying to drown out the Salvationists and each other, the battling bands no longer took turns. At the end, a brass trio prevailed with "There'll Be a Hot Time in the Old Town Tonight."

This rare interior view of a box-house theater shows the orchestra and staff at Ed Dolan's Eagle Hall and Casino in Grays Harbor County. After taking their turn on stage, the actresses hustled drinks to customers at the bar or in curtained boxes on the balcony. Dolan managed similar establishments in Pioneer Square. Photo by Charles Pratsch. Washington State University Libraries, 107

Buoyed by cheering onlookers, the Salvation Army marched off with a few converts. The all-male crowd divided and followed the musicians into the theaters.

Unlike his competitors, Considine created two separate job categories for females: waitresses, who hustled liquor to customers on the floor and in curtained boxes on the balcony, and performers. The recognition of actresses was a small but important step that paved the way from the box-house toward legitimate theater. Each evening, the house band accompanied a variety of performances, including magicians, slapstick comics, singers, dancers, gymnasts, minstrel shows, or animal acts. A lascivious throng packed the People's for its grand opening starring Little Egypt, a belly dancer whose strip-

tease on a New York stage had made her the most famous burlesque queen of the day.

In 1897 the People's presented a motion-picture clip of the Corbett-Fitzsimmons fight, which introduced the silent screen to the raucous crowd—and to Seattle. Again, Considine was at the forefront of the entertainment industry. A year later, entrepreneur Dell Lampman opened Seattle's first movie theater, a block west in the dusty basement of G. O. Guy's Drugstore. Alaska-bound prospectors lined up at the door to buy ten-cent tickets. When everyone was seated, Lampman turned off the lights and hand-cranked a series of celluloid strips through the miracle projector. Half a century later, he recalled that each film lasted only a few seconds. "One might depict a man walking, . . . another a horse trotting, or a few local scenes, gulls against the skyline, a steamer puffing to dock."

Another box-house owner, John Cort, cleaned up acts from his Standard Theater and used them to launch the Palm Garden, north of Yesler Way. In a move toward propriety, he was the first to test a liquor-free market with special Saturday-afternoon matinees that catered to ladies and children. Cort's venture was a failure, and the Palm Garden closed within its first year for lack of business. When it reopened in 1900, it advertised free admission and sold alcoholic drinks throughout the house at bar prices.

But by the turn of the twentieth century, moral factions were making progress. Considine and Cort continued to move in the direction of propriety, expanding their holdings beyond the Tenderloin and converting bump-and-grind acts from their box-houses into variety theater.

Considine also recognized the redeeming qualities and economic potential of silent film. He bought an interest in Edison's Unique Theatre, which opened in 1903, advertising "Moving Pictures, Illustrated Songs, Dissolving Views and Colored Slides: Refined Entertainment for Ladies, Gentlemen and Children." In 1911 he and two partners opened the lavish Orpheum Theater at Third and Madison (not to be confused with the later landmark structure at Fifth and Westlake). Liquor-free and designed for family entertainment, the Orpheum offered programs that combined the nickelodeon with live acts, some of which had simultaneous billings at the notorious People's. Recruiting the best actors from traveling road shows, the promoters soon transformed variety theater into more sophisticated vaudeville.

As in the earlier California gold rush of 1849, theater in Seattle's Tenderloin was characterized by what historian Nancy Allison Wright calls "a laughing irreverence for the ways of the world."

Vaudeville's irreverence, vitality, and love of life stand as a lasting legacy in American theater. Wright says, "It was because of Seattle's Skid Road box-houses that American vaudeville in the West attained Paul Bunyan proportions."

Real estate magnate Henry Broderick recalled that by 1907, Considine's Lyric Theatre (which he had acquired from John Cort south of Yesler Way at Washington and Occidental) was "the only place in town where one could [still] be in a theater and a bordello at the same time." In the meantime, respectable crowds lined up in front of the Orpheum's ticket booth. Admission prices were low and performances were brief, with several each day and evening. This translated into high turnover and profit. So that he could import big-time acts, Considine built a circuit, opening theaters in Victoria and Vancouver, British Columbia; Bellingham, Spokane, Yakima, and Everett, Washington; and Portland, Oregon. He billed it as "the first legitimate, popular-priced vaudeville chain in the world: admission ten cents." John Cort, meantime, reinvested his profits from Seattle box-houses, buying up theaters in towns throughout the Northwest.

In 1902 Pericles "Alexander" Pantages entered the scene, opening the Crystal Theater on Second Avenue. A Greek immigrant who could neither read nor write, he had a genius for organizing entertainment that appealed to the general public. He was a veteran of the Alaska gold rush, where he had won the heart and the partnership of Kate Rockwell, a showgirl and hostess. Her fans called her "Klondike Kate" or "Queen of the Yukon," and when she danced, adoring prospectors tossed coins and pouches of gold at her feet. Together, Kate and Pantages mined the dance halls of Dawson City and Nome rather than the goldfields.

In Seattle, Kate performed in regional vaudeville circuits to grubstake her lover's business.

Vaudevillians, ca. 1912. Courtesy of Rod Slemmons

Sophie Tucker, Will Rogers, Fred Astaire and his sister Adele, the Great Houdini, Sarah Bernhardt, John Barrymore, Al Jolson, and a host of others. West Seattle's June and Rose Havoc (the latter known later as Gypsy Rose Lee) got their start as child stars with appealing song-and-dance acts. In its heyday, a typical vaudeville program opened with an orchestral overture followed by seven acts and a finale that featured a motion picture of current news events.

Movietown U.S.A.

In 1904 the new Pantages Vaudeville opened, followed by a rapidly expanding empire that would earn him millions. But just as the business began to boom, Pantages married another woman. The newspaper headlines screamed, "Uses Her Money, Then Jilts Girl." Kate sued but eventually settled for less than $5,000. She continued performing her famed erotic flame dance in Considine's rival establishments, twirling yards and yards of bright red chiffon across the stage.

In the first two decades of the twentieth century, three major vaudeville circuits controlled a lucrative industry that reached from coast to coast. Considine teamed up with a New York financier and politician, big Tim Sullivan. Both the Sullivan/Considine and the Pantages circuits began in Seattle, while the Orpheum circuit grew out of San Francisco. The owners built opulent theaters with an average seating capacity of 1,400. In its heyday, Seattle boasted more than twenty-five vaudeville theaters. At Considine's blocklong Coliseum (not to be confused with the later movie house now home to the Banana Republic), sellout crowds bought ten- to seventy-five-cent tickets twice a day.

Vaudeville featured popular animal acts and big-name performers, including W. C. Fields,

Vaudeville flourished until the late 1920s, when "talking pictures" and the Great Depression dealt it a double blow. By this time, both the Considine and Pantages families had moved to Los Angeles, where John Considine Jr. later married Alexander Pantages' daughter, Carmen. The Considines, father and son, launched successful careers as motion-picture producers. In many ways, the movies were rooted in their vaudevillian forebears. Audiences across the country continued to go to the grand theaters, now dominated by Hollywood. The stars included familiar actresses and actors, who not long before had performed live on the stage. That stage was now replaced by the big screen. It too had roots in vaudeville, which had always featured the technological marvels of film.

Live acts with clean scripts and decent performers remained popular in theaters such as the Alhambra in Pioneer Square. But Seattle's former vaudeville audiences transferred much of their enthusiasm for the stage to the screen. In the 1970s, all three of the nation's major television networks, along with *The New York Times,* the *Washington Post,* and the *Boston Globe,* took their turns proclaiming Seattle "Movietown U.S.A."

Until the 1980s, almost all of the city's movie

The basement of the Metropole Building at Second and Yesler is where moving pictures made their Seattle debut. Washington State Archives, Puget Sound Regional Branch

theaters were owned by two homegrown chains, Sterling and Seven Gables. Like the earlier vaudeville circuits, the Sterling got its start on the Skid Road, when John Danz opened his first movie theater in 1913. It was located at Second Avenue South and Washington, the same intersection where Considine had launched his People's Theater and introduced silent films to a raucous crowd some two decades earlier.

Eagles Soar

Through trial and error, the Skid Road also propagated lofty ideals that rivaled its vaude-villian legacy. For instance, it was there that the Fraternal Order of Eagles was founded. In 1898 the Musicians Mutual Protective Union went on strike for higher wages against Considine's People's Theater, John Cort's Palm Garden, H. L. Leavitt's Bella Union, and other box-house theaters. The owners held a secret meet-

ing on a waterfront wharf, where they agreed to stand together, abolish their orchestras, and make do with player pianos. They formed an organization they called the Seattle Order of Good Things, with the motto "Skin 'em."

A month later, the strike was over and the bands were back. The owners met again in a more magnanimous spirit and decided that their organization would be a workingman's lodge, open to any man of goodwill. They drew up bylaws and a constitution, changed the name to "Fraternal Order of Eagles," and adopted a new secular motto: "Not God, heaven hereafter, but man, earth now." Their creed espoused liberty, justice, truth, and equality. Initially they encouraged memberships from bartenders and theater people, who were often excluded from other organizations.

The founders formed Seattle Aerie No. 1 as the first lodge. Through theater circuits, they established lodges in other cities, including

When lodges held conventions, they promoted themselves with parades. Here the Odd Fellows march south from Yesler Way on Second Avenue South. The Walla Walla delegation carries matching umbrellas. Photo by Asahel Curtis. MSCUA, *University of Washington Libraries, A Curtis 16171*

Spokane, Portland, Tacoma, and San Francisco. Historian Eugene Clinton Elliott notes that by the turn of the twenty-first century, there were "aeries" in more than a hundred cities across the nation, with some forty thousand members. The Eagles sponsored America's first workmen's compensation law, along with old-age pension legislation.

Beginning on the Skid Road, the original Grand Aerie had several temporary homes. In 1925 throngs turned out to celebrate the opening of its ornate temple at Seventh and Union

(recently restored as the home of A Contemporary Theater), said to be the finest fraternal building in America. Members and their guests gathered in the magnificent ballroom for plays, movies, traveling exhibitions, and dances with big bands. The downstairs was equally lavish, with a grand hall especially equipped for lodge rituals. In 1935 U.S. President Franklin D. Roosevelt invited Eagles delegates to witness his signing of the Social Security Act and presented them with a pen. Walter Winchell later proclaimed the Eagles as America's greatest contributor to philanthropic organizations. According to historian JoAnn Roe, Seattle claimed nine aeries in 1995, and there were more than four thousand nationwide.

John Cort and John Considine, Seattle's premier vaudeville impresarios, remained active in the Fraternal Order of Eagles, frequently serving as delegates to national conventions. Once again, the seed that they had planted on the Skid Road grew to local and international prominence.

Free Speech Corner

In the early twentieth century, burlesque acts continued to draw crowds to the Lyric Theater at Occidental and Washington. Outdoors, Free Speech Corner provided a different kind of performance that attracted street-side audiences. Soapbox orators ran the gamut from political radicals to Holy Roller Christians, from promoters of snake-oil cures to crackpots with an ax to grind. Through the World War I era, the corner was a magnet for loggers and sailors wanting to get into a good fight. Police generally left it alone but sometimes drove up in the "Black Maria" (paddy wagon) and made a few arrests to break up a melee. As for the orators, everyone understood that if things got out of hand, they were on their own.

The 1919 General Strike that shut down the city had given Seattle a national reputation as a haven for left-wing politics (see chapter 6). Radicalism escalated with the stock market crash of 1929 and the onslaught of the Great Depression. At Free Speech Corner, prophets of doom lambasted the capitalistic system, striking a resounding chord with their unemployed listeners (see chapter 7). College students from other parts of the city joined the crowd, intrigued by the radical ideas. Some paused to

listen before slipping into the Lyric; others had come to the Skid Road to check out food bars, where a nickel would buy a bowl of soup, a roll, and coffee, or to get a heaping strawberry ice cream sundae at the Washington Cigar Store.

In the late 1930s, both Free Speech Corner and the Lyric Theater faded into obscurity, not because of outside efforts to close them down, but because times were changing. But in many ways, the legacy of free expression had become a tradition that would continue to characterize the neighborhood south of Yesler Way. In ensuing decades, the Skid Road's openness to unconventional ideas, fringe groups, and cultural diversity created a climate that was conducive to the arts and artists.

Elizabeth Gurley Flynn, shown here in Spokane, was a Wobbly who fired up crowds at Free Speech Corner and around the Northwest. She often landed in jail, becoming the inspiration for Joe Hill's hit tune "Rebel Girl." MSCUA, *University of Washington Libraries,* UW 341

A Place for Artists

Today's thriving arts community has a direct link to the Great Depression, when the Works Progress Administration introduced the Federal Art Project with subsidized jobs for artists. One of those artists was twenty-year-old Bill Cumming, who began working at the low wage of $66 per month and who still paints and teaches art in the Seattle area. The job introduced him to established artists Kenneth Callahan and Morris Graves, as well as the now-famous Northwest School of art, of which he is the last surviving member. In the 1930s Cumming roamed the Skid Road, making abstract sketches of burlesque theater, prostitutes, dockworkers, soapbox orators, and the down-and-out who languished around the Victorian pergola at Pioneer Place. The sketches were the basis for his characteristic warm silhouettes, painted in deep orange and yellow tempera.

In his memoirs, Cumming writes about artists who moved into abandoned lofts in the Howard Building, on First Avenue next door to the Pioneer Building. A priest from Seattle College (now Seattle University) had given one of them a cadaver, which they kept in a claw-foot bathtub half full of alcohol. Cumming's "great studio" was on the top floor. It had formerly housed a photographer and was "unbelievably bright," with a skylight and white cardboard covering the floor, ceiling, and walls.

In the depths of the Depression, Cumming became a "Red." In an interview with the *Seattle Times* on July 29, 2001, he explained, "We were naive. We talked about things we knew nothing about, and we believed it. So when the Revolution turned into an outburst of murder, I went through the usual disillusionment." During the McCarthy era, he was blacklisted. By the late fifties, he was bored with the Left and tired of censorship from the Right. He moved to Pocatello, Idaho, to head the School of Art at Idaho State College.

Literary Luminaries

Like Cumming and the new wave of Bohemian artists, there were others with deep roots in the Skid Road culture, which often provided inspiration for their work. A few of them have gained prominence in the American literary scene.

Carlos Bulosan

A prolific writer, Carlos Bulosan was the first Filipino to bring the concerns of his people to national attention. In the Philippines he had peddled fish and vegetables in his family's business and had attended American schools, where he absorbed idealistic lessons about equal rights and opportunities in a democratic society. In 1930, at age seventeen, he immigrated to Seattle, only to have his dreams shattered by the realization that equality did not extend to people of color.

He joined the small, largely male Filipino community that bunked in Skid Road hotels and socialized in dance halls and cafes near Second Avenue South and Main. In the depths of the Great Depression, he worked as a migrant laborer, encountering horrific working conditions and race discrimination that was sometimes violent. He later wrote, "I know deep down in my heart that I am an exile in America. I feel like a criminal running away from a crime I didn't commit. And this crime is that I am a Filipino in America." By 1935 he became involved in the labor movement, organizing unions to protect his people. When he contracted tuberculosis, he devoted his two years in a hospital to intensive reading and writing.

During World War II, a shift in attitudes

created demand for his articles, poems, and books. In the Philippines, Americans fought side by side with Filipinos against Japanese invaders, and on the homefront, names such as "Corrigador" and "Bataan" became household words. President Franklin D. Roosevelt chose Bulosan to write "Freedom from Want," which was one of the "Four Freedoms" articles published in 1943 in the *Saturday Evening Post.* Bulosan's satirical book *Laughter of my Father* hit the best-seller list in 1944 and was translated into several languages, with excerpts read on wartime radio. In 1946 *Look Magazine* named his semiautobiographical novel *America Is in the Heart* one of the fifty most important American books ever published. In it, he brings to life the immigrant Filipino of the 1930s and 1940s by telling stories based on his own and his friends' experiences.

In the postwar era, Bulosan's work fell out of vogue and faded into obscurity. He and other union activists were blacklisted as radicals and threatened with deportation. Continuing his activism, he edited the 1952 yearbook of Local 37 of the International Longshoremen's and Warehousemen's Union, which was headquartered at Second Avenue South and Main. Bulosan died of pneumonia in 1956, still in his forties.

A resurgence of interest in his work began in the early 1970s, when *America Is in the Heart* was republished and became a cornerstone of the Filipino-American identity movement. Along with Bulosan's book, University of Washington Press republished John Okada's 1957 novel, *No-No Boy.* Both have become mainstays of Asian-American studies programs and are now required reading in college courses across the nation.

John Okada

In 1923 John Okada was born in the Merchants Hotel near First and Yesler, which was managed by his immigrant parents. He attended Bailey Gatzert Elementary School, Broadway High School, and the University of Washington before the bombing of Pearl Harbor in 1941 and the subsequent evacuation of people of Japanese descent from the West Coast. At the camps where they were interned, he and most of the other American-born young men, to prove their patriotism, enlisted when U.S. Army recruiters came.

After serving on the Pacific front, Okada received an honorable discharge. He returned to the Skid Road, where his parents had resumed managing hotels that they owned. In his artistic family, John focused on literature and writing, while his younger brother, Frank, laid the groundwork for a successful career in painting. John earned a degree from Columbia University, then married and worked at the Seattle Public Library to support his wife and children.

At the time, most members of the Japanese community had already taken an unspoken vow of silence to try to put the upheavals of the recent past behind them and get on with their lives. Unlike their immigrant *Issei* (first-generation) parents, who were ineligible for citizenship, the *Nisei* (second generation) were citizens who dreamed of assimilating into the American mainstream, with a promising future for themselves and their children. John Okada wanted to preserve and interpret the unique and conflicted heritage of his generation. He turned to fiction and wrote his only published novel, *No-No Boy.*

His main character, Ichiro, returns to the Skid Road after four years' absence—two in an internment camp and two in federal prison. In deference to his mother's romanticized view of her home country, Ichiro had refused to sign an oath disavowing allegiance to the emperor of Japan. In the U. S. Army's eyes, this constituted draft evasion. Okada weaves together complex themes, including race discrimination, the outrageousness of the internment camps, the fractured lives of Japanese-American men—whether they had said yes or no to the draft—and their struggles to assimilate into a changed society. The characters come alive through blunt dialogue, evocative descriptions of *Issei* and *Nisei* mannerisms, and a vivid sense of time and place. To Okada's surprise, when his book was published his own people rejected it.

In 1970 Jeff Chan found a copy in a San Francisco bookstore and passed it around to literary friends, including David Ishii, Frank Chin, and Shawn Wong of Seattle. In Okada's book, they found "a living force among us," and they hailed him as the first Japanese-American novelist. His work filled a void in their literary heritage by boldly confronting the identity crisis and challenges of racism and assimilation felt by numerous Asian Americans in the years surrounding World War II.

In 1971 some of the friends tracked down Okada's wife to ask for permission to republish the book, only to learn to their sorrow that they had just missed him. He died of a heart attack at age forty-seven, still believing that Asian Americans had no interest in his work. Pooling their resources, the friends organized the Combined Asian American Resources Project, Inc., which published two small paperback editions of *No-No Boy* that sold out; they later transferred the rights to University of Washington Press.

Gary Snyder

Another writer with links to the Skid Road is Gary Snyder, a Pulitzer prize–winning poet. Snyder grew up in the Seattle area, where he climbed nearby mountains, worked in rugged outdoor jobs, and took pride in his radical her-itage. His grandfather had preached the Wobbly gospel from a soapbox at Free Speech Corner prior to the devastating antiradical purges that followed World War I.

In the late forties and early fifties, Snyder regaled fellow students at Reed College in Portland with songs from the IWW's *Little Red Songbook* and with stories about how radical labor had helped shape the history of the Northwest. Writer John Suiter tells how Snyder was blacklisted by the Federal Bureau of Investigation in 1954 for being "suspicious," in part because of his affection for the then moribund IWW. Snyder was fired from his federal job as a ranger in the North Cascades, and his passport was invalidated, forcing him to cancel plans to study in Japan.

The next year Snyder, Jack Kerouac, and Allen Ginsburg were part of a small group of American writers who launched the Beat Generation in San Francisco. Their underlying philosophy was visionary enlightenment, Zen Buddhism, and Amerindian culture. They rejected prevailing academic approaches to poetry and instead felt that it should be brought to the people with readings, often accompanied by jazz. A common theme was withdrawal from and protest against prevailing middle-class values. Almost overnight, some of the pioneer Beats rocketed to fame.

Suiter recounts a story of Snyder and Ginsburg, who hitchhiked to Seattle to give a reading at the University of Washington. Snyder took his friend on a tour of the Skid Road, beginning at the Colman Dock, where Wobblies on board the steamship *Verona* had returned from the notorious Everett Massacre in 1916, then had been marched up Yesler Way to the county jail to await trial. Tracing their footsteps, Snyder sang Wobbly songs that had been part of the scene. At Fourth and Yesler, he and Ginsburg entered the old IWW Hall. Inside, they talked with a few elderly Swedes and Finns who were playing cards and took note of yellowed slogans and photos of legendary Wobs such as Joe Hill that were on the walls. Both poets incorporated the experience into their work.

Within a short time, the McCarthy era was over and Snyder was free to travel to Japan to study with a Zen master. Strongly influenced by Eastern thought, his work later expanded far beyond Beat poetry to a still radical vision that includes a wilderness ethic and concepts of humanity's place in the cosmos. As of this writing, he teaches at the University of California Davis and is widely regarded as one of the foremost literary figures of the twentieth century.

Traditions and Beyond

Along with immigrants and radical labor organizations, Native Americans also gathered in the Skid Road neighborhood. By the 1950s, they constituted one of its major ethnic groups. The Washington State Intertribal Council recognized the pressing needs of urban Indians and concluded that they could best be addressed by tribal members who understood the value of Native cultural traditions. The council conceived the idea of the American Indian Women's Service League (AIWSL), which was chartered in Seattle in 1957. The next year, it established the Seattle Indian Center, with Pearl Warren of the Makah tribe as the first director. In an April 1967 interview with *Seattle Magazine,* she explained that its mission was "to make Indians part of the community they live in and to get non-Indians to recognize us as an Indian group." The Seattle Indian Center provided a variety of programs and services and a respectable gathering place for the city's estimated five thousand Indians. Non-Indian visitors were always welcome.

While promoting education and job train-

ing, AIWSL members encouraged urban Indians to rediscover, celebrate, and share their cultural traditions. The center's Indian arts and crafts shop enabled traditional artists to display and sell their work. In the early 1970s, the AIWSL and the Seattle Indian Services Commission purchased the Broderick Building and contracted with Jones & Jones to redesign it as the new home for the Seattle Indian Center.

In 1982, when it sold the building to Martin Smith, Inc., the AIWSL negotiated a long-term lease for its Traditions and Beyond shop, whose roots make it Pioneer Square's oldest arts and

According to ancient legends, Tsonoqua was a female giant and "nightmare bringer" whom mothers called to scare naughty children into obedience. Her image is part of a group of four dramatic totems in Occidental Park carved by Duane Pasco, a modern master of traditional Indian art in the Northwest Coast style. Gallery owner Richard White presented them as a gift to the Pioneer Square Association in the late 1980s. Photo by Karin Link.

crafts gallery. Kenny Alhadeff purchased the building in 1992 and continues to honor the lease. The AIWSL is headquartered in the shop, where it maintains a collection of treasured artifacts, including intricate baskets and beadwork that were gifts from each of the AIWSL's one hundred charter members. The collection is a rare example of regional Native American art in Seattle.

James Rasmussen, a member of the Duwamish Tribal Council and owner of Bud's Jazz Records in Pioneer Square, explains that Puget Sound tribal art did not include totem poles—they were a Northwest Coast tribal tradition. He notes that when Chief Seattle signed treaties, his rationale was in part to protect his people from fierce raids by Northwest Coast tribes. Rasmussen says that, ironically, the northern tribes are still raiding, not with weapons, but with their art. The totem pole at Pioneer Place

Detail from Edgar Heap of Bird's "Day and Night," next to the Chief Seattle fountain. The two-sided panels present Lushootseed symbols on one side, translated into English on the other. Photo by Karin Link

is from the Tlingit Island of Tongass in Alaska (see chapter 5). In the late 1980s, art gallery owner Richard White donated the dramatic ensemble of totems that stand in Occidental Park, between South Washington and Main Streets. They were carved by Native artist Duane Pasco in the tradition of coastal tribes in northern Washington and British Columbia.

The public artwork that strikes the most resounding chord among members of Puget Sound tribes was meant to be a temporary installation. "Day and Night" is a series of panels created by Edgar Heap of Birds in 1989 for Washington state's centennial celebration. Located near the Chief Seattle fountain at Pioneer Place, the panels display Native Lushootseed symbols on one side, translated into English on the other. Voices of the Duwamish chief's descendants seem to address his watchful bronze bust, sculpted by James Wehn in 1909. The messages convey loss and struggle, but with it a sense of ongoing pride and determination to survive. An example: "Chief Seattle, now the Streets Are Our Home." This is the site of an ancient Duwamish village that has always been a meeting place for the Native people (see chapter 1).

All That Jazz

In the post–World War II era, others began bringing their dreams to the Skid Road. Attracted by cheap rents and colorful old buildings, entrepreneurs leased derelict taverns and saloons, cleaned them up, and moved in with bongo drums, beatnik poetry readings, and, later, Dixieland and modern jazz. Changes in liquor laws enabled bartenders to serve drinks by the glass. Illegal speakeasies were a thing of the past. Another factor was the integration of black and white musicians' unions and a consequently young, racially mixed customer base.

Pete Barbas, a visionary twenty-year-old jazz fan, opened Pete's Poop Deck in 1957. Historian Paul de Barros calls it "the first self-consciously styled modern jazz club in Seattle." Located next to the viaduct on South Main Street, it had a "beatnik pad" decor with apple-crate tables, peanut shells on the floor, and a maritime motif of fishnets and floats. Poets recited their work while artists hung their paintings on the walls and sketched in the corners. Barbas tended bar and hired the best jazz groups in Seattle and also from out of town. He was one of the first to lure black musicians out of the Central Area's lively after-hours clubs, where jazz legends Quincy Jones, Ernestine Anderson, and others got their start. With a knack for promotion, Barbas got regular notices in local newspapers and drew enthusiastic crowds.

Several other modern jazz clubs followed in Pioneer Square, including the Penthouse, the posh Parnell's, and the Pioneer Banque, which was owned by Barbas's cousin, Gus Boutsinis. The latter employed another cousin, Dimitriou, who later opened his famed Jazz Alley in the University District.

While Barbas launched the jazz scene, Jimmy Manolides, then in his late teens, began playing and singing in groups such as the Frantics and the Dynamics, which brought rock and roll to Skid Road clubs. After a hitch in the army, Manolides returned in 1968. He says that Richard White, then the new owner of the Globe Building, "kicked out the ABC Junk Company" on the main floor and let him have the space "dirt cheap at $10 a month" to open his Contemporary Crafts Gallery, later renamed the Manolides Gallery. Manolides gave a back room to Ned Neltner and Butch Ormsky for Third Alliance Music, a small publishing company that produced records for his rock group, Junior Cadillac. Following numerous performances, tours, and recordings, the group won

popular acclaim as "Seattle's favorite band." In 1991 Junior Cadillac was accepted into the Northwest Area Music Hall of Fame.

Like jazz and rock venues, the Blue Banjo in the Pioneer Building drew visitors to the Skid Road. In the late 1950s, Jack Fecker, Joe Rutten, and Jerry Koch opened the rollicking beer and wine club, where a brass and banjo band performed antics reminiscent of vaudeville. The owners teamed up with Elroy Pettyjohn to open Elroy's, an alcohol-free eatery and ice cream parlor famed for singing waitresses. Located in the Mutual Life Building on the west side of Pioneer Place, it replaced the derelict Brittania Tavern. Elroy's stayed open until late at night, catering to teenagers who dropped in after the movies. Downstairs, Wally and Harry Toner opened a coffee shop that became a popular neighborhood gathering place.

The 1962 Century Twenty-one Exposition brought nationally known jazz musicians to Seattle who shared bookings at the Seattle Center fairgrounds with local performers. Visitors and residents alike discovered lively and diverse nightclubs in the old Skid Road district. While the Space Needle pointed toward the future, the city's fledgling historic preservation movement was taking root in Pioneer Square.

Beginning of a Renaissance

In the early 1960s, architect Ralph Anderson rehabilitated the Capitol Brewing Company building, also known as the Jackson Building, at First and Jackson. He persuaded Allen Salsbury to move his prestigious interior-design display room into the ornate space of the former Tumwater Tavern. The store was a lightning rod that attracted well-to-do customers. Anderson's offices were on the second and third floors; sculptor John Geise's studio was in the basement; Richard White's gallery fea-

Bill Speidel and daughter Sunny, who has followed in his footsteps as head of the Underground Tour (see chapter 3) and other Pioneer Square businesses. Photo by Paul Dorpat. Courtesy of Bill Speidel Enterprises

tured antiques and oriental carpets; J. Michael Johnson's gallery dealt in primitive art; and Bill Speidel leased an office, where he wrote and published the weekly *Seattle Guide* to entertainment.

Many an aspiring entrepreneur did not wait for building renovations. At First and Yesler, Clodall Wilson stripped four layers of paint off the red brick walls of the Yesler Building, transforming a former dingy tavern into a clothing boutique, where her distinctive custom designs were in demand. Her neighbor Polly Friedlander had to restore electrical wiring, the staircase, and the front door before she could open her art gallery on the second and third floors. At first she featured one-artist shows with an opening every three weeks.

The Skid Road was fertile ground for people of widely different backgrounds who had cut loose from the corporate job market to start one-of-a-kind small businesses. Antique shops, flower shops, a woodworkers' gallery, oriental rug galleries, a kite shop, crafts shops, and specialty bookstores opened next door to missions, loan shops, and taverns. The new proprietors developed a strong sense of camaraderie, working together on cleanup days and on promotional projects that attracted customers.

The Greening of the Square

Seeing where she could help, Jean Claire Salsbury invited some of her affluent women friends to an elegant tea in her husband's display room in the Jackson Building. She told them about a previous generation of ladies bountiful who had successfully lobbied the city for tree planting after the Great Fire in 1889. Inspired by their forebears, the friends took up the torch for greenery in Pioneer Square. They organized as the philanthropic Committee of Thirty-three to donate funds for trees in public spaces and along the streets. Shirley Speidel recalled that they encouraged neighbors throughout the square "to plant window boxes, trees, hanging baskets—anything that grew." On Occidental Avenue between Jackson and Main, committee members planted seasonal flowers and trees until the city took over the planning in 1970.

Jones & Jones was named landscape architect for Occidental Square and Pioneer Place parks (see chapter 9). Seeing the parks as centers of community life, Ilze Jones proposed a plan that linked them with the neighborhood and its gateways via tree-lined streets and a boulevard on First Avenue South—then part of a truck route that veered west on Yesler Way and continued north on Western Avenue to the Pike Place Market. The controversial plan sparked opposition from White River Valley farmers, who had transported their produce along the route for decades.

The iron and steel pergola at the Washington Street Boat Landing designed by D. R. Huntington, 1920, housed the city's harbormaster and served as a port of entry for foreign seamen. In 1970 the Committee of Thirty-three provided funds to restore it. The Port of Seattle created a small public park on its south side, linking it to Pier 48, which served the Alaska Marine Ferries System from 1967 to 1989. Despite the Alaskan Way Viaduct, right, community activists envisioned a revitalization of Pioneer Square's historic waterfront gateway. Photo by Karin Link

Arthur "Art" Skolnik, the city's Pioneer Square district manager, spearheaded a campaign for the proposed greenery. In response, the City Council redirected the truck route to Alaskan Way and sanctioned the conversion of First Avenue South to a pedestrian-friendly, tree-lined boulevard with traffic controls and a median planted with shrubs and flowers. The greening coincided with installations of the district's signature three-globe street lamps, modeled after the historic five-globe lamps at Pioneer Place.

Culinary Arts and Influence

In 1969 Francois and Julia Kissel gave the district's promoters a decisive boost when they took over the old Pittsburgh Lunch in the basement of the Pioneer Building. They cleaned up the grime and transformed it into one of Seattle's most interesting restaurants and gathering places of the '70s. Considered a culinary marvel in its day, the Brasserie Pittsbourg featured authentic French cuisine and lent a taste of the Parisian Left Bank to Pioneer Square. The restaurant opened just before the Boeing bust, when drivers heading south on Highway 99 encountered a billboard with the message "Will the Last Person Leaving Seattle Please Turn Out the Lights?"

As property values plummeted, the Brasserie filled with a creative cadre of community activists, including architects and historic preservationists who had moved into the old buildings and politicians who came down from City Hall. One of the contentions of this lively group was that the revival of Pioneer Square was a key to Seattle's future. On the butcher-paper tablecloths, the Kissels' customers drafted many a scheme for city improvements while relishing

The Blue Banjo Band heralds a group of public officials and history lovers gathered at the Mutual Life Building in January 1961 to discuss the first historic preservation ordinance. Identified are, top row from right, Dick Miller, Carl Gould Jr., Hans Lehman, Anne Gould Hauberg, and Langdon Simons; second row from right, unknown, Amnee Costigan, Jacquetta Freeman, two unknowns, Mayor Gordon Clinton; and front row, right Helen Marie Wyman. Courtesy of Bill Speidel, the Underground Tour

French meals served cafeteria-style at lunch and formally at dinner.

Other intriguing restaurants opened nearby, making the district the center of fine dining in Seattle. Peter Cipra's Prague Restaurant, later renamed Labuznik ("gourmet" in Czech), was rated one of the city's best. At Main and Occidental on the new pedestrian mall, Marvin Timberlake opened Das Gasthaus and introduced Seattle to European-style sidewalk dining.

One of the district's historic restaurant venues is in the Frye Hotel. It debuted as the lavish Rose Room in 1911, featuring banquets and vaudeville stars such as "Klondike Kate." In the 1960s, Ellensburg rancher Stuart Anderson leased the space and hired architects Bystrom and Greco to redesign it for his "gay nineties"

Gold Coast restaurant, the precursor of his popular Black Angus chain. Diners packed the house for full-course steak dinners at the bargain price of $2.95. In the mid-seventies, Dean and Doris Yari transformed the space into their still-popular Togetsu Restaurant. Dean had mastered traditional culinary and design arts in the couple's native Japan. His traditional decor creatively integrates Anderson's hanging stained-glass medallions into the ceiling.

In 1975 the Kissels opened a second restaurant, the opulently appointed City Loan Pavilion, designed by architect James Daly. A crystal chandelier from the former Orpheum Theater beckoned guests into the greenhouse dining room and entrance that extended across the alley from Occidental Park. Born in Vietnam, Francois Kissel sponsored the resettlement of several refugees from his homeland, including eleven who worked at the pavilion. The casual menu of chic salads and one-course meals featured traditional French dishes, some of which showed a Vietnamese influence. While the pavilion garnered rave reviews, there was a drawback: women in high heels often avoided the cobblestones that at the time covered the entire surface of the park.

Between the Brasserie's debut in 1969 and the City Loan Pavilion's in 1975, more than thirty restaurants had opened in Pioneer Square, and several were doing well. In 1976, *Seattle Times* columnist John Hinterberger summed up the significance of Kissel's legacy: "He proved that an authentic French restaurant could be moved into a formerly squalid basement beanery . . . and attract the gentry. Perhaps more important, the Brasserie proved that the concept of upgrading the Skid Road was feasible, that a cross-cultural transplant would take." The article quotes Kissel, who said, "This much is certain, the area has become a quality area, and those places that began with quality and retained it are still in business."

When the Kingdome opened in 1976, waves of sports fans flooded Pioneer Square, creating traffic congestion and a lack of parking spaces that alienated many diners. Many of the acclaimed restaurants eventually closed or moved to other neighborhoods. One that successfully catered to the new sports clientele is Mick McHugh's F. X. McRory's Steak, Chop and Oyster House, located at Occidental and King.

Another that has become a neighborhood mainstay is the Trattoria Mitchelli, which opened in 1978 featuring casual Italian fare. Dany Mitchell's establishment replaced the old OK Cafe at Post Alley and Yesler Way in the Traveler's Hotel building. The building's new owner, Jones & Jones, waived the first three

months' rent so that he could clean up the place and restore its historic horseshoe-shaped oak counter. In the tradition of the OK Cafe, Mitchell opened at 4:00 A.M. with doughnuts and coffee for farm laborers, who came to the Washington State Employment Office on the Western Avenue side of the building, then waited for buses to pick them up for a day's work in the fields. Neighbors and visitors gathered around the counter for breakfast and lunch.

When Mitchell added dinner, his low-priced Italian specialties drew an evening crowd. He expanded, taking over the space of Helen's Pup Tavern next door in the building and later the employment office. The Trattoria stayed open twenty-two hours a day, closing only between 4:00 and 6:00 A.M. Today it remains one of Pioneer Square's most popular restaurants and meeting places, and the horseshoe-shaped oak counter continues to attract convivial guests from early morning until late at night.

Trattoria Mitchelli. Note the historic oak counter and dessert display case. Limited edition print by Billie King, 1989; courtesy of owner Dany Mitchell and the artist

Related to the neighborhood's restaurant scene are more casual venues. The Grand Central Bakery, founded in the early 1970s by Gwen Bassetti, introduced artisan breads to Seattle and has made the Grand Central Arcade an ongoing meeting place for neighbors and visitors and a destination for arts groups. Other popular gathering places are casual restaurants such as Sedat Uysal's Cafe Paloma; espresso bars, including the Bizzarri brothers' original Torrefazione Italia and Zeitgeist, with its art shows and experimental music performances; and taverns including the Central and McCoy's Firehouse. For Seattle's literary community, the book-lined Elliott Bay Cafe serves as a constant hub.

Literary Culture

In 1971 Walter Carr leased space on South Main Street in the Marshall Building (also known as the Globe Building) for his Elliott Bay Book Company. From his window, he watched a bulldozer pulling a mammoth proof roller onto the bumpy surface of the parking lot across the street—all that remained of former buildings that had been demolished because of damage from the 1949 earthquake. The sole survivor was the small one-story structure that housed the California Tavern.

On the building's alley side, Rick Simonson, an enterprising college student, was setting up a sandwich shop. When the heavy equipment

Inside the Elliott Bay Book Company. Photo by Karin Link

began leveling the lot for conversion to Occidental Park, neighboring buildings shook, the California Tavern collapsed, and Simonson's would-be sandwich shop sank into the basement. Taking pity on a fellow entrepreneur, Carr offered him a job in the bookstore. The outcome proved fortuitous.

Carr and Simonson went to work building bookshelves and an inventory that quickly expanded to thousands and thousands of titles. As owner of the Marshall Building and the sister Walker Building next door, Jones & Jones broke through the separating wall to combine them as the Marshall-Walker Block. Carr leased the entire ground floor and basement, transforming it into a wood-and-brick warren with floor-to-ceiling books, reading nooks, and a cozy basement cafe.

A prolific reader, Simonson rose to chief book buyer. He became the guiding spirit behind the acclaimed series of author readings held downstairs in a casual space next to the cafe. In a March 9, 1997, profile of Simonson, *The Seattle Times* noted that the program of one or more literary talks a day had become the largest and one of the most influential in the nation. Typically, Simonson's introductions of the writers and their work are as memorable as the readings. His excitement about an undiscovered Northwest book can launch its author on a regional or even national tour. The *Times* article quoted Gigi Bradford, literature director for the National Endowment for the Arts, who said of the reading series, "It's a tremendous contribution not only to the Seattle area, but to all of American literature."

The popularity of the bookstore's author readings has been a catalyst for related regional programs that began in Pioneer Square. In 1987, with Sherry Prowda as founding executive director, Seattle Arts and Lectures (SAL) launched its hallmark literary lecture series,

bringing distinguished cultural thinkers and writers to local audiences. Novelist Francine Prose, who spoke in the 2002–2003 series, observed, "The audiences . . . are not only, in my experience, shockingly large but also informed, generous, responsive, and loyal to this valuable series." For years, SAL's offices have been in rooms above the Elliott Bay Book Company in the Globe Building, where owner Jones & Jones waives the rent.

In addition to the lectures, SAL brings professional writers into the Seattle Public Schools to work with students and organizes seminars for teachers. It also presents programs for the public with a wide range of opportunities to meet writers and engage in intellectually stimulating discussions about literature and society.

An organization with a related mission is Northwest Bookfest, which hosted its first annual two-day fall book festival in 1995 in the funky, cavernous space of Pier 48 at the foot of South Washington Street. With major support from *The Seattle Times* and the Washington Commission for the Humanities (then housed in the Lowman Building at Pioneer Place), the festival's founding executive director, Kitty Harmon, orchestrated nonstop author presentations and book signings, children's activities, a book-arts exhibition, and more than two hundred bookseller and publisher booths. In addition, the festival raised grant funds to distribute to some fifty literacy organizations throughout the five-state Pacific Northwest region. Staffed by hundreds of volunteers, the free event drew more than twenty-five thousand people of diverse ages and cultural and socioeconomic backgrounds. When the city declared the pilings of the old waterfront pier unsafe, the festival was moved to other venues and continued through 2003 as the largest and most diversely programmed literary event in the Pacific Northwest.

Together, Elliott Bay Book Company, Seattle Arts and Lectures, and the Northwest Bookfest have tuned in to a local passion for reading, providing the community with interactions among writers and readers that contribute to the cultural richness of our region. Sponsors of the events believe that their programs have contributed to a more educated, informed, engaged, and democratic community. It is no surprise to them that Seattle has recently been ranked among the most literate cities in the United States.

In 1999, when Walter Carr retired from the helm of his Elliott Bay Book Company, Jones & Jones was determined to perpetuate it, crafting a new lease with partners Ron Sher and Peter Aaron. While Sher provided the business with a needed infusion of cash, Aaron took over management, retaining most of the caring and knowledgeable staff. Today Simonson continues as chief book buyer with, in *The Seattle Times'* words, "a reputation that speaks volumes."

As a regular stop for literary residents and visitors, Elliott Bay Book Company has enhanced business for some of its long-term neighbors, including Wessel and Lieberman's antiquarian books, Michael Maslan's shop featuring historic photographs, and David Ishii's used and rare bookstore, which became the Grand Central Arcade's first tenant in 1972. Today these and related shops in the Historic District continue to cater to a steady stream of browsers, collectors, readers, and writers.

Artists and Galleries

While literary entrepreneurs and others opened one-of-a-kind shops, artists continued to gravitate to Pioneer Square, where they found live/work spaces in buildings that did not meet city codes. Landlords charged rock-bottom rents, leaving improvements and maintenance up to the tenants. City building inspectors usually did not investigate unless someone filed a complaint. By the mid-sixties, the district was home to Seattle's first arts community. Until then, there were only a few independent galleries in the city, including one in the University District and another on Capitol Hill.

Richard White moved his gallery from its original space in the Jackson Building to 311 Occidental South, where he specialized in Native American art. He later partnered with Don Foster to promote traditional Northwest art and artists. In 1967 Virginia (Mrs. Bagley) Wright opened First Editions in the same building, becoming the first of several women gallery owners. She specialized in prints by American artists, including Robert Rauschenberg, Roy Lichtenstein, and Andy Warhol. In January 9, 1972, the *Seattle Post-Intelligencer* hailed First Editions as "Seattle's first exposure to New York." When asked about the Skid Road's ubiquitous "population of disreputable-looking individuals," Wright noted that she had never had a bad experience. She said, "I'm very fond of the area, and wouldn't consider moving."

In the early 1970s, Linda Farris entered

Richard White left hosts an opening at his gallery. Museum of History and Industry, 86.53819.1

the scene at Second Avenue South and Jackson. With astute instincts and flamboyant public relations, she established herself as Seattle's "avant-garde gallery." She discovered and sustained contemporary Northwest artists, showing their work in concert with an impressive smattering of nationally known artists. In his November 8, 1995, article in the *Seattle Weekly,* gallery owner Greg Kucera wrote, "She changed forever the nature of being an art dealer in Seattle. . . . Linda put her artists on the cocktail circuit, entertained them with their collectors, opened their studios, and removed much of the intimidating mystery of the artistic presence. . . . Suddenly, the modest quietude of Northwest expression exploded into riotous celebration which demanded to be heard and noticed."

The Linda Farris gallery became a respected showplace for a slowly changing stable of local artists, among them Randy Hayes, Marsha Burns, Dennis Evans, Norie Sato, Sherry Markovitz, Julie Speidel, Alfred Harris, and glass artists Ginny Ruffner and Ann Gardner. Challenging theme shows, such as "My Neighbor the Kingdome," drew public attention.

The gallery scene evolved in the late 1970s and early 1980s with a new crop of dealers. Mia McEldowney specialized in folk art, while Don Foster and Bill Traver made transitions to spotlight shimmering Pilchuck glass. Larry Reid's Rosco Louie Gallery was a venue for new youthful attitudes and expressions, including neodada and punk. It served as a springboard for local new-wave artists such as Lynda Barry and Matt Groening (creator of *The Simpsons),* who skyrocketed to international fame.

In 1983 Kucera negotiated cheap rent with absentee landlord Sam Israel for a storefront in a run-down building a block north of the Smith Tower. The Greg Kucera Gallery soon became Seattle's primary venue for contemporary prints and has since moved into its own space at Third Avenue South and Washington. Kucera's shows have featured established print artists, including Richard Diebenkorn, Robert Motherwell, Helen Frankenthaler, Jasper Johns, and Roy Lichtenstein, as well as younger stars such as Susan Rothenberg, Kiki Smith, and Terry Winters. In addition, he showcases established Northwest artists and provides a venue for experimental work. His retrospective of Frank Okada's work, now internationally known, recalled the artist's nearby roots and the influence of his immigrant parents' generation on his late paintings (for a discussion of his older brother, novelist John Okada, see Literary Luminaries earlier in this chapter).

Kucera's theme shows have won national recognition. In an April 19, 1996, interview with the *Seattle Post-Intelligencer,* he said, "I try to figure out what's happening in art that wasn't happening 10 years ago and use that as a curatorial theme." Examples are "Natural Selections" (1989), about art that manipulates the natural world; "This Is My Body (1994), about art that features the artist's own body; and "God and Country" (1990), about art that incorporates patriotic and religious themes.

First Thursday Gallery Walk began in 1981 as a cooperative business venture among mostly smaller art dealers in Pioneer Square. One of the seventeen founders, Larry Reid recalls that Sam Davidson was the only "big" gallery owner to participate. The group printed a handout map, chipped away at promotion, and on the first Thursday of each month painted footprints on the sidewalks leading visitors to their doors. As crowds bypassed major galleries, their owners "burned." In 1982 the holdouts joined in. The monthly round of openings accompanied by white wine and cheese cubes became a highlight of the local arts scene.

Although initially lukewarm to the idea,

Artists paid dirt-cheap rent for abandoned rooms like this one and converted them into live/work space. Photo by Dave Potts, 1971. Museum of History and Industry, Seattle Post-Intelligencer Collection, 86.5.54389, 6

Linda Farris became Gallery Walk's often-photographed "poster girl," sporting sexy fashions, outlandish glasses, and sparkling tiaras. In the *Weekly* article, Kucera credited her with keeping the monthly event exciting for the public in its early years: "Pretty soon Linda's gallery on a First Thursday became a competition of outfits and attitudes. Everyone from art mavens to impressionable teenagers donned their elf boots, push-up bras, leggings, and black tights and pranced out to the openings to model their outfits on the fashion runway of First Thursday."

Along with the galleries, other shops, restau-rants, and bars welcomed the schmoozing crowds for the monthly fun-filled social event, while sidewalk artists and street vendors vied for attention. Art lovers and collectors often planned to come back at a quieter time for a closer look at new and intriguing work.

The 1990s witnessed a noticeable shift in the type of buyer that prowled the galleries. In 1995 Patterson Sims, then curator of modern art at the Seattle Art Museum, observed: "Enormous wealth has been generated in this area in the last 15 years, and there is much more collecting going on." Young, intellectually savvy collectors had homes and office buildings with ample wall space to fill. They started out with a commitment to collect the very best, including works by emerging Northwest artists, and they were in a position to pay high prices to get what they wanted.

Some of Pioneer Square's artists and galleries made unprecedented gains but at a price. New residential and commercial developments, described in chapter 9, have exacted the inevitable toll on the Bohemian community, including displacement of low-income residents and many a small business. The Washington Shoe Building at Second Avenue South and Jackson was the district's last large enclave of "starving artists." Although it was zoned for business and not residential use, many of the artists lived in their studios there. The building's cooperative gallery gave tenants a chance to showcase their work with the potential of being discovered as a rare new talent. When the Shoe was renovated in 2000, almost all of the artists had to leave Pioneer Square.

As of this writing, established artists still rent studio space in a handful of unrenovated buildings along Jackson Street and in former warehouses on Western Avenue. Jim Leong, whose paintings are exhibited in major galleries throughout the world, is one of the district's few remaining long-term artist/residents. He considers himself fortunate, since the owner of the building has not yet targeted his cavernous, light-filled loft for restoration. A former Seattle Arts Commissioner, Leong regards the downtown environment as essential to an artist's economic well-being. When prospective buyers view his work in local galleries, they can visit his studio to see more.

Leong and his former neighbor, Catherine Vandenbrink, now a member of the Seattle Arts Commission, have become leading advocates for the value of artists as contributors to the downtown community. While her husband, Michael Fajans, continued his career as an acclaimed painter, Vandenbrink put her jewelry art on hold to work for Pioneer Square's community organizations. Thanks to this support as well as public/private partnerships, a few recent and forthcoming rehabilitation projects include live/work space for low-income artists. One of them, now owned by the Pioneer Square Community Association, is the historic Tashiro-Kaplan Building, which combines the former Tashiro Hardware Building and the Kaplan Warehouse on Prefontaine Place. Vandenbrink is widely credited with moving the project from concept to reality.

Support for artists' housing is in keeping with the 1998 Neighborhood Plan, which underscores the community's commitment to retaining its artists and small businesses. In addition, a mandate in the Historic District requires the involvement of artists in new development projects and city planning.

Public Art Program and Projects

The Public Spaces Forum and the Seattle Arts Commission produced the 2001 "Pioneer Square Public Arts and Legends Program," a sequel to the Neighborhood Plan that was created by nationally known public artist B. J. Krivanek and local historian Mildred Tanner Andrews. The program recognizes the value of artistic interpretation in a community dealing with such weighty issues as shifting demographics, the need to balance preservation and new development, and the desire to embrace prosperity without forgetting the powerless. To address the district's diversity, the authors divided it into seven thematic areas, with historic, social, and cultural polarities that could provide inspiration for artists. In addition, they suggested concepts for various forms of visual and performance art. The Seattle Arts Commission encourages the use of the program "by every planner, every developer, every community leader whose decisions will impact the future character of Pioneer Square."

Even as the program was being developed, new public artworks in the neighborhood shared its philosophy and served as models of its viability. Fortson Square at Second and Yesler had deteriorated into a place targeted by city and neighborhood coalitions concerned with public safety, hygiene, and appearance. The small triangle caught the eye of people in buses and cars on Yesler Way and of thousands more who exited the downtown transit tunnel at the Pioneer Square Station across the street.

Under lead sponsorship of the district's Community Development Organization (CDO), the 2001 sculptural "ruin" by artist Elizabeth Conner and landscape architect Cliff Willwerth took center stage in the cleanup initiative. Half-buried remnants of buildings reflect the neighborhood south of Yesler Way, where Seattle's original downtown fell into decline. Inscriptions on paver stones recall Seattle's original Skid Road (now Yesler Way) to the lumber mill, a log chute that later became a metaphor for the district to the south; a cable-car stop next to a horse-and-mule market; Wyatt

Earp's saloon; Seattle's first Chinatown and a multiethnic immigrant community decimated by the Second Avenue Extension; the city's first gay bars; and more from the area's intriguing past.

The work attracts visitors and residents who mingle in the square. In addition to discovering entertaining historical nuggets, they learn about traditions of social, economic, and cultural diversity unique to the area. The work provides a sense of ongoing traditions and challenges for those pondering ways to balance today's missions, low-income housing, and social services with small businesses, high-tech firms in the Smith Tower, and waves of tourists and commuters.

In 2000 the Weller Street pedestrian "Bridge Between Cultures" crossed the railroad tracks south of King Street and Union Stations, physically linking Pioneer Square and the International District, while connecting the historic districts with contemporary developments in transportation, sports stadiums, and office complexes. Artists Fernanda D'Agostino and Valerie Otani created playful and provocative metal cutouts along the bridge's side rails to invoke historic themes from the area, some of which are ongoing while others have faded into the past. Examples are Indians in dugout canoes, abundant salmon, tumbling cascades of railroaders' pocket watches, Asian game pieces, and balls from various sports. As a study in continuity and change, the work gives hope for a future that integrates the area's cultural heritage with new trends and development but that also cautions preservationists to protect what they value.

In 2002 the Friends of Post Alley celebrated the completion of "Pioneer Square Pals," an outdoor wall mural on the side of the Post Building at Post Alley and Yesler Way. The ad hoc neighborhood group, spearheaded by Dany

Mitchell with Ilze Jones and Kevin Carl of Jones & Jones, planned the project to add flavor to the pedestrian experience at the historic alley's south end. Having lived and worked in the district for thirty years, artist Billy King derived his inspiration from the old Skid Road, where strangers swapped stories and helped each other out. The Billy King mural is a milestone that introduces public art and historic interpretation into the revitalization of the district's alleys.

The colorful and engaging mural is at the vanguard of efforts to convert Pioneer Square's narrow, brick-lined alleys from havens for vagrants and drunks into clean, safe, historic treasures. Related programs include the city's removal of dumpsters from the alleys and the establishment of CleanScapes, an independent corporation that began as a program of the Pioneer Square Community Council to keep outdoor spaces clean for property owners who contracted for their services.

The Friends of Post Alley gather in October 2002 at the donor reception to dedicate "Pioneer Square Pals" by the artist Billy King. The outdoor mural is painted on the rolling steel wall panel of the Post Building. Photo by Doug Vann. Courtesy of the photographer and the artist

The Club Scene and Popular Culture

Billy King and most of the Friends of Post Alley were witnesses to an earlier phase of revitalization that launched the district's club scene. In 1971 Bob Foster and Jim Anderson left hectic jobs at the Boeing Company and bought the Central Tavern, on First Avenue South between Washington and Main, which billed itself Seattle's "oldest second-class tavern." They spent three months cleaning up the grime of the derelict Skid Road venue and bringing it to borderline respectability and beyond. *Seattle Times* columnist John Hinterberger characterized it as "a cozy headquarters of slum chic, a beat up period piece gone fashionable, and a gathering place for a whole battalion of countercultural types who grew up there and decided to stay." They championed a range of causes, including antiwar activism, saving the whales, a ban against litter in the natural environment, and historic preservation in Pioneer Square. Tiny Freeman made an unsuccessful run for Congress from one of the Central's barstools.

In the same period, Stan and Harry Poll purchased and carefully restored the J & M Cafe next door at First and Washington. It was another local gathering place that, unlike the Central, continued its long tradition of hosting card games. Named for its founders, Joe and Mary McGonigle, it lays claim to being Seattle's oldest tavern.

Bob Foster was reportedly in the J & M on a gloomy winter night when he came up with an idea to spark the February business doldrums—"a great big party, like Mardi Gras!" Foster pulled together an impressive Fat Tuesday Committee, including Norman Langill, whose One Reel Vaudeville was a popular show that toured the region in a big delivery truck. In 1977 the first weeklong bacchanal got a tremendous boost from the filming of the "running of the beers" Rainier Brewery ad in Pioneer Square, in which people in bottle costumes with legs mimicked the running of the bulls in Pamplona, Spain; a crowd of thousands turned out.

Music, bunting, balloons, and zany costumes were everywhere, day and night. Costumed revelers staged a parade between the Pike Place Market and Pioneer Square. When the expected five hundred participants mushroomed to fifty thousand, altercations broke out with city police assigned to the event.

In subsequent years the parades, the zaniness, and the confrontations continued. Revelers gladly paid the joint cover charge that admitted them to most of Pioneer Square's clubs. There were eat-offs, face-offs, and, in later years, Spam carving, launched by Ruby Montana, who sold kitschy Western collectibles at her legendary Pinto Pony shop.

But from the early years, the week of party madness was marked by moments of violence. Many revelers did not confine their drinking to clubs, and minors imbibed on the streets. Critics objected to the lax enforcement of liquor laws, pointing out that predominantly non-Catholic Seattle had no basis for a pre-Lenten carnival. In February 2001, a combination of a mostly underage rioting mob and a police force that stood on the sidelines resulted in several injuries and the tragic death of Kristopher Kime. A subsequent task force appointed by Mayor Paul Schell outlined plans for a future midwinter festival that would be family-oriented with strict enforcement to curtail underage drinking and violent behavior.

Theatrical Debuts

Over the years, Pioneer Square's clubs and taverns have been gathering places for a devoted neighborhood theater crowd. In the 1970s and

1980s, Skid Road Theater staged popular performances in the City Club Building, on First Avenue South between Yesler and Washington, and later in a basement theater at First and Cherry, giving numerous actors and playwrights their start. Its founders were Lauralee Johnson and Robert Leroy "Yankee" Johnson, who at one time served as director of the King County Arts Commission. Like many other artists, they were active in the Pioneer Square community and counted their neighbors among their staunchest supporters.

Jean and Greg Falls, founders of A Contemporary Theatre (ACT), had their office in the Globe Building when they helped establish the new Empty Space Theater in the early 1970s, with Burke Walker as artistic director. A decade later, the Empty Space moved into a dream home in newly renovated Merrill Place, with an agreement to begin paying rent after a year. But when expenses proved too high, the company moved again, taking refuge in the old Occidental Avenue South quarters that had been vacated by the defunct Pioneer Square Theater.

Before rocketing to grunge fame, Nirvana, the Presidents of the United States of America, and Pearl Jam performed, along with many other jazz and punk bands, at the O.K. Hotel. The O.K. continued to roll with rock until the 2001 Nisqually Earthquake shut it down. At present, the upper floors, which have been vacant for decades, are being renovated for low-income housing, including live/work space for artists. Washington State Archives, Puget Sound Regional Branch

The Velvet Elvis Theater at 115 Occidental South—John Considine's early-twentieth-century Star Theater—was the scene of the 1983 opening of the punk-rock parody *Angry Housewives,* about four frustrated suburban moms who made a hit record called "Eat Your Fuckin' Cornflakes." The show later moved to the Pioneer Square Annex Theater, a former burlesque house next door to the Smith Tower. It ran for a record six and a half years, entertaining a mainstream Seattle audience that sometimes viewed punk rock as a menace and on other occasions saw it as a quaint oddity to be laughed at.

The Birth of Grunge

Angry Housewives was appropriately staged in Pioneer Square, where punk was the rage and where Seattle grunge got its start in the seminal period of 1983–1986. At first there were live shows in venues such as the Metropolis, Gorilla Room, and Rosco Louie.

In 1985 the City Council passed a controversial Teen Dance Ordinance, which, according to grunge historian Clark Humphrey, made it financially impossible or illegal to hold all-age live rock shows "anywhere bigger than a basement or smaller than an arena."

Larry Reid, who closed his successful Rosco Louie Gallery, went on to open a new gallery called Craven Image at Third and Washington, on the outskirts of the neighborhood. He welcomed young high-school musicians to his basement, which became a rehearsal and gathering space that spawned a unique combination of music, fashion, dance, art, and politics. The bands performed at Craven Image and in nearby teen clubs, including the Metropolis and Ground Zero, in environments that would put Seattle on the map as the birthplace of grunge. Some of the now-famous groups were Pearl Jam, Mudhoney, and Nirvana.

When Steve Freeborn and Tia Matthews opened the long-abandoned O.K. Hotel in 1988, they created a popular grunge and alternative music venue for underage fans. The September 21, 2001, *Seattle Post-Intelligencer* noted that their venture was not profitable until they opened a bar in one of the storefronts. Matthews said, "At the time we got liquor, our booking agent thought that it would be a disaster. He thought nobody would respect us any more. It turned out to be completely untrue." The O.K. bar and the Central Tavern drew an older crowd with an insatiable appetite for grunge and punk rock. After rolling with rock for more than a decade, the O.K. was slammed by the 2001 Nisqually Earthquake and forced to close.

Pioneer Square has a tradition of social and cultural diversity with new beginnings that include Seattle's gay community. Its history and the local "coming out" can be viewed in the context of national gay and lesbian history. The sidebar Out of the Closet illustrates how a former fringe group gained a toehold in the district before merging into the mainstream of Seattle culture.

Out of the Closet

by DANA COX

By the turn of the twentieth century, Pioneer Square, distant as it was from the fleshpots of the urban eastern seaboard, had become Seattle's equivalent of the Bowery District in New York and the Barbary Coast in San Francisco. Seattle had honed its skills in fleecing greenhorns on their way to the goldfields of the Klondike and soldiers fresh off the farm going off to the Spanish-American War. Pioneer Square was certainly the area of Seattle that attracted men, straight or gay, to drink, gamble, and find sex.

George Chauncey, while conducting research for his excellent book *Gay New York,* found evidence in police records that steam baths in that city were considered safe "gay space" as far back as the 1890s. Oral histories collected by the Northwest Gay Lesbian Transgender History Museum Project (NWGLTHMP) indicate that the South End Steam Baths (formerly the Turkish Baths at the Northern Hotel) in the Terry-Denny Building, on First Avenue South between Yesler and Washington, were frequented by gays at least as far back as the 1920s. This was one of several public baths in the district since the 1890s. Given that the ratio of men to women in Pioneer Square was sometimes estimated at fifteen to one during the gold rush era, it should not be too great a stretch to understand the possibilities of male-male inti-

macy in the darkened corridors of an anonymous steam-bath environment.

Female impersonators performed in floor shows at speakeasies in Seattle in the 1920s, and oral histories indicate that they were in chorus lines at least as far back as the Klondike gold rush, whether the audience knew it or not. Evidently the proprietors felt no need to announce that there were female impersonators in their shows.

Payoffs and Protected Places

Pioneer Square served as an incubator for a gay and lesbian community, as it did for other marginalized groups and businesses. As the business district migrated farther north, the district south of Yesler Way went into a gradual decline. The character of its businesses shifted to the shadier side. Seattle's notorious police payoff system created a sort of haven or protected environment in the bars in the district that allowed a gay culture to begin to emerge. The owners made payoffs to protect their performers and clients from harassment—which is not to say that one didn't look both ways before darting into a doorway or a stairwell. Entering a known gay establishment before the 1970s was in a sense a political act. But as historian Don Paulson says in his book *An Evening in the Garden of Allah,* being "out" in Pioneer Square was "a giant step toward having the confidence to form political groups, challenge police authority and pound on the doors of City Hall."

The Double Header Tavern, which opened in 1934 after the repeal of Prohibition, is considered by some to be the oldest gay bar in America. Although it has always been straight-owned, it has always been gay-friendly. The Double Header was one of the more popular venues in town during the World War II–era population boom. It is remembered for drag shows and an all-female oompah band called the Cracker Barrels. In the basement of the Double Header was another popular place officially named the Casino (the marquee is still there today). This space had previously been John Considine's box-house theater, the People's Theater. The Casino, an after-hours club, was affectionately known as Madame Peabody's Dancing Academy for Young Ladies, or the Dance—one of the few places on the West Coast where same-sex dancing was allowed. Gays were also welcome across Washington Street at Mattie's, where McCoy's Firehouse is today, and a couple doors west at the Columbus Tavern, opened sometime before WWII.

Female Impersonators and Cabarets

In 1946 the Garden of Allah opened in the Arlington Hotel on First Avenue at University Street, now the site of the Inn at Harbor Steps. Although it was a few blocks north of Pioneer Square, the Garden of Allah is relevant to the district because, as Don Paulson opines, the opening of the Garden of Allah in 1946 was a monumental step for the gay community. Pioneer Square was where strides were made toward creating a gay community, and it was the scene of the majority of the gay bars. The Garden, open from 1946 to 1956, quickly became part of the national circuit for cabarets that featured female impersonators. Others were

Finocchio's (a fixture in San Francisco's nightlife through the 1980s), the Beige Room in Los Angeles, the Chi Chi in Palm Springs, and the 440 in New York City.

Female impersonators in this era were different from today's drag queens. They didn't lip synch; they actually sang and performed. Most of the performers at the Garden of Allah had honed their skills, including striptease, in vaudeville and burlesque theaters.

The big-name acts at the Garden of Allah were Bill de Voe, Jackie Starr, Hotcha Hinton, Francis Blair, and Kenny Bee. The first four performed in drag. Kenny, who was house comedian, often emceed at the Garden. A popular number was called "Hold That Tiger." The big three at the Garden were Jackie, Hotcha, and Francis. When Jackie was on stage, "she" reputedly had such presence that you could hear a pin drop. "She" won national recognition when Walter Winchell called her the "prettiest boy

Skid Road sidewalk scene, 1950s. The Double Header Tavern opened in 1934 with a straight owner who has always welcomed gays and a mixed clientele. MSCUA, University of Washington Libraries, UW 6562

in America." Winchell may have referred to one of the times, beginning in the 1930s, when Starr reportedly stood in for Gypsy Rose Lee in Manhattan. Hotcha was known for "her" foul mouth, especially when dealing with hecklers. Francis Blair was the only one in the group who was homegrown. Blair got "her" training in Seattle's cabarets and burlesque houses in the '30s.

Soldiers and sailors were a significant part of the Garden's audiences in the post–WWII era, when they were on leave or off duty. Tourists also liked to come down to stare at the queers. They sometimes got more than they had bargained for. Gays sometimes referred to the straights as "trade."

Some venues in Pioneer Square served gay clientele through several changes of name and ownership. One such establishment was a gay bar at Yesler Way and Occidental Avenue called Cimbre's during the sixties; it became the 107 Club, a gay all-ages hangout, in the seventies. Next door was yet another gay bar, the Dollhouse.

A block away on the west side of Second Avenue between Washington and Main Streets was the Golden Horseshoe. In the 1960s, it was the first regular-hours bar where men could openly dance with one another. One of its owners, MacIver Wells, tired of paying the police for protection, cooperated with the FBI in an investigation that eventually helped break Seattle's notorious payoff system.

Organization and Action

The Mocambo, a class H, hard liquor bar on Fortson Square, operated from 1951 to 1978. It was more upscale than most of the other bars in the neighborhood—cleaner, better equipped, with better interior design. As it was class H, it served food and was patronized by business-

people and employees from the nearby King County Courthouse. In the sixties, gay political and social groups, including the Gay Business Council (which became the Greater Seattle Business Association) and the Ebony Council (an association of gay African American men) used the space to hold meetings. The Court of Seattle created cross-dressing events that paid tongue-in-cheek homage to the worlds of cotillions and beauty pageants. It met at the Mocambo, as did the Dorian Society.

Members of the Dorian Society spoke at Seattle-area high schools and also helped found the Seattle Counseling Services for Sexual Minorities. One of the group's founders, Peter Wichern, appeared on the cover of *Seattle Magazine* in 1967. The cover proclaimed: "This is Peter Wichern. He is a local businessman. He is a homosexual." This was a brave act in the pre-Stonewall era. The Stonewall Riots in Greenwich Village, often considered the seminal event of the gay rights movement, would not happen for another two years.

In 1973 Seattle enacted specific civil-rights protections prohibiting discrimination in employment on the basis of sexual orientation. In 1975 the city broadened the protection to include housing codes. In 1978, inspired by Anita Bryant's Save Our Children Crusade in Florida, Seattle police officers Dennis Falk and David Estes and their far-right supporters launched Initiative 13 to repeal the Fair Housing and Employment Ordinance.

Opposition to the initiative galvanized Seattle's gay community to action. Two factions emerged: one a conservative, business-oriented, mainstream group that saw the referendum as an issue of privacy; the other a more in-your-face radical faction that defined the debate as a direct attack on gays. On November 7, 1978, Seattle voters rejected Initiative 13 decisively, by nearly two to one.

Gay Pride

In 1973 Shelly's Leg, Seattle's first discotheque, opened at the foot of Main Street and Alaskan Way. It had a large sign visible from the street that proclaimed Shelly's Leg a gay bar for gay guests and their friends. Wildly popular with both gays and straights, it was perhaps Seattle's first openly gay business and a model for the future. It publicly demanded to be accepted by the straight world on its own terms. Shelly's Leg succeeded in part because of the gay-rights movement and in part because of the trendy, energetic disco atmosphere.

The club's name came from the owners' macabre sense of humor about a Seattle Bastille Day accident that injured one of them. Shelly Bowman was standing in front of a cannon on a float that was to shoot confetti over the crowd. Unfortunately, the confetti had been turned into a compacted plug (probably from beer poured down the barrel), so that when fired, the cannon's ensuing explosion took Shelly's leg. The $330,000 insurance settlement financed the opening of the club. Like many of the customers, Shelly Bowman was straight.

In 1974 Mayor Wes Uhlman decreed the city's first Gay Pride Week. The *Seattle Post-Intelligencer* reported that about two hundred attended a picnic at Occidental Park in Pioneer Square. Entertainment included music and a "Gayrilla theater." Banners from the stage read "[P]roud to be lesbian, [P]roud to be gay." The evening street dance featured music by Blue Moon and Sue Isaac.

On June 28, 1974, the Gay Community Center at 1726 Sixteenth Avenue East on Capitol Hill held a grand opening. Seattle's gay organizations and gathering places were moving

The original Shelly's Leg sign is on display at the Museum of History and Industry. It was rediscovered by the Northwest Gay Lesbian Transgender History Museum Project. Courtesy of NGLTHMP

out of Pioneer Square. Capitol Hill was attractive, since many gays and lesbians resided in the neighborhood. The gay, lesbian, bisexual, and transgender community was also emerging from the shadows. Along with society's increasing acceptance of gays, the community was becoming more diverse. There was a desire for a more visible and broad-based community with more than just bars and baths. But Pioneer Square remained gay-friendly. Some of its current residents and business owners helped organize the original Gay Pride Week and have also supported the historic preservation movement (see chapter 9).

Preservation and the Era of Civic Revival

Karin Link

In the mid-1950s, charismatic publicist Bill Speidel was one of the first tenants of the Jackson Building, the former Capitol Brewing Company building, located at the northeast corner of First Avenue South and South Jackson Street. Speidel began exploring the forgotten underground city that was Seattle's birthplace. The original streetscape had been buried after the Great Fire of 1889, when city engineers raised the streets to improve sanitation and relieve chronic flooding (see chapter 3).

With his wife, Shirley, Speidel scoured historical archives and city records. His newspaper stories about the labyrinthine passages and their colorful history sparked great interest in Seattle's subterranean cityscape. At one point, Bill and Shirley Speidel received 300 letters and numerous phone calls urging them to give tours of Seattle's underground. They were helped by enthusiastic student volunteers from Cleveland High School, who cleaned out "tons of debris" in order to create a safe route for tourists. The first tour, in May 1965, offered at a "buck a head" and sponsored by the Seattle Chamber of Commerce as part of "Know Your Seattle Day," was a rousing success. Bill Speidel later wrote: "the Square was jam-packed with people holding dollar bills. We took 500 people on tours that day."

From the start, the Underground Tour was

a magnet for tourists and residents alike. Today Sunny Speidel (sister of artist Julie Speidel; see chapter 8) heads the organization that her parents founded. She and her spirited crew of trained guides regale visitors with lighthearted stories based on her father's original script. These colorful tales describe the special charms of Seattle's underground as well as Seattle's past.

In Bill Speidel's hands, the mystique of underground Seattle had tremendous potential for galvanizing public interest in the preservation of Pioneer Square; but tours of Seattle's underground streetscape were not enough to protect the aboveground historic buildings and streets. It would take a tenacious group of citizens, described as a group of "do-gooders and architects" by architect Victor Steinbrueck, to salvage the birthplace of downtown and transform it into one of the city's most cherished treasures.

Politics and Preservation

In the 1950s and 1960s, Pioneer Square was described as a very blighted area and shunned by most of Seattle's citizens, but the effort to save and preserve the district had really already begun in the 1950s. Victor Steinbrueck, on the architecture faculty at the University of Washington and for a time the department's chairman, was a modernist architect who played a pivotal role in preserving Seattle's historic legacy, in Pioneer Square as well as in the Pike Place Market. In the October 3, 1965, *Seattle Post-Intelligencer,* Steinbrueck wrote:

The city began at Pioneer Square. It has lived here and time may demonstrate whether or not it will end here, as well. Yesler's mill and cookhouse, the center of activity, was located here for the first thirty five years of Seattle's life. Later when Seattle's modern downtown burned to the ground in 1889, the regrowth took place here again, with the present buildings providing the environment for commercial activities for many years.

Much of the history of Seattle is visible in Pioneer Square. If the city can find a way to sympathetically restore its "home place," there is good basis to believe that it will continue to live. If places of distinctive character and historic association are not retained, then the city as we know it will not endure and even such buildings as the elegant Norton Building are doomed also. . . .

Taken separately the Pioneer Square buildings are not great architecture, but as a group of buildings of similar character, scale and material of the same era, a total environment is created that is the most architecturally successful within the central business district.

The care and hard work of other architects such as Ralph Anderson, Alan Bumgardner, Ibsen Nelsen, Fred Bassetti, Ilze Jones, and Grant Jones among others, as well as developers such as Alan Black, Richard White, and Marvin Burke, spearheaded a movement to preserve and rehabilitate Seattle's early birthplace and give it a new and interesting life.

Pioneer Square's battle to preserve not only its buildings but to define its continuously changing character has been difficult. It remains so to this day. There is still much political infighting in Pioneer Square, with certain factions

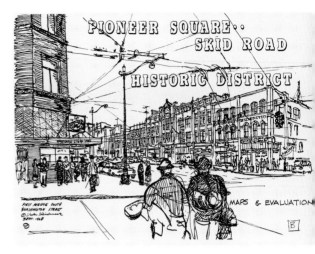

Victor Steinbrueck sketched First Avenue South, looking south from Washington Street in 1968, and used it as a cover for the architectural and historical survey that he prepared for the Seattle Planning Commission. His antigentrification stance comes through in depictions of people in casual conversation and in the inclusion of appealing Skid Road features, such as signage for the J & M Cafe and the ad for soft ice cream at the Washington Cigar Store. MSCUA, University of Washington Libraries, Acc. 3252–3, Box 2, Folder 38

hoping for a much more upscale neighborhood while others see the district's value as a neighborhood that should continue to provide more low-rent housing, offices, art galleries, and artists' live/work spaces as well as decent and

Victor Steinbrueck as a young architect sketching outdoors. MSCUA, University of Washington Libraries, 366

*Five architects who were instrumental in saving
Pioneer Square, from left to right: Ralph Anderson,
Al Bumgardner, Ibsen Nelsen, Fred Bassetti, and
Victor Steinbrueck. Photo by Mary Randlett,
August 1984. © Mary Randlett. MSCUA, University
of Washington Libraries*

better shelter for the homeless population. Of
course, many people fall somewhere between
these two points of view.

Pioneer Square has also had to deal with
the forces of nature. The February 28, 2001,
Nisqually Earthquake, estimated at 6.8 on the
Richter scale, hit the neighborhood with some
force. A few buildings were obviously damaged
as parts of their facades crumbled. As of this
writing, the structural damage to many of the
buildings is still being repaired. The 2001
Nisqually Earthquake is the greatest temblor
to affect Seattle since the 1949 one, measuring
7.1 on the Richter scale, which also took its
toll on Pioneer Square. It was during the 1949
earthquake, for instance, that many of the
historic building cornices fell or were later
removed as a precautionary measure.

The 1950s and 1960s:
Early National Preservation Laws

In general during the early 1950s and 1960s,
there was little appreciation for historic buildings and older, often blighted areas within
American cities. The handful of early preservationists had no legal recourse or support.

While several federal laws sought to establish
the importance of historic buildings or archaeological sites, they also had little clout. The
Historic Sites Act, passed by Congress in 1935,
created the National Historic Landmarks
Program but did not really protect privately
owned historic properties from any destruction
their owners cared to inflict. The National Trust
for Historic Preservation, chartered by Congress
in 1949 and operating with donated funds, was
authorized to administer historic buildings, sites,
and objects.

Neither of these laws had any value below
the federal level and therefore were of little help
to local preservationists in the late 1950s and
early 1960s. A few historic districts had been
created on an individual basis as far back as the
1930s: in Charleston, South Carolina, in 1931
and at the Vieux Carre in New Orleans in 1936,
as well as in Massachusetts, Connecticut, North
Carolina, and Florida in the 1950s and 1960s.
There were no official mechanisms, however,
for creating historic districts until 1966.

The National Historic Preservation Act of
1966, administered by the National Park Service,
created the National Register of Historic Places,
a list of "sites, buildings, objects, districts and
structures" of historical significance at the
national, state, or local level. It also established
an Advisory Council on Historic Preservation
that approved modifications to be made to historic properties and administered grants-in-aid
programs for registered properties. Ultimately,

the National Historic Preservation Act would have an important influence on Pioneer Square, but even by the late 1960s these mechanisms for nominating a historic district to the National Register of Historic Places were very new.

As in many American cities, it was grassroots citizen outrage or support that forced the issues. In New York, for instance, it is generally felt that the destruction of Pennsylvania Station signaled the importance of maintaining the best of the historical built heritage. In Seattle, the demolition of the Seattle Hotel in 1961 and its replacement by the "sinking ship" garage was a sign to many that strong action needed to be taken to preserve the rest of Pioneer Square.

The issues of preserving Pioneer Square—how much should be preserved, how it should be redeveloped if not preserved, what guidelines, laws, and ordinances should be put in place for its complete preservation—have all been hotly contested. From the outset, Pioneer Square as we know it today came fairly close to being demolished. Political as well as natural and physical forces have frequently threatened its existence—and continue to do so.

Pioneer Square's Key Players

Several key players helped shape what would become the Pioneer Square Historic District. The Central Association was founded in 1958; a forerunner of today's Downtown Seattle Association (DSA), it was concerned with the development of a thriving downtown business district. The Central Association's membership consisted of what were then considered Seattle's top business leaders. Its first office and meetings were in the Olympic Hotel, still one of Seattle's most elegant hotels in the downtown business district, north of Pioneer Square. The Central Association had strong ties with the Seattle City

Council, which in 1963 adopted the Central Association's "Central Business Plan." This recommended the building of two ring roads around the business district, an outer ring to allow traffic to bypass it and an inner ring that would feed cars directly into a series of parking structures near its perimeter. Within Pioneer Square, Main Street would have been used for eastbound traffic and Washington Street for westbound traffic. The eastern part of the ring would have been at Fifth Avenue. In the final stage of the scheme, both streets would connect by ramps to a two-level viaduct, sited parallel to the Alaskan Way Viaduct. Thankfully, none of this was built, but it does show the increasing emphasis on traffic infrastructure as a basis for urban design in Seattle (as well as in other American cities) in the 1950s and 1960s. The notion of building a ring road continued to influence subsequent plans for the city and specifically Pioneer Square through the 1960s.

Another player was the Pioneer Square Association, an organization of local Pioneer Square business owners and a forerunner of the Pioneer Square Community Council and today's Pioneer Square Community Association. In the 1950s, this group was friendly to the Central Association. In fact, in those years it was not uncommon for members of the Pioneer Square Association to be members of the Central Association. By the late 1960s, however, these two groups' respective political stances concerning the fate of Pioneer Square were markedly different. Among other factors, the local Pioneer Square businesspeople often already had a vested financial interest in the renovation rather than the demolition of their properties.

In addition to these business groups, there were the idealistic and visionary citizens, developers, and architects (mentioned above), often identified with Allied Arts of Seattle, the Seattle chapter of the American Institute of Architects, and, particularly, Action/Better City. Founded informally as the "Beer and Culture Society" in 1952, Allied Arts was known for its many civic contributions, including its support in 1955 for the creation of the Municipal Art Commission (succeeded in the 1970s by the Seattle Arts Commission) and its role in the campaign to save the Pike Place Market in the early 1970s. Action/Better City, originally an offshoot of the Seattle chapter of the American Institute of Architects, took a strong preservationist stance and had creative visions for the revitalization of Pioneer Square. These civic-minded groups cared deeply about Seattle's development and saw real value in both Pioneer Square and the Pike Place Market.

The Late 1950s: An Early Planning Study

In 1959 the Seattle Planning Commission and the Central Association produced one of the earliest planning studies of Pioneer Square and presented it to the Seattle City Council. It described two projected fates: continued deterioration of the already blighted neighborhood and eventual demolition of most of its buildings; or rehabilitation of the area. In fact, the study recommended rehabilitation of the buildings, which would create an economically viable tourist attraction and an artistic and cultural center.

One of the major suggestions of the 1959 planning study was to close down Pioneer Place and enlarge the park. The report also stated clearly the stance of the Central Association: the preservation of buildings was a worthy endeavor, but in no way should it ever interfere with individual profit or business interests. A 1960 *Seattle Times* article entitled "Association Pushes Pioneer Square Restoration" stated:

A project of prime interest to the Central Association of Seattle is the restoration of Seattle's birthplace—Pioneer Square. . . .

The association points out that Pioneer Square can be to Seattle what the French Quarter is to New Orleans. Instead of an area of increasing blight, the Square can become a tourist attraction, an historic entertainment center. . . .

A plan for the enlargement of Pioneer Place Park by converting "Pioneer Place" . . . has been developed by the Seattle Park Department and other city departments. Funds for the improvements are available from the park bond issue passed this year by Seattle voters.

However the key to the restoration of Pioneer Square is action by the neighboring property owners in restoring their buildings to attract new restaurants, shops, clubs and other tourist and entertainment oriented businesses, say the leaders of Seattle's Central Association.

The Central Association

In the late 1950s and early 1960s, the Central Association saw itself as pro-preservation. Issues of the *Central Association Newsletter* from 1960 to around 1964 usually carried items referring specifically to preservation efforts in Pioneer Square. The February 1, 1960, issue, for instance, speaks very approvingly of the new Allied Arts Pioneer Square Committee. It goes on to suggest:

Action in restoring historical areas in cities like New York, San Francisco, Albuquerque, Philadelphia etc., points the way for Seattle. Our Pioneer Square Chairman, Langdon Simons, will visit two similar projects on the coast in the next few weeks—Olvera Street in Los Angeles and Jackson Square in San Francisco.

The August 16, 1963, newsletter with the title "Another Building Restoration 'Success Story'" describes the rehabilitation of the old Capitol Brewing Company building, now known as the Jackson Building, by Ralph Anderson. This building has had many names and associations, as the following passage indicates:

The opening of Interior Designer Allen Salsbury's Studio at First and Jackson recently, signaled what may be an important new trend in south-end building restoration. This adds another successful "Case History" to the Central Association's Building Restoration program. Without divulging the cost and income figures, we can report that this appears to be an excellent business investment for architect Ralph Anderson. This was the former Garrett-Schafer Building, built in 1905, and originally housed the historical Tumwater Tavern. The second and third floors will be used for architec-

The original owner of the Jackson Building was the old Capitol Brewing Company, which commissioned the ornate cross-vaulted ceiling for its tasting room. Catering to a different kind of taste, the space is now an art gallery. Photo by Karin Link

The Jackson Building at First and Jackson was one of the first buildings restored by architect Ralph Anderson. Photo by Karin Link

tural offices of the owner, and other offices in allied fields.

While the Central Association's views concerning preservation were always based on preservation making good business sense and not on the idea of preservation for preservation's sake, this attitude became even more firmly entrenched as doubts regarding the profitability of rehabilitating all of Pioneer Square's buildings surfaced. This stance colored later studies and debates.

From 1960 to 1964, the Central Association's discussions and activities remained mostly unremarkable and uncontroversial. The "Pioneer Square Rehabilitation Economic Study," published in October 1961, suggested restoring all of Pioneer Square as a reminder of gold rush–

era Seattle, with many improvements to be made by the opening of Seattle's World's Fair in April 1962.

By 1964, judging from its newsletters, the Central Association's boosterism was showing troubling signs from a preservationist point of view. A special issue of the November 1964 newsletter, called the "Downtowner's Newsletter," describes in glowing terms the "Nine Major Downtown Projects Underway." One was the Pike Plaza redevelopment project:

[a] 12.5 acre, $58 million urban renewal project to revitalize the west side of the Retail Core. . . . prime sites for tower apartments, a major new Downtown hotel, parking for 2,000–3,000 cars, a 3–block waterview park and a restored or rebuilt Market. At least two major new prestige office buildings. . . . Transit terminal for 17 lines.

Very little of the Pike Place Market, as we know it today, would exist if such a project had been effected, but that is another preservation story. The description of the "Pioneer Square Redevelopment" is less upsetting, depending on what is meant by "redevelopment," but the mention of a feasibility study similar to the Pike Plaza project's study was perhaps a first sign of the battle to be fought between the Central Association and Seattle preservationists:

Property in the Pioneer Square and "South of Yesler" area offers an excellent opportunity for redevelopment of the City's greatest concentration of blight. This area redeveloped can provide magnificent sites for office buildings, expanded commercial activity in a "green belt" setting. A preliminary feasibility study (similar to that undertaken in the past year for the Pike Plaza Project) . . .

The proposed Graham Plan for redevelopment of Pioneer Square also galvanized the local preservation movement. From John Graham and Company, Architects, Pioneer Square Redevelopment, *Seattle 1966. Courtesy of the DLR Group*

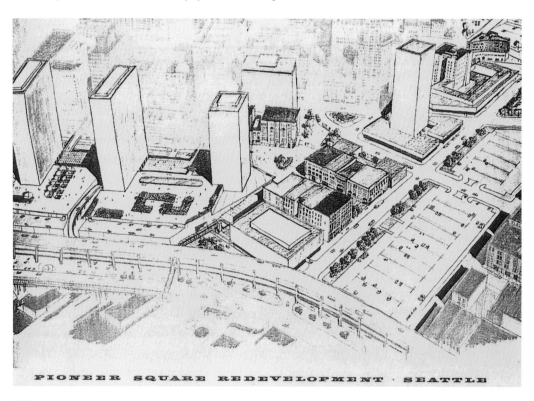

PIONEER SQUARE REDEVELOPMENT · SEATTLE

The Early 1960s:
The Seattle Hotel Demolished

Many architects and other local citizens were shocked by the demolition of the Seattle Hotel in 1961. Built in 1889 as the Occidental Hotel at Second and James, it had replaced its predecessor, which was destroyed during the Great Fire, and became a symbol of elegance in early Seattle. It weathered the economic Panic of 1893, when it was temporarily turned into an office building. By the late 1890s, thanks to the Klondike gold rush, it once again knew prosperity and was renamed the Seattle Hotel. Around 1906 or 1907, its interiors were refurbished at great expense. By World War II, the building was somewhat run-down.

Around 1960, a contractor inspecting the building insisted that he had seen an exterior wall moving back and forth and that the building was about to collapse. His observation was enough to justify demolition at a time when the understanding of historic buildings and methods of their restoration were far from sophisticated. In 1961 the local papers continued to carry nostalgic pieces describing the elegance and history of the Seattle Hotel. Its demolition and replacement by the "sinking ship" garage, considered a real eyesore, is credited with spurring local preservation sentiment. Citizens, and especially a suddenly determined group of architects, were indeed alarmed.

The Late 1960s: The Graham Plan

In the "Advance Planning and Feasibility Study—Pioneer Square Redevelopment" produced by John Graham Architects Planners and Engineers, which appeared in February 1965, the chief interest is a map showing buildings considered "questionable" or "substandard" in the Pioneer Square area. Few were considered "standard." This study provided preliminary information about buildings upon which the more well-known 1966 study, entitled "Pioneer Square Redevelopment," was based. More commonly referred to as the "Graham Plan," it defined urban renewal as a "means of removing blighting conditions, clearing obsolescent buildings, acquiring land at a write-down, and guiding redevelopment in accordance with an overall plan."

However, it acknowledged that the Municipal Art Commission, subsequently the Seattle Arts Commission, considered the following buildings of historic significance: the Maynard Building (northwest corner of First Avenue South and South Washington Street), the Cascade Hotel (the Olympic Block at First and Yesler, which collapsed dramatically in 1972), the Mutual Life Building (also at First and Yesler), the Pioneer Building at Pioneer Place, and the Washington Building, as well as the Colman Building, now on the edge of the Historic District at First and Columbia. It also mentioned that the Preservation Committee of the local chapter of the American Institute of Architects had added the Terry-Denny Building, the City Club Building (both on First Avenue South between Yesler and Washington), and the Interurban Building (Yesler and Occidental) as being significant.

The Graham Plan would have demolished most of what we now know as the Pioneer Square Historic District. It would have retained Pioneer Place and its surrounding structures such as the Lowman Building, Pioneer Building, Mutual Life Building, and Maynard Building (First and Washington) and those buildings facing Yesler Way from First to Western. The Frye Hotel (Third and Yesler) and the Prefontaine Building (between Prefontaine Place and the southwest corner of Yesler Way and Fourth Avenue South) would have been rehabilitated. All of the buildings on the west side of Western Avenue would now be surface parking lots. A large parking structure would have replaced the historic structure at the northeast corner of First and Cherry. The rest of the area would be given over to superblock towers and surface parking lots.

A system of bridges would have connected the superblocks so that "pedestrians within the eleven block area bounded by the waterfront on the west, Second Avenue on the east, Marion Street on the north and Washington Street on the south would be able to reach any other point in this entire area without crossing a street at-grade." This plan also appropriated the Ring Road idea, originally proposed in the 1963 "Central Business Plan." Again, Main Street was proposed as the "eastbound couplet of the Ring Road." The 1966 plan also stated that "two blocks bounded by Washington, the Alaskan Way Viaduct, Main and Occidental will be utilized by on-and-off ramps." In other words, the streets themselves would have been given over to auto traffic, with pedestrian traffic discouraged. What has been one of the liveliest areas near Main Street and Occidental, at least for the last fifteen years, would never have existed.

Resistance to the Graham Plan

Thankfully, a group of activists, led by architect Victor Steinbrueck and including Ben Masin of Masin's Furniture as well as many other businesspeople from the local Pioneer Square Association, were instrumental in stopping the Graham Plan. From 1967, there were serious attempts to create a Pioneer Square Historic District and an ordinance that would guide the efforts to rehabilitate and preserve its buildings as an ensemble. The idea was an unusual one for the late 1960s and early 1970s. It met with clear and consistent opposition from the Central Association,

Pioneer Place in December 2002, with the newly reconstructed pergola and the Chief Seattle fountain in the foreground. Buildings in the background, from left to right: a portion of the new Olympic Block; the Maynard Building (Albert Wickersham), 1892; the Terry-Denny Building, formerly known as the Northern Hotel (Charles W. Saunders), 1889; the Schwabacher Hardware Company Building (Bebb and Mendel), 1905; and the Yesler Building (Elmer Fisher), 1890. Photo by Karin Link

which stated that such an ordinance would infringe on the rights of Pioneer Square property owners.

For several years, the Central Association was successful in its attempts to stop the Seattle City Council from approving a preservation ordinance. In July 1968, when Phyllis Lamphere, a propreservation city councilmember, called for a study of the possibilities for a historic district, the conclusions were pessimistic, but by the end of 1968, when Mayor Dorm Braman was presented with a petition of 100,000 signatures put together by Bill Speidel supporting a Pioneer Square Historic District, it was clear that the wind was changing.

In 1969 Victor Steinbrueck produced "An Architectural and Historical Survey and Study of the Pioneer Square–Skid Road Historical District" for the Seattle Planning Commission. The study described the historical and architectural significance of the Pioneer Square area, building by building. It was a carefully researched and very convincing document and the first step to designating Pioneer Square as an official historic district. Steinbrueck's architectural and scholarly background was the basis of his political strength. On a more purely political front, in December 1969 a member of the Pioneer Square Association stated categorically: "We want no more ball and chain activity here at present." The fight between the Central Association and the forces of preservation continued to be fierce.

1970: The Pioneer Square Historic District Is Created

Mayor Wes Uhlman was a great supporter of the proposed ordinance and historic district. In March 1970, he made his stance clear to the Seattle City Council: "The basic purpose of this ordinance is to maintain the integrity of the old

Bill Speidel and Mayor Wes Uhlman battle cobwebs on a tour of the Underground. Courtesy of Bill Speidel, the Underground Tour

Seattle and the Pioneer Square District and to help provide a sense of architectural and historical continuity in the development of Seattle."

The ordinance was passed by the Seattle City Council on April 6, 1970. The local historic district is officially known as the Pioneer Square Preservation District. It is better known both locally and nationally as the Pioneer Square Historic District. It was originally bounded by Alaskan Way to the west and Columbia Street to the north. The eastern edge was a complicated zigzag line that included a line between First and Second Avenues running north-south from Columbia to Cherry Streets, which zigzagged to another eastern boundary line between Second and Third Avenues running from Cherry Street to Yesler Way. From here, the eastern boundary followed a north-south trajectory mid-block between Second Avenue Extension and Third Avenue South until "75 feet north of Washington Street," then zigzagged out again to Third Avenue South for about a block. It then more or less followed the

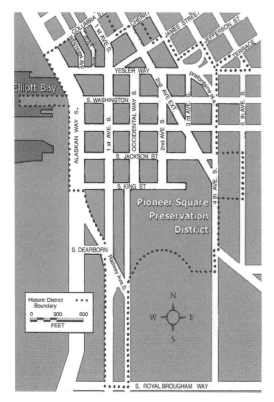

Map of Seattle's Pioneer Square/Skid Road Historic District. Courtesy of Department of Neighborhoods, with edits by Karin Link

eastern edge of Second Avenue to the southern boundary, located one half block south of Jackson Street. Since 1970 the district boundaries have been modified several times, with the last changes made in 1988.

At the same time that the ordinance was passed, the Pioneer Square Historic District Preservation Board (now succeeded by the Pioneer Square Preservation Board) was created to ensure that all restoration and building efforts, as well as signage, would be compatible with the historic and architectural character of the district. The passage of the ordinance and the creation of the board were important milestones in the urban history of Seattle and continue to have a far-reaching effect in Pioneer Square. As Victor Steinbrueck noted in an interview with Donald Schmechel in the 1980s,

when the Pioneer Square Historic District was first created and the ordinance passed, there was not even a City Landmarks Board. Creating a historic district in 1970, particularly in Seattle, was a momentous event with only few precedents in the United States. In 1970 the district was also listed on the National Register of Historic Places as the Pioneer Square Skid Road National Historic District.

1973: Special Review District Established

In 1973 the Pioneer Square Preservation District, along with the International District, became "Special Review Districts." The Seattle City Council established these districts for further protection against undesirable effects from automobile traffic and the Kingdome. The city imposed restrictions on a variety of sports-related activities as well as traffic and parking regulations.

While the original Pioneer Square Preservation District was a twenty-block area, the Pioneer Square Special Review District was a much larger forty-block area extending to Fourth Avenue South and from King Street to Columbia Street. Pioneer Square Special Review District guidelines set preservation standards concerning any changes to the exterior facades of buildings, with special attention to the location and design of signs and awnings. The guidelines also encouraged ground-level uses that would stimulate pedestrian activity.

The former Pioneer Square Historic District Preservation Board became the Pioneer Square Special Review District Board. This new board made sure that the guidelines were enforced and also took on the added role of reviewing building uses. Currently called the Pioneer Square Preservation Board, it is composed of volunteer members who are Pioneer Square residents or representatives of district businesses. Many of the members have expertise or interest in historic preservation, history, architecture, landscape architecture, or related fields.

Private Projects:
Politics and Energetic Solutions

Along with key players and political forces that helped create the Pioneer Square Historic District, independent people continued to work tirelessly on their own projects, restoring key buildings. These early efforts, before and after the passage of the ordinance in 1970, are still some of the crowning achievements in the history of the Pioneer Square Historic District. The rehabilitation of buildings, the restoration of Pioneer Place, and the creation of Occidental Park created a cohesive set of spaces and buildings, a spine for the district. In turn, this early work created the impetus to inhabit, visit,

restore, and care for the district. Through all of this period, Seattle Mayor Wes Uhlman contributed his support, a huge boost to local preservation efforts.

In the early 1970s, the City of Seattle Building Department began to focus on the nascent renovation activity in the Pioneer Square area and developed rules about earthquake resistance, including parapet tiebacks and reinforcement, all extremely important requirements today. At that time, few building officials or even architects had an understanding of historic buildings or construction. Pioneer Square is extremely lucky for the sensitivity and persistence of those involved in the early restoration projects.

Capitol Brewing Company Building

One of those who has described the 1961 demolition of the Seattle Hotel as a turning point

The infamous "sinking ship" garage rose on the site of the once grand Seattle Hotel. The vacant lot on the right was the home of the Olympic Block before it collapsed in 1972. A new building, designed to blend in with its historic neighbors, now stands in its place. In the foreground, an Underground Tour group follows its guide to the catacombs. Photo by Paul Dorpat

The northwest corner of the Globe Building, which houses the Elliott Bay Book Company. On the sidewalk, the Earl Layman Clock is dedicated to Seattle's first historic preservation officer. It was moved from its original location at Fourth Avenue and Pike Street in 1984. Photo by Karin Link

in his understanding of the value of the preservation of Pioneer Square's buildings is Ralph Anderson. He worked alongside Richard White, Alan Black, and Marvin Burke on the restoration of many historic structures in Pioneer Square. Anderson's involvement with Pioneer Square began early, with the restoration of the Capitol Brewing Company Building (now the Jackson Building) at First and Jackson in 1963.

Union Trust Building

In 1965 Anderson bought and restored the Union Trust Building, on the southwest corner of Occidental Avenue South and South Main Street. He also moved his office there. The restoration was done on a piecemeal basis. As the work progressed, various compromises with city building officials had to be made. The building's tenants, including artists, craftspeople, and others, also did a considerable amount of work on their own particular spaces.

The Globe Building

In 1968 Richard White purchased the Globe Hotel, the northern part of the former Marshall-Walker Building corresponding to the portion of the building originally developed by Marshall. Designed by William E. Boone in the 1890s, the building's two portions had been jointly developed by two owners, Marshall and Walker, who separated their respective portions with a brick wall. Subsequently, in the 1980s, Jones & Jones broke through the brick wall, connected the two parts, and restored the interior of the building. The entire ensemble is now called the Globe Building.

Jones & Jones is also well known for its work in the early 1970s in transforming many of Pioneer Square's open spaces. Originally founded by Grant Jones and Ilze Jones (Johnpaul Jones, no relation, joined the firm later), Jones & Jones today is also known for sensitive projects that combine careful site and landscape design, environmental considerations, and architecture. Their offices are housed in the Globe Building, as are a variety of other independent and creative businesses, notably Elliott Bay Book Company, which was founded on the ground floor in 1973.

Grand Central Building and Occidental Park

In 1971 Alan Black, Richard White, and Ralph Anderson bought the Squire-Latimer Building, on the northeast corner of First Avenue South and South Main Street, across the street from the Globe Building. Originally designed for offices by Nelson Comstock and Carl Troetsche in 1889, it housed the Grand Central Hotel from the time of the Klondike gold rush. The entire building was called the Grand Central Hotel from the 1930s onward. By 1971 the build-

ing was severely run-down and known as a white elephant. Others had tried to renovate it but had abandoned it.

In 1971 and 1972 Anderson took on the job of restoring the building. Both Allied Arts, as a preservation advocate, and Bill Baillargeon of Seattle Trust and Savings Bank lent support to the project. The upper floors were converted back to office space. A main interior ground-floor space was created. It boasted wrought-iron and glass doors, exposed brick walls, chandeliers salvaged from the King County Courthouse, and an intriguing warren of shops. Among these, the Grand Central Bakery drew many customers and visitors.

The area to the east of the Grand Central Building was a parking lot, the site of yet other demolished buildings. Federal funds were obtained to develop this open area into a park, now known as Occidental Park, and developed

Interior of the Grand Central Arcade. The Grand Central Building as built as the Squire-Latimer Block in 1889. Photo by Karin Link

Vaulted areaways from the underground were exposed before city engineers filled in Occidental Avenue to make it part of Occidental Park. Courtesy of Jones & Jones Architects and Landscape Architects

by Jones & Jones. Ilze Jones designed the cobblestoned and brick paved open spaces as well as the modern pergola and fountain. The design of the Occidental Park pergola was inspired by both the industrial nature of the district, its fire escapes, and its water towers as well as the Washington Street Boat Landing. The new pergola's glass canopy was a way of tying the newly created park with Pioneer Place and its glass-covered pergola.

The Grand Central Building and Occidental Park became one of the important focal points of the district, continuing to draw locals as well as tourists. Originally, a single row of London plane trees were planted down the middle of Occidental Street to underscore the Jones & Jones plan for a building to frame Occidental Park to the east at the site of a parking lot. To

date, this building has not been built, although it is still called for in the latest Pioneer Square Neighborhood Plan.

The Pioneer Building and Pioneer Place

Following the Grand Central project, Ralph Anderson and Partners was hired to renovate one of the great gems of Pioneer Square, Elmer Fisher's Pioneer Building. Located prominently on Pioneer Place, it was originally designed by Fisher and built by Henry Yesler in 1890–1891. By the early 1970s, the building had suffered twenty-five years of neglect; project architect Ron Murphy described it as "sound, but deteriorating fast."

The restoration was based on the original drawings, kept in the archives of the University of Washington's Northwest Collection. The project included adding a new roof, replacing the roof skylights and rotted joists, cleaning the exterior masonry, and repointing the mortar joints. The building's open atrium was maintained, as well as such details as its cage elevator and its marble wainscoting. The building's interior, as it stands today, is particularly wonderful. This very sensitive renovation keeps much of the historic detailing and fabric.

As part of the open space plan sponsored by the City of Seattle (which also commissioned the design of Occidental Park), Jones & Jones was asked to develop Pioneer Place and to restore the historic pergola, then in a decrepit state. The city appropriated $150,000 and James Casey, the founder of United Parcel Service, donated $100,000.

In researching the pergola, Ilze Jones found useful information in the Webster & Stevens photograph collection. Interviews with older Seattle architects also revealed much. It became clear, for instance, that the sheet metal–covered canopy had originally been of glass with a metal frame. Further details became evident when original drawings were found. This kind of painstaking research, which is necessary for historical projects, allowed a reconstruction of the pergola with attention to its original detailing. New detail drawings were also created based on old photographs and research. New castings were made and special care was taken in the reconstruction of the hollow metal lamps, which originally served as vents for the still-closed underground restroom. It was a delicate and difficult project, and it restored Pioneer Place to a long-lost elegance.

Many years later, on January 15, 2001, a U.S. Xpress Enterprises truck turned a corner too sharply and accidentally snagged the pergola, which fell into a shattered heap. U.S. Xpress unhesitatingly offered to pay for the

full reconstruction. Once again, the pergola's reconstruction relied on historic photographs and drawings. The pergola's scattered parts were painstakingly gathered, analyzed, and reassembled by Seidelhuber Iron and Bronze Works. Most of the cast-iron pieces were reused, while a relatively small number of ornamental pieces were recast. A new earthquake-resistant structural skeleton of steel-pipe columns is now hidden inside the "original" hollow cast iron and is welded to steel plates embedded in the concrete slab underneath the pergola.

The reerection of the pergola was also difficult because the original cast-iron construction had few real right angles and also apparently sat unevenly on its site. This recent reconstruction was successfully completed and celebrated, with some fanfare, including a Dixieland band play-

Detail of the central bay of the Pioneer Building. Photo by Karin Link

The Occidental Square parking lot on April 1, 1970, when architect Ralph Anderson presented a proposal to the city to convert it into a public park. Museum of History and Industry, Seattle Post-Intelligencer *Collection, 86.5.52038*

ing "The Ballad of the Pergola," on August 17, 2002.

Another milestone in the preservation of Pioneer Place was the restoration of the totem pole in 1972. It had been severely burned and was deteriorating. Bill Holm hired carvers from the Tsimshian tribe of northern British Columbia to repair and refinish it. It was trucked to Seattle Center, where John C. Hudson Jr., a Seattle longshoreman as well as a traditional Tsimshian carver, took charge of the work. Jones & Jones also worked with Bill Holm and detailed the supporting structure—a steel

I-beam embedded deep into the ground and hidden inside the totem.

The Merchant's Cafe Building

Across the street from the historic pergola and totem pole of Pioneer Place, the 1889 Merchant's Cafe Building's ground floor was also restored in 1972. Special attention was paid to the exterior glass canopy, the restaurant interior with its period bar carved in wood, and the ornamental ceiling. A more recent restoration, including seismic strengthening, was completed in 2002 by Kovalenko Hale Architects, with minimal intervention in the historic restaurant on the ground floor.

The Early 1970s: Challenges

One of the most controversial aspects of these early efforts was that some of the poorer and predominantly male population who had inhabited buildings such as the Grand Central had to move out so that renovations could be made. Preservationists including Victor Steinbrueck consistently pointed out that the district should continue to welcome and house the poorer population. Complete or even partial gentrification of the area was never endorsed and was frequently decried. This continues to be a controversial issue in Pioneer Square.

The Pioneer Square Historic District faced several other immediate challenges in the early years after the passage of the ordinance. One was the dramatic collapse of the historical Olympic Block, also called the Cascade Hotel, at the corner of First Avenue and Yesler Way, in 1972. A construction worker had been working on the building when part of it collapsed. There are reports that Earl Layman, Seattle's first historic preservation officer and head of the Office of Historic Preservation, heard some odd creaking noises the evening before the collapse, while he was at a meeting at the Brasserie Pittsbourg, a neighborhood meeting place housed in the Pioneer Building.

Many criticized the City of Seattle for not making a greater effort to save the original Olympic Block. Many, including Victor Steinbrueck, also criticized the early designs for its modern replacement, which was seen as incompatible with the district's historic architecture. It was a controversial issue. The new Olympic Block, designed by architects Olson Walker and Hewitt Isley, was eventually built in 1984.

In 1972 another big fear for many preservationists was the effect that the construction and presence of the new King County Domed Stadium, known as the Kingdome, would have on the newly established historic district. The city chose the location immediately south of Pioneer Square on the site of abandoned freight yards that had once served the railroads. In

The pergola under reconstruction at Seidelhuber Iron and Bronze Works in 2002. Photo by Karin Link

Yesler Way, looking south from Pioneer Place left to right: the sandstone Interurban Building, the three-story Korn Building, the Merchant's Cafe Building, and a partial view of the modern Olympic Block. Photo by Karin Link

addition, there were also plans to build a convention center next to the Kingdome. Local art gallery owners such as Polly Friedlander, vice president of the Pioneer Square Association at the time, feared in particular the influence of the "quick buck type investor" and of increased parking demands. On the other hand, according to a June 12, 1973, *Post-Intelligencer* article, a Pioneer Square Special Review District Board member stated that the board was strong enough to prevent the tastes of the stadium–convention center supporters from turning the district into a "honky-tonk plastic old town."

While the Kingdome did have a strong impact, attempts to save Pioneer Square from "honky-tonk plasticity" have so far been successful. The Washington State Convention and Trade Center's siting was also a highly contested issue for more than a decade. In the end it was not built near the Kingdome or close to the Pioneer Square Historic District.

Influential Preservationists in the City Administration in the 1970s

With the many challenges faced by the Pioneer Square Historic District, a guiding hand was clearly needed to steer it in the right direction. A dynamic and extremely positive force in its early development was Arthur Skolnik, an architect and urban designer hired by the city to serve as Pioneer Square Historic District manager in 1973. He had originally chaired Mayor Wes Uhlman's task force that had established programs that transformed the district. Within two years of his appointment as Pioneer Square Historic District manager, Skolnik is credited with turning a $250,000 municipal investment into $2 million worth of capital improvements. He also directed the district through the creation of the Pioneer Square Special Review District.

Skolnik guided the formulation of the

"Pioneer Square Historic District Plan," produced in 1974 by Makers Architecture and Urban Design. The plan described a series of recommendations, first for the period from 1974 to 1976, the United States Bicentennial, and then for the period from 1977 to 1986.

For the first period, topping the list were capital improvements such as sidewalk replacement, particularly along First Avenue South between Yesler Way and South Washington Street; the addition of three-globe light standards throughout the district; and the restoration of the Washington Street Boat Landing. Other ambitious projects included:

◆ Development of a 400–room hotel between Main and Washington Streets, on the lot east of Occidental Park

◆ A special bicentennial project: building a trolley line along First Avenue, connecting Pike Street, Pioneer Square, and the Kingdome

◆ Restoration of the comfort station underneath the Pioneer Place pergola

◆ A housing project, built near City Hall (now the King County Courthouse), of 200 low-income units as well as 50 to 100 upper- and middle-income units

◆ Initial design work to turn Union Station into a transportation terminal, either for the Metropolitan Transit Authority (Metro) or for a multimodal transportation hub

Important on the list of capital improvements for the 1977–1986 period was installation of brick paving on major streets, particularly on Occidental Mall, and street furniture, particularly along First Avenue as well as Jackson Street. Major projects were also conceived:

◆ A 1,500–unit mixed-income housing development east of Fifth Avenue between Yesler Way and Main Street to serve Pioneer Square and the International District

◆ Replacement of the "sinking ship" garage with a public-use theater or historical interpretive center

◆ Rebuilding of the Butler Hotel, including the

Panorama from the Pike Place Market shows the massive Kingdome, which drew crowds in excess of fifty thousand for Seahawks games, boat shows, Billy Graham crusades, and other events. Mount Rainier is in the background, ca. 1978. Seattle Municipal Archives, Pike Place Market Collection, Item 29981

three upper floors, which had been dismantled following earlier earthquake damage

◆ Extension of the First Avenue trolley to the International District

◆ Replacement of the Olympic Block, which had collapsed in 1972, at the southeast corner of First Avenue and Yesler Way

◆ Relandscaping of the park near City Hall at Third and Yesler

◆ Projected for after 1986, replacement of the Alaskan Way Viaduct by an underground expressway

While the landscaping and street furnishing improvements seem to have been accomplished according to the plan and the Olympic Block was replaced by a new building in 1984, many of the major recommendations either have not yet come to pass or have been implemented differently. Today the trolley runs along the waterfront to Broad Street to the north and also connects Pioneer Square to the edge of the International District. Union Station became a transportation hub in the 1990s. Housing has been encouraged in all subsequent plans, but the emphasis on low-income housing is now less strong. In the late 1990s, interest in restoration of the pergola comfort station surfaced once again but is still in the discussion stage. As of this writing, the "sinking ship" garage has still not been replaced and, of course, the Alaskan Way Viaduct, for now, is still aboveground. The 400–room hotel was never built, although a plan to build housing on the lot east of Occidental Park is being encouraged. If nothing else, the ideas presented in the 1974 "Pioneer Square Historic District Plan" show an energetic originality that still influences current ideas and plans. This is not only a credit to Makers Architecture and Urban Design and to the many Pioneer Square denizens and designers who contributed to the study, but also to the hard work and leadership of the former Pioneer Square Historic District manager.

The position of Pioneer Square Historic District manager was eliminated after Arthur Skolnik's three-year tenure. To administer the Pioneer Square Historic District, as well as other historic districts designated subsequently, the City of Seattle created the Office of Historic Preservation, at various times of its existence called the Office of Urban Conservation. The Office of Historic Preservation (now part of the Department of Neighborhoods) oversees the Pioneer Square Preservation Board, charged with ensuring that all restoration and building, including signage, meet architectural and historical guidelines.

Earl Layman was Seattle's first historic preservation officer, at the helm of the Office of Historic Preservation from 1973 to 1982. His accomplishments were major, including the designation of more than one hundred and fifty properties as city landmarks and the creation of an inventory of Seattle's historic buildings and resources. His leadership is in great part responsible for ensuring that the Pioneer Square Historic District was developed in the 1970s and early 1980s with special sensitivity to its historic integrity.

The Mid-1970s

The second half of the 1970s was marked by a number of restoration projects that changed the nature of the Pioneer Square Historic District. The struggle for funds was often difficult, but new incentives encouraged restoration projects. For instance, the Federal Tax Reform Act of 1975 provided an investment tax credit of 10 percent on the rehabilitation of historic commercial structures.

In 1974 Richard White and Ralph Anderson

bought the Maynard Building; Olson/Walker Architects restored it. Also in 1974 and 1975, Jones & Jones restored the Broderick Building, at the northwest corner of Second Avenue and Cherry Street. In 1977 James Casey donated the block and money for Sasaki and Associates' design of Waterfall Park at Second Avenue South and South Main Street. The park was built on the location where in 1906 Casey had founded the American Messenger Company, which became United Parcel Service. By 1979 the Travelers/Post Mews Building, originally the Travelers Hotel, at Yesler and Post Alley was restored by Grant Jones and Ilze Jones. It became Seattle's first mixed-use condominium

The Maynard Building. Photo by Karin Link

building, with Trattoria Mitchelli in the former location of a greasy spoon on the ground floor. The trattoria is now one of the oldest businesses in Pioneer Square. Other restorations from this period include the McKesson-Robbins Building (home of F. X. McRory's, a popular steak and lobster house), the Interurban Building, and the First and Cherry Building.

One obstacle to the continued restoration of Pioneer Square, but with a definite silver lining, was that several major property owners maintained their buildings at minimum or basic levels. Artists, who paid low rental prices for space in these properties, moved to the district and created a vibrant arts community. The buildings also housed art galleries and small offices in fields including graphics, architecture, and law.

The 1980s

By the 1980s, there was an additional wave of building restoration. Major projects included the restoration of the Alaska Building in 1982 by Stickney Murphy Architects, the 1983 restoration of the Mutual Life Building by Olson/Walker Architects, and the 1982 restoration of the Heritage Building (historically the Wax and Raine Building, located at the southeast corner of First Avenue South and Jackson Street) by NBBJ. The Heritage Building became the home of this internationally prominent architecture firm formerly known as Naramore Bain Brady and Johanson. In 1983 the Ruggles-Lucknow Building, located next to Waterfall Park near the northwest corner of Second Avenue South and Main Street, was restored by Downey/Monson Associates and Stickney Murphy Architects. In 1984–85 Ralph Anderson's firm, at the time called Anderson Koch and Duarte, created the Court in the Square on Second Avenue South, between South Jackson and

Ilze Jones redesigned the old Travelers Hotel as the Travelers/Post Mews Building, with condominium entrances and gardens in the mews. Courtesy of Jones & Jones Architects and Landscape Architects

South King Streets, by linking two buildings (the Northcoast Building and the Goldsmith Building) with a glass-canopied lobby.

Moving away even more from pure restoration was the development of Merrill Place, at First Avenue and Jackson Street. This ambitious project by architects Olson/Walker and NBBJ combined the remodel of the Hambach Building, originally by Saunders and Lawton (1913); the Seller Building, originally by A. Warren Gould (1906); the Schwabacher Hardware Company Building, originally by Charles Bebb and Louis Mendel (1905); and a fourth structure by Bebb and Gould. An alley courtyard was

created by replacing the original back wall of the Seller Building with a stepped glass facade that faces an open plaza and reflecting pool.

The Early 1990s

Most of the early 1990s saw less dramatic physical changes to the buildings in Pioneer Square. Nevertheless, much thought was given to the development of the Pioneer Square Historic District. "The Pioneer Square Plan Update," considered an update of the 1974 "Pioneer Square Historic District Plan," was produced in 1990 under the direction of Denice Hunt, the late head of the local chapter of American Institute of Architects, and John Chaney, now the executive director of Historic Seattle (a nonprofit group devoted to the preservation of Seattle's historic buildings). The plan update set further urban design goals for Pioneer Square.

The updated plan discussed the challenges faced in terms of housing, transportation, and Pioneer Square's traditional role in the area of human services. It stressed a commitment to a "comprehensive downtown health and human services delivery system," adequate comfort stations, a hygiene center, and a community recreation facility serving all income levels. High on the list of goals was the creation of a mix of housing for all income levels, artists' studios and housing, pedestrian uses, and modes of transportation other than the automobile, in addition to increased public safety.

A special section of the Pioneer Square Plan Update, based on a 1978 study by Jones & Jones, dealt with the upkeep of the areaways. These had been created below the existing sidewalks and buildings when the district's streets were raised in the 1890s. The updated plan also discussed the importance of maintaining the

Northwest corner of the Mutual Life Building. The basement and first floor were designed by Elmer Fisher in 1890–91 and upper floors by Emil DeNeuf in 1892–93, with a later western addition by Robertson and Blackwell. Restored by Olson/Walker Architects in 1984. Photo by Asahel Curtis, 1903. MSCUA, University of Washington Libraries, A Curtis 94100

historical glass prisms as part of the sidewalks. In addition, it addressed desired urban design features, such as the appropriate choice of streetlights, benches, drinking fountains, and other features, and the nature of open spaces and parks in the district.

Although many of the recommendations were implemented, some are still being worked on or have proved controversial. Perhaps inspired by a 1988 *Seattle Times* article by Richard Larsen, many local businesspeople and residents still feel that too many human services have been concentrated in the district. On the other hand, in the late 1990s a special Open Space Committee of the Pioneer Square Community Council was formed to consider further changes to the district's open spaces. Their deliberations and discussions have been fruitful: in 2001, enamel

panels describing the history of Pioneer Square were added to the base of the modern pergola in Occidental Park. Further changes, particularly for Occidental Park, are also being envisioned.

Boots and Buildings

One of the controversial but definitely important influences in Pioneer Square since the 1940s has been the Samis Land Company. Since the death of its owner, Sam Israel, in 1994, the Samis Land Company has been overhauling and sprucing up its holdings; but during most of Sam Israel's lifetime, his personal influence was of a different nature.

Born on the Aegean isle of Rhodes, Sam Israel apprenticed there as a shoemaker. He and his family immigrated to Seattle at the beginning of the twentieth century, becoming part of Seattle's Sephardic Jewish community. He arrived in Seattle in 1919 at age twenty and worked for a Greek shoemaker. Sam Israel soon set up what became a thriving shoemaking business in the Collins Building, located on the southeast corner of Second Avenue and James Street. One particularly lucrative contract involved the repair of a large number of boots for the U.S. Army during World War II.

After the war, he focused his energies on real estate and was able to buy buildings inexpensively because they were extremely run-down. He founded the Samis Land Company in 1946, eventually amassing a huge real estate portfolio, including fourteen properties in Pioneer Square, major holdings around the Pike Place Market and Belltown in Seattle, and properties in Eastern Washington, including his home and surrounding property near Soap Lake as well as a good portion of downtown Ephrata, Washington. Considered a strong personality, he is known for acquiring this vast amount of real estate and refusing to maintain it at anything but minimal levels, although he usually ensured that the roofs of his buildings were in good repair.

Real estate developers, local building officials, and many in building-related professions found his administration of real estate properties puzzling, neglectful, and sometimes even downright frightening. Some of these people were interested in developing the buildings themselves, but Sam Israel rarely agreed to sell any of them. Others felt that his dogged insistence on minimally maintaining his properties was in large part responsible for the historic integrity of Pioneer Square. And Sam Israel seems to have had a real affinity for many artists and creative denizens of the district, who benefited from the extremely low rents he charged

and other acts of generosity. In fact, some also credit him for being the driving force behind the reinvention of Pioneer Square as a creative haven, particularly in the 1970s and 1980s, and behind the district's reputation in arts communities as far away as Greenwich Village and Soho in New York City.

In 1987, seven years before his death, Sam Israel created the Samis Foundation. It supports Jewish education and cultural programs in Israel and Washington state, promotes Jewish refugee resettlement, provides assistance for widows and orphans in Israel, and supports archaeology and wildlife preservation. In the late 1980s, the Samis Foundation was already in place to create the financial backing the foundation needed, but it became more proactive about obtaining a monetary return on its real estate holdings. About two years after Sam Israel's death, William Justen, a former head of the Seattle Department of Construction and Land Use (now the Department of Planning and Development) who exhibits business and political savvy as well as, not surprisingly, a fine-tuned knowledge of building codes, was picked to head the Samis Land Company. He put into effect an ambitious plan to upgrade the properties, including the buildings in Pioneer Square.

Soon the Corona Building and the Collins Building, as well as the Smith Tower, which was acquired by the Samis Foundation after Sam Israel's death, were transformed into state-of-the-art office buildings. Visitors to the Smith Tower can enjoy the newly refurbished, hand-operated elevators, the restored lobby, and the ornate Chinese Room, long a popular tourist attraction as well as a venue for many festive Seattle parties and gatherings. Above the ground floor, the main hallways were kept as they were, while the office space was redesigned to accommodate larger offices, reflecting a trend in new office building design. On the northwest corner of Second and James Street, the ground-level remains of the once-elegant Butler Hotel, now the Butler Building, were converted to street-level shops and several floors of parking. Across the street, at the southeast corner of Second and James, the Collins Building, where Sam Israel made shoes and boots, now houses the law offices of Cairncross and Hempelmann, a prestigious law firm. These transformations have definitely changed the flavor of the district.

The Arts Community in the Late 1990s

In great part because of the recent conversions to higher-priced offices and condominiums, the consensus in the local arts community is that the district—and, indeed, Seattle—is no longer a haven for artists. In the 1990s, however, there was a small successful push to re-create artists' housing. Kovalenko Hale Architects designed artists' live/work spaces in the old Harbor Light Building, also known as Leighton Center, on Fortson Square between Yesler Way and South Washington Street, in an attempt to improve that part of the neighborhood. Fortson Square itself was redesigned and endowed with a sculptural "ruin" by artist Elizabeth Conner and landscape architect Cliff Willwerth. Not far from Fortson Square, at Second Avenue Extension and South Main Street, landscape architect Kenichi Nakano and sculptor Bill Will created a public landscaped square.

A project under discussion since the very end of the 1990s is the renovation of the Tashiro-Kaplan Building, located on Third Avenue South between Yesler Way and South Washington Street, by Artspace Projects Incorporated, a nonprofit artists' housing developer. (They have also developed artists' live/work space projects in Minneapolis, St. Paul, and Duluth, Minnesota; Chicago; Pittsburgh; Galveston, Texas; Reno; and Portland, Oregon.) The Tashiro-Kaplan renovation, designed by Stickney Murphy Romine Architects (formerly Stickney Murphy Architects) and scheduled for completion in 2004, will include fifty artists' residential/work spaces, as well as spaces for arts organizations and related businesses.

The historic water tower located on the roof of the Washington Shoe Building was included in the 2000 restoration, thanks to local preservationists. Photo by Karin Link

Developments at the Edge of the District in the Late 1990s and After

Other large construction projects also contributed to changes in the neighborhood in the 1990s. To the south of Pioneer Square, Seattle's state-of-the-art Safeco Field was designed for the Mariners baseball team by NBBJ, with architectural features that recall historic ball fields as well as Pioneer Square. It also showcases artwork with baseball themes by many local artists. On July 15, 1999, a crowd of 47,000 attended the inaugural game against the San Diego Padres, who beat the Mariners 3–2.

Not long after the completion of Safeco Field, the Kingdome—Seattle's older sports stadium—was dramatically imploded in March 2000. Droves of fascinated onlookers converged on Pioneer Square to catch one final glimpse of the toppling structure as other citizens fled the area to avoid ear-breaking noise and impending confusion. But the Kingdome has never really quite disappeared: 97 percent of the Kingdome rubble has been recycled; 35 percent of it was used as fill in the new Seahawks Stadium, completed on the site of the former stadium in 2002.

Union Station Associates, a partnership between Nitze-Stagen and Vulcan Northwest, restored Union Station on the eastern edge of the district, then donated it to Sound Transit for $1. NBBJ was the architect. The restoration was complete in February 2001, when the Nisqually Earthquake caused major damage, most notably to its grand interior vaulted ceiling, which was partly glazed. The building still won a National Trust Award, but a further restoration, also completed by Union Station Associates, was necessary. Major plans have also been in the works since the 1990s to restore the present train depot, King Street Station, to its original elegance. The interior of the building has long been something of an eyesore. One part of the projected restoration plans envisions removing the suspended ceiling from the waiting room, exposing the long-hidden ornamental plaster above it, and re-creating much of the ornamental cladding that once graced the walls below. Lack of funding has been the main obstacle to this project.

Planning for the Late 1990s and Beyond

Many of the physical changes in Pioneer Square were encouraged by the 1998 "Pioneer Square Plan." This document resulted from citywide neighborhood planning efforts involving the input of Seattle citizens in the late 1990s. The 1998 "Pioneer Square Plan" builds on the early 1990s "Pioneer Square Plan Update" and outlines a whole series of short-term and long-term objectives for the district. High on the list are the following goals:

◆ Encourage housing development, using incentive packages to develop middle-income housing

◆ Develop the lot north of the Kingdome with a substantial housing element, parking, and retail

◆ Improve "public safety and cleanliness and behavior standards," including service by the Seattle Police Department and enforcement of civility laws (prohibiting behavior construed as loitering), and encourage cleanliness of public spaces by promoting CleanScapes, a private/public enterprise originally founded in Pioneer Square and devoted to cleaning and maintaining urban spaces

◆ Identify and install street furnishings compatible with the historic nature of Pioneer Square, as well as landscaping

◆ Strengthen Pioneer Square's economic base by implementing a marketing and public relations campaign

◆ Strengthen the neighborhood's historic char-

The Kingdome's implosion on Sunday, March 26, 2000, made way for the new Seahawks Stadium. Photo by Michael Fajans

acter and arts identity by the creation of the "Arts and Legends Program," which describes existing and potential public art sites and a network of historic sites marked with interpretive elements and tied to a companion book and walking tour, and by the creation of a way-finding system for visitors, including directional signs, maps, and informational kiosks

◆ Improve access to Pioneer Square during events (such as ball games in the nearby sports arenas) and create a community parking facility

◆ Develop the open area, currently parking space, on the east side of Occidental Park with a building (a notion mentioned frequently since the 1970s)

The 1998 "Pioneer Square Plan" also expresses the goals of residents and business owners who are trying to create a more even income mix, with middle-income housing that bridges the gap between high-end condominiums and the neighborhood's low-income apartments and shelters for the homeless.

The Twenty-first Century

During the economic boom of the 1990s, many dot-com companies began to fill available office space (usually of the inexpensive kind) in Pioneer Square. For awhile, an interesting subculture of techies filled the district, particularly in cafes and restaurants at lunchtime. With the subsequent economic downturn, the Nisqually Earthquake on February 28, 2001, and the attack on the New York World Trade Center on September 11, 2001, the dot-coms—as in other parts of the United States—went bust, leaving a big real estate void in Pioneer Square, which, as of this writing, has not been filled.

The Nisqually Earthquake continues to produce all sorts of shocks and social aftershocks. In postearthquake battles, members of the Pioneer Square community, the Pioneer Square Preservation Board, and Historic Seattle worked to prevent the demolition of the Cadillac Hotel, severely damaged by the earthquake. On February 28, 2002, the first anniversary of the Nisqually Earthquake, Historic Seattle bought the Cadillac Hotel to ensure its survival and restoration. The Klondike Museum is scheduled to move into the ground floor and basement of the newly restored building in 2005.

Several businesses, such as McCoy's Firehouse, a popular watering hole at Second and Washington, were seriously damaged. McCoy's Firehouse is now back in business, thanks to the hard work of the owners, staff, and neighbors, in addition to loans from Historic Seattle Preservation and Development Authority and the Seattle Community Capital Development Corporation, an independent company that provides loans and technical support to Seattle's small businesses. Meanwhile, the new owner of the O.K. Hotel, which also suffered extensive earthquake damage, has restored it for low-income housing. For the same reason, many of the social service agencies, including the Union Gospel Mission, the Bread of Life Mission, and the Compass Center, have taken great care to restore their buildings. The Low-Income Housing Institute (LIHI) is also restoring the Frye Apartments.

On the other hand, some owners of Pioneer Square buildings have been reluctant to spend the energy and money to ensure that their buildings are seismically safe. This is cause for great concern, since another earthquake of the same magnitude as the Nisqually Earthquake may cause serious harm and damage.

The Alaskan Way Viaduct and the Impact of the Waterfront

Another structure close to Pioneer Square severely impacted by the Nisqually Earthquake is the Alaskan Way Viaduct. The Washington State Department of Transportation has produced several alternatives, including a "preferred alternative" that calls for rebuilding the seawall along the shore of Elliott Bay and making the portion of the viaduct that currently runs aboveground along the western edge of Pioneer Square, from King Street to Pike Street, an underground tunnel. (A similar idea was suggested in the 1974 "Pioneer Square Historic District Plan.") Another alternative suggests rebuilding the Alaskan Way Viaduct, more or less at the same height aboveground and in its current location but wider. Another scheme, the "surface option," calls for demolishing the viaduct and designing Alaskan Way to absorb a higher volume of traffic. A scheme also suggests the full retrofitting of the old structure (originally built in 1953), but as more and more structural problems have become obvious, it appears to have been shelved. The seawall itself is falling apart and much of the fill near or under the viaduct is spongy, so remedying these problems properly is extremely important.

These alternatives have been showcased and discussed at length among community groups, engineers, planners and urban designers, architects and landscape architects, and real estate developers. The final decision on the design alternative for the viaduct is scheduled for the winter of 2004. Whatever choice is made will impact Pioneer Square, particularly the buildings along its western edge. Any construction or reconstruction efforts—or delays in remedying the problems, for that matter—could have far-reaching effects on the historic district. The situation along the waterfront, and the possibility that the viaduct may no longer be elevated aboveground along the edge of the Pioneer Square area, has inspired a series of designs. Some of them are mainly centered around Pier 46, but in some cases they also propose changes for Pioneer Square itself or the entire waterfront.

Designs for Future Living

In February 2003 a group of Pioneer Square property owners—including the Samis Land Company, Nitze-Stagen, No Boundaries Inc., Vulcan Northwest, Mackensay Real Estate Services, Pioneer Square Properties, and the Gregory Broderick Smith Real Estate Company—organized as the Major Property Owners Group. The MPOG unveiled an ambitious design that, in keeping with the 1998 "Pioneer Square Plan," would dramatically increase the amount of housing in Pioneer Square but also increase the built density along the adjacent waterfront.

A rendered sketch of the proposed scheme shows major development west of Seahawks Stadium on the eighty-acre container yard at Terminal 46, with an auto ferry south of it and a hotel at Pier 48. Terminal 46 and Pier 48 are currently owned by the Port of Seattle. More specifically, the MPOG design concept includes a mixed-use complex, a central park, and a lake as well as residential and commercial buildings, all at Terminal 46; retail and parking topped by playfields on the Seahawks Stadium north parking lot (long slated for housing in previous schemes, when the Kingdome was on the site);

and smaller residential buildings in place of existing parking lots within the Pioneer Square Historic District itself. The design also identifies sixteen buildings within the district as candidates for rehabilitation. The entire scheme would create 12,000 multifamily housing units and 4 million square feet of commercial space for retail, office, and institutional use.

More recently, citizens, planning and design professionals, and City of Seattle urban designers and planners have renewed the conversation, one that has been held at least since the 1970s, concerning the urban design of the entire waterfront. What shape the design will take will also have an impact on Pioneer Square itself. Decisions about the design of the waterfront's open spaces and the west-east connections from the waterfront to the district are particularly important points of consideration.

CityDesign, established in 1999 within the City of Seattle's Department of Construction and Land Use (now the Department of Planning and Development), oversees the urban design of the city. One of its important projects is the urban and environmental development of the waterfront, which includes considerations about changes to the waterfront and its relation to adjacent neighborhoods. In February 2004, a waterfront *charrette,* a two-day design workshop sponsored by CityDesign, attracted 300 participants (including representatives of community groups, urban designers, architects, landscape architects, engineers, local developers, environmentalists, and fish and wildlife experts), from not just Seattle but all over the world. A host of visionary ideas that, in particular, develop or modify Piers 46 and 48 and waterfront areas that tie in with Pioneer Square were produced.

One of the most interesting design schemes, and very different from the MPOG proposal, was produced by Ilze Jones, the designer of many of Pioneer Square's open spaces in the

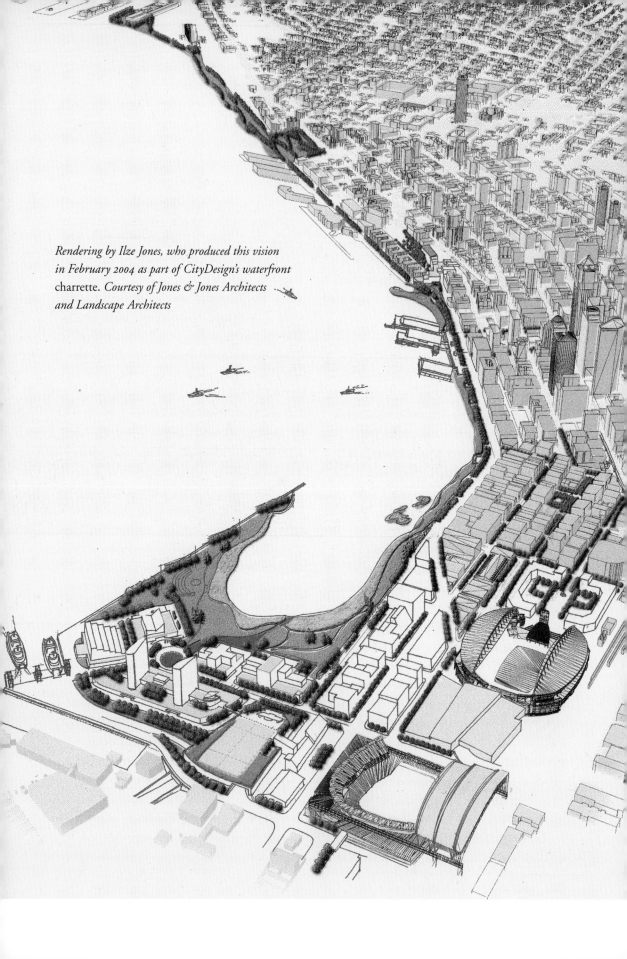

Rendering by Ilze Jones, who produced this vision in February 2004 as part of CityDesign's waterfront charrette. Courtesy of Jones & Jones Architects and Landscape Architects

Graphic of vision by Major Property Owners Group. Rendering by Bill Hook, 2003; courtesy of MPOG

1970s and a key player in debates about the future of Seattle's waterfront. In fact, this is a scheme she has been refining at least since 1995, and as she has suggested herself, it gets better every time she produces a new version. Jones sees the current situation along the waterfront as a "perfect storm," an unprecedented opportunity to reverse effects of more than a century of dredging, filling, toxic contamination, and other abuse along the shores of Elliott Bay. She envisions a healthy marine ecosystem along a creatively designed seawall that provides shallow-water habitats and beaches, so that all of Puget Sound's diverse creatures can find their niches. Along a continuous bayshore greenway with areas of restored nearshore habitat, people too would have ample opportunity to access the water; or they could peer over a downtown railing to see seastars, birds, and anemones. Jones sees a green bayshore and a healthy bay as keys to future economic and cultural opportunities for a truly great city. In 2003 she said, "We need to fundamentally address the waterfront for what it is—our connection to Puget Sound. And we need to articulate a vision for Elliott Bay itself, to grasp the opportunity at hand—

Detail from the Interurban Building's entrance.
Photo by Karin Link

to achieve a healthy bay *and* to reach our transportation, economic, and urban design goals at the same time."

In April 2004 there was a public presentation and discussion of all the designs and visions produced at the waterfront *charrette*. While these schemes are now only drawings, they too are poised to have impact not only on adjacent waterfront areas, but on Pioneer Square and its connections to other neighborhoods.

But, at the beginning of the twenty-first century, only time and circumstance will tell which visionary or not-so-visionary plans for Pioneer Square will really be built and what these changes will ultimately bring.

Epilogue: The Unfinished City

Change—both positive and negative—has been a constant feature of Pioneer Square's colorful history. But Pioneer Square has always shown continuity with the past. The district has often been described as the city's heart. It also remains a backdrop for Seattle's achievements and failures and its hopes for the future. For more than a century, the district has been the place where the creative and the enterprising, the practical and the visionary, the down-and-out and the prosperous have gathered to create a Northwest metropolis. Through it all, the buildings that arose in the wake of the Great Fire of 1889 have remained remarkably intact, as has the spirit of renewal. But in many ways this unique experiment is unfinished. Pioneer Square continues to face man-made challenges and the forces of nature. But it has always weathered adversity with incredible gusto. Pioneer Square still embodies the Seattle spirit, proud of its past but always with an eye to the future.

BIBLIOGRAPHY

Adcock, Joe. "Fillin' the Space for 30 Years: Theater Company Has Had a 'Charmed Life.'" *Seattle Post-Intelligencer,* October 28, 1999, sec. D, p. 1.

Adney, Tappan. *The Klondike Stampede of 1897–98.* Seattle: University of Washington Press, 1995.

Advisory Committee on Social Security to King County Board of Commissioners. "Single Homeless Men on Relief in King County, Washington." Seattle: King County, November 1937.

Alhadeff, Kenny. Interview by Mildred Andrews, 2000.

Anderson, Ralph. Interview by Donald Schmechel. Tape recording. Seattle Public Library, May 25, 1987.

———. Interview by Mildred Andrews and Karin Link, 2000.

Anderson, Ross. "A Culture Slips Away." In series "150 Years: Seattle By and By." *The Seattle Times,* May 27, 2001, sec. A, pp. 1, 18.

Andrews, Mildred Tanner. *Washington Women as Path Breakers.* Dubuque, Iowa: Kendall/Hunt Publishing Company with Junior League of Tacoma, 1989.

———. *Woman's Place: A Guide to Seattle and King County History.* Seattle: Gemil Press, 1994.

Andrews, Mildred Tanner, ed. *Judge J. T. Ronald: Reflections Along the Wayside of Life.* Shoreline, Wash.: Shoreline Historical Museum, 2003.

Armbruster, Kurt E. *Orphan Road: The Railroad Comes to Seattle.* Pullman: Washington State University Press, 1999.

Arnold, William. "A Century of Movies in Seattle." *Seattle Post-Intelligencer,* November 16, 1998, sec. D, pp. 1, 3.

"Association Pushes Pioneer Square Restoration." *The Seattle Times,* October 30, 1960, sec. C, p. 3, col. 2–5.

Austin, G. W., and H. S. Scott. *The Great Seattle Fire of June 6, 1889.* Tacoma: Puget Sound Printing Company, 1889.

Avner, Jane. *Historic Jewish Seattle: A Tour Guide.* Seattle: Washington State Jewish Historical Society, 1995.

Bagley, Clarence. *History of Seattle from the Earliest Settlement to the Present Time.* 3 vols. Chicago: S. J. Clarke Publishing Co., 1916.

———. *Pioneer Seattle and Its Pioneers.* Seattle: S. J. Clarke Publishing Company, 1928.

Bass, Sophie Frye. *When Seattle Was a Village.* Seattle: Lowman and Hanford, 1947.

Beaton, Welford. *The City That Made Itself: A Literary and Pictorial Record of the Building of Seattle.* Seattle: Terminal Publishing Company, 1914.

Berner, Richard. *1900–1920: From Boomtown, Urban Turbulence, to Restoration.* Vol. 1 of *Seattle in the Twentieth Century.* Seattle: Charles Press, 1991.

———. *1920–1940, From Boom to Bust.* Vol. 2 of *Seattle in the Twentieth Century.* Seattle: Charles Press, 1992.

———. *Seattle Transformed: World War II to the Cold War.* Vol. 3 of *Seattle in the Twentieth Century.* Seattle: Charles Press, 1999.

Berton, Pierre. *Klondike: The Last Great Gold Rush, 1896–1899.* Rev. ed. Toronto, Canada: McClelland and Stewart, 1997.

Black, Alan. Interviews by Mildred Andrews, 1998, 1999.

Boswell, Sharon, and Lorraine McConaghy. *Raise Hell and Sell Newspapers: Alden Blethen and The Seattle Times.* Pullman: Washington State University Press, 1996.

Brandenfels, Kathryn S. "Down on the Sawdust: Prostitution and Vice Control in Seattle, 1870–1820." Master's thesis, Hampshire College, Amherst, Mass., 1981.

Brewster, David. "Can They Put Pioneer Square Together Again?" *Argus* 80, no. 32 (August 17, 1973), p. 1.

Brewster, David, and David M. Buerge, eds. *Washingtonians: A Biographical Portrait of the State.* Seattle: Sasquatch Books, 1989.

Brians, Elizabeth Ann. *Indomitable Pioneer Square.* Master's thesis, University of Washington, 1973.

Brown, Kirby. Interview by Mildred Andrews, 1999.

Buerge, David. "Seattle before Seattle." *The Seattle Weekly,* December 17, 1980.

———. "The King County Wars." *The Seattle Weekly,* February 14, 1984.

———. *Seattle in the 1880s.* Seattle: Historical Society of Seattle and King County, 1986.

Building of Seattle. Seattle: Terminal Publishing Company, 1914.

Burger, Steve. "Jim Casey Revisits Pioneer Square." *Pioneer Square Gazette* 3, no. 2 (summer 1982), p. 2.

Buttnick, Meta. Interview by Mildred Andrews, 2000.

Buttnick, Morris. Interview by Mildred Andrews, 2000.

Central Association. Newsletters, particularly 1960–1965. MSCUA, University of Washington.

Chambliss, William J. *On the Take: From Petty Crooks to Presidents.* 2d ed. Bloomington: Indiana University Press, 1988.

Chauncey, George. *Gay New York: Gender, Urban Culture, and the Making of the Gay Male World, 1890–1940.* New York: Basic Books, 1994.

Chew, Ron. Interviews by Mildred Andrews, 1999–2000.

Chew, Ron, ed. *Reflections of Seattle's Chinese Americans: The First 100 Years.* Seattle: University of Washington Press, 1994.

Chin, Doug. "The Rise and Fall of Old Chinatown." *The International Examiner,* September 1976, p. 8.

Clark, Norman. *The Dry Years: Prohibition and Social Change in Washington.* Seattle: University of Washington Press, 1965.

Cleveland High School Students. *The Duwamish Diary.* 2d ed. Seattle: Cleveland High School, 1996. First published 1946.

Clever, Dick. "Pioneer Square Renaissance Buffs Worry About Stadium." *Seattle Post-Intelligencer,* June 12, 1973, sec. A, p. 3.

Collins, Bertrand. "Doomed Hotel Was Link to Seattle's Early Days." *The Seattle Times,* September 4, 1960, pp. 4–5.

Conner, Elizabeth. Interview by Mildred Andrews, 2000.

Cooper, Jerry. Interview by Mildred Andrews, 1999.

Cordova, Dorothy. Interview by Mildred Andrews, 2000.

Cordova , Fred. *Filipinos: Forgotten Asian Americans.* Dubuque, Iowa: Kendall/Hunt Publishing Company with the Demonstration Project for Asian Americans, 1983.

Crowley, Walt. *National Trust Guide: Seattle.* New York: John Wiley and Sons, 1998.

Crowley, Walt, and Heather MacIntosh. *The Story of Union Station in Seattle.* Seattle: Sound Transit, 1999.

Cumming, William. *Sketchbook: A Memory of the 1930s and the Northwest School.* Seattle: University of Washington Press, 1984.

Daniels, Kevin. Interview by Mildred Andrews, 1999.

De Barros, Paul. *Jackson Street After Hours: The Roots of Jazz in Seattle.* Seattle: Sasquatch Books, 1993.

"The Disaster of Pioneer Square: Olympic Block Falls; Restoration Obstacles Told." *Seattle Flag* 1, no. 3 (April 12, 1972), p. 7.

Dorpat, Paul. *Seattle—Now and Then.* 3 vols. Seattle: Tartu Press, 1984–1989.

———. Interview by Mildred Andrews, 1998.

Dorpat, Paul, and Genevieve McCoy. *Building Washington: A History of Washington State Public Works.* Seattle: Washington Chapter of American Public Works Association, 1998.

Downey, Roger. "The Shock of the New: A Fresh Crop of Art Dealers Meets the Challenges of Seattle's International Art Market." *The Seattle Weekly,* August 16, 1995, pp. 25–27.

"Effect of the Gold Rush on Seattle." *Seattle Daily Times,* November 25, 1897, p. 8.

Elliott, Eugene Clinton. *A History of Variety—Vaudeville in Seattle from the Beginning to 1914.* Seattle: University of Washington Publications in Drama, 1944.

"Eye of an Architect: Earl Layman and Pioneer Square." *Pioneer Square Gazette* 3, no. 2 (summer 1982), pp. 1, 11.

Facts for Klondykers. Seattle: Yukon Publishing Company, n.d.

Farley, Kristi Langlow. *A Primer: Preservation in Seattle.* Seattle: City of Seattle, 1977.

"Filling the Tideflats of Elliott Bay." *Sunset Magazine,* November 1907, p. 31.

Gage, Ted, and Carol Tobin. "Pioneer Square: The Politics of Preservation." Manuscript, Seattle Public Library, 1976.

"Gold! Gold! Gold!—Sixty-Eight Rich Men on the Steamer Portland." *Seattle Post-Intelligencer,* July 17, 1897, p. 1.

Halpin, James, and Roger Sale. "Square Dance." *The Seattle Weekly,* June 17, 1992, pp. 25–36.

Hartnett, Gary. Interview by Mildred Andrews, 1998.

Hawthorne, Julian, ed. *History of Washington, the Evergreen State: From Early Dawn to Daylight.* New York: American Historical Publishing Company, 1893.

Hill, Kris. Interview by Mildred Andrews, 1998.

Hinterberger, John. "It's Hard to Know Whether to Eat, Gawk." *The Seattle Times,* August 21, 1976, sec. E, p. 4.

———. "A Remembrance of Laughter." *The Seattle Times,* March 7, 1979.

Holden, Ronald. "Pioneer Square: Half-Way Back." *The Seattle Weekly* 4 (May 23, 1979), pp. 10–15, 32.

Horton, John. "The House Graham Built." *The Seattle Scroll,* August 4, 1997, pp. 4–6.

Humphrey, Clark. *Loser: The Real Seattle Music Story.* Portland: Feral House, 1995.

Hunt, Denice, and John Chaney. "Mayor's Recommended Pioneer Square Plan Update." Report. Seattle: Department of Community Development, City of Seattle, 1990.

Hutchison, Susan. "Advice on Pioneer Square Renovation." *Seattle Post-Intelligencer,* February 28, 1969, p. 15.

"Inside Three Historic Buildings." *The Seattle Times,* April 16, 1972, pp. 16–22.

Ishii, David. Interviews by Mildred Andrews, 1999–2003.

Ito, Kazuo. *Issei: A History of Japanese Immigrants in North America.* Seattle: Japanese Community Service, 1973.

John Graham and Company, Architects Planners Engineers. "Advance Planning and Feasibility Study—Pioneer Square Redevelopment." Report. Seattle, February 1965.

———. "Pioneer Square Redevelopment." Report. Seattle, July 1966.

Jones, Grant. Interviews by Mildred Andrews, 2003.

Jones, Ilze. Interviews by Mildred Andrews and

Leonard Garfield, 2000, and by Mildred Andrews, 2003.

Jones & Jones Architects and Landscape Architects. "Pioneer Square Areaway Right of Way Guideplan." Report. Seattle, 1978.

Kaplan, Bob. Interview by Mildred Andrews, 2000.

Kelly, Jim. "Pioneer Square: A Place for Artists." *Seattle Arts* 21, no. 1 (January 1998).

King, Billy. Interview by Mildred Andrews, 2003.

Klondike: The Chicago Record's Book for Gold Seekers. Chicago: The Chicago Record Co., 1897, pp. 47–48.

Koob, Marlene. Interview by Mildred Andrews, 1998.

Kreisman, Lawrence. *Made to Last: Historic Preservation in Seattle and King County.* Seattle: University of Washington Press, with Historic Seattle Preservation Foundation, 1999.

Krivanek, B. J. Interviews by Mildred Andrews, 2000–2001.

Kucera, Greg. "Art-world Diva." *The Seattle Weekly*, November 8, 1995, pp. 33–37.

———. Interview by Mildred Andrews, 2001.

Label, David. Interview by Mildred Andrews, 1999.

Lachman, Donald. Interview by Mildred Andrews, 1999.

Larry Smith & Company. "Demand Analysis Summary and Preliminary Financial Analysis, Pioneer Square Project, Seattle, Washington." Report. San Francisco, 1966.

Layman, Earl, and William R. Daniel. "Proposed Expansion, Pioneer Square Historic District." Seattle: Department of Community Development, May 1973.

Leong, Jim. Interview by Mildred Andrews, 1999.

Lerner, Barron H. *Contagion and Confinement: Controlling Tuberculosis along the Skid Road.* Baltimore: The John Hopkins University Press, 1998.

Lyke, M. L. "Seattle's Legacy." *Seattle Post-Intelligencer,* March 22, 2001, sec. E, p. 1.

Mahoney, Sally Gene. "A Rebirth Reborn—Pioneer Square's once again the site of a rush to renovate historic buildings." *The Seattle Times,* August 14, 1983, sec. D, p. 7.

Makers Architecture and Urban Design. "Draft Environmental Impact Statement for the Pioneer Square Historic District Plan." Report. Seattle, 1974.

———. "Pioneer Square Historic District Plan: a public improvement study." Report. Seattle, 1974.

Malone, Michael P. *James J. Hill, Empire Builder of the New Northwest.* Norman: University of Oklahoma Press, 1996.

Manolides, Jimmy. Interview by Mildred Andrews, 2000.

"Marvin Burke: A Profile of Historical Progress." *Pioneer Square Gazette* 1 (May 6, 1980), p. 1.

McConaghy, Lorraine. "Seattle in the First Person: Henry L. Yesler." Lecture given at the Museum of History and Industry, Seattle, April 9, 2003.

McWilliams, Mary. *Seattle Water Department History, 1854–1954.* Seattle: Dogwood Press, 1955.

Mejia-Giudici, Cynthia. "Filipino Americans in Seattle." Seattle: Historylink.org, 1998.

———. "Carlos Bulosan." Seattle: Historylink.org, 1999.

Mighetto, Lisa, and Marcia Babcock Montgomery. *Hard Drive to the Klondike: Promoting Seattle during the Gold Rush.* Seattle: University of Washington Press, with Northwest Interpretive Association, 2002.

Mitchell, Dany. Interview by Mildred Andrews, 2003.

Moody, Fred. "Art and the Aesthetic Salesman." *Seattle Weekly,* April 9, 1986, pp. 35, 42.

Morgan, Murray. *Skid Road: An Informal Portrait of Seattle.* Rev. ed. Seattle: University of Washington Press, 1982. First published 1951 by Viking.

Morgan, Murray, Lane Morgan, and Paul Dorpat.

Seattle: A Pictorial History. Virginia Beach, Va.: Donning Company, 1982.

Morse, Minna. "The First Empire Builder of the Northwest." *Smithsonian,* November 1999, pp. 130–44.

Mumford, Esther Hall. *Seattle's Black Victorians, 1852–1901.* Seattle: Ananse Press, 1980.

————. Interview by Mildred Andrews, 1999.

Murtagh, William J. *Keeping Time: The History and Theory of Preservation in America.* New York: John Wiley and Sons, 1997.

Museum of History and Industry. "Salmon Stakes: People, Nature, and Technology." Seattle: Museum of History and Industry, 1997. Exhibit.

National Archives. Letters received by the Office of Indian Affairs, 1824–81. Roll 909.

Nelsen, Ibsen. Interview by Donald Schmechel. In "Video history of Prominent People of the Pacific Northwest." Seattle Public Library, 1988.

Nesbit, Robert C. *He Built Seattle: A Biography of Judge Thomas Burke.* Seattle: University of Washington Press, 1961.

Newell, Gordon, and Don Sherwood. *Totem Tales of Old Seattle.* Seattle: Superior Press, 1956.

Nodell, Bobbi. "Rebuilt Pergola 'a gift' to History and Civic Pride." *The Seattle Times,* August 18, 2002, Seattle Times Web site.

Nomura, Gail. "Tsugiki, a Grafting—A History of a Japanese Pioneer Woman." In *Women in Pacific Northwest History: An Anthology,* ed. Karen J. Blair. Seattle: University of Washington Press, 1988.

Norris, Frank B. *Legacy of the Gold Rush: An Administrative History of the Klondike Gold Rush.* Anchorage, Alaska: U.S. Department of the Interior, National Park Service, Anchorage System Support Office, 1996.

Northwest Gay Lesbian Transgender History Museum Project. Oral history archives, Seattle, n.d.

"Northwest Magazine," February 1891. Special Collections, University of Washington.

O'Brian, Tim. Interviews by Mildred Andrews, 1999–2000.

Ochsner, Jeffrey Karl. " Neither Scientist nor Bricoleur." *Column 5, Journal of Architecture* (University of Washington), vol. 5, 1992.

————. *Shaping Seattle Architecture: Historical Guide to the Architects.* Seattle: University of Washington Press, 1994.

————. Proceedings, Marion Dean Ross Chapter of the Society of Architectural Historians. Portland, Ore., October 1997.

————. "Seeing Richardson in His Time: The Problem of Romanesque Revival." In *H. H. Richardson: The Architect, His Peers and Their Era,* ed. Maureen Meister. Cambridge: MIT Press, 1999, pp. 102–45.

Ochsner, Jeffrey Karl, and Dennis Alan Andersen. *Distant Corner, Seattle Architects and the Legacy of H. H. Richardson.* Seattle and London: University of Washington Press, 2003.

Okada, John. *No-No Boy: A Novel.* Seattle: University of Washington Press, 1976.

Olin, Laurie. *Breath on the Mirror: Seattle's Skid Road Community.* Seattle: n.p., 1972.

"$100,000 for Pioneer Square." *Seattle Post-Intelligencer,* January 7, 1972, p. 1, col. 5.

Parkinson, John. Parkinson Archives. Available from Web site http://www.parkives.com.

Paulson, Don, and Roger Simpson. *An Evening at the Garden of Allah: A Gay Cabaret in Seattle.* New York: Columbia University Press, 1996.

Peavy, Linda, and Ursula Smith. *Women in Waiting in the Westward Movement.* Norman: University of Oklahoma Press, 1994.

Pieroth, Doris. "Bertha Knight Landes, the Woman Who Was Mayor." In *Women in Pacific Northwest History: An Anthology,* ed. Karen J. Blair. Seattle: University of Washington Press, 1988.

Pioneer Square Gazette 1, no. 2 (summer 1982), p. 1.

"Pioneer Square: Renew or Tear Down?" *Argus* 73, no. 5 (February 4, 1966), p. 4.

"Pioneer Square: A Report by the City Planning Commission and the Central Association of Washington." Seattle, 1959.

"Pioneer Square—Restoration Supported in Planning Effort." *The Seattle Times*, November 10, 1967, p. 16.

Pioneer Square Task Force. "Report." Seattle Public Library, October 11, 1977.

Rasmussen, James. Interviews by Mildred Andrews, 2000–2001.

"Reclaiming the Tidelands." *Sunset Magazine*, July 1912.

Reid, Larry. Interview by Mildred Andrews, 2000.

Roblee, Robert. Interview by Mildred Andrews, 2001.

Roe, JoAnn. *Seattle Uncovered*. Plano, Texas: Seaside Press, 1996.

Roy, F. "Hooverville: A Study of a Community of Homeless Men in Seattle." Master's thesis, University of Washington, 1935.

Sale, Roger. *Seattle, Past to Present*. Seattle: University of Washington Press, 1976.

Sanger, S. L. "A Landmark Bites the Dust." *Seattle Post-Intelligencer*, March 3, 1974, sec. A, p. 3, col 3.

Sayre, J. Willis. *This City of Ours*. Seattle: Seattle School District No. 1, 1936.

Schmid, Calvin F. *Social Trends in Seattle*. Seattle: University of Washington Press, 1944.

Schultz, Marcia. "Women Pioneering Old Seattle." *The Seattle Times*, January 9, 1972.

Schwantes, Carlos Arnaldo. *Hard Traveling: A Portrait of Work Life in the New Northwest*. Lincoln: University of Nebraska Press, 1991.

———. *Railroad Signatures Across the Pacific Northwest*. Seattle: University of Washington Press, 1993.

———. *The Pacific Northwest: An Interpretive History*. Rev. ed. Lincoln: University of Nebraska Press, 1996.

Seattle Chamber of Commerce. "Leading Seattle." In *Seattle Illustrated*. Chicago: Baldwin, Calcutt and Blakely [1890?]. Special Collections, University of Washington.

Seattle Department of Engineering. "Pioneer Square, Areaway Study, Phase II." Report. Seattle, ca. 1976.

"Seattle a Hot Town." *Seattle Daily Times*, October 7, 1897, p. 5.

Seattle Post-Intelligencer. June 20, 1889, p. 3, col. 1; June 21, 1889, p. 3, col. 1; June 22, 1889, p. 4; July 2, 1889, p. 3, col. 1; July 3, 1889, p. 3, col. 1, and p. 4, col. 5; July 5, 1889, p. 4, col. 5; July 7, 1889, p. 7; July 10, 1889, p. 4; August 1, 1889, p. 4; August 6, 1889, p. 1, col. 5, and p. 2; October 30, 1921.

Seattle Office of Economic Development. "Pioneer Square: An Economic Evaluation." Report. Seattle, April 1974.

Seibert, Paul. "Can Pioneer Square Be Saved?" *Puget Soundings*, January 1960, pp. 14–15, 24.

"Shining Sendoff for Pioneer Square Park." *Seattle Post-Intelligencer*, February 24, 1973, sec. A, p. 3.

"A Siege of Petty Larceny." *Seattle Daily Times*, November 7, 1897, p. 5.

Simonson, Rick. Interview by Mildred Andrews, 2001.

Sone, Monica. *Nisei Daughter*. Seattle: University of Washington Press, 1979.

"Special District Delay Voted Down." *Seattle Post-Intelligencer*, August 14, 1973, pp. 1–4.

Speidel, Bill. "Is Pioneer Square?" *Seattle Business Journal*, June 2, 1964, pp. 1–2.

———. *Sons of the Profits*. Seattle: Nettle Creek Publishing Company, 1967.

———. *Doc Maynard: The Man Who Invented Seattle*. Seattle: Nettle Creek Publishing Company, 1978.

Speidel, Sunny. Interviews by Mildred Andrews, 1998–2003.

Steinbrueck, Victor. "Pioneer Square." *Seattle Post-Intelligencer*, October 3, 1965, sec. "Northwest Today," p. 6.

———. "An Architectural and Historical Survey and Study of the Pioneer Square–Skid Road Historical District." Seattle: Seattle Planning Commission, 1969.

———. Interview by Donald Schmechel. 3 videos. Seattle Public Library, ca. 1984.

Stipe, Robert E., and Antoinette J. Lee, eds. *The American Mosaic: Preserving a Nation's Heritage.* Washington, D.C.: US/ICOMOS, 1987.

Stockton, Paysha. "Pergola Rising in Pioneer Square." *The Seattle Times,* June 19, 2002, Seattle Times Web site.

Suffia, David. "Pioneer Square Plan Receives Council's OK." *The Seattle Times,* April 21, 1970, sec. A, p. 11.

Suiter, John. *Poets on the Peaks: Gary Snyder, Philip Whalen and Jack Kerouac in the North Cascades.* Washington, D.C.: Counterpoint, 2002.

Sweeney, Michael. "Historic Model for the Nation." *Seattle Post-Intelligencer,* April 3, 1974, sec. A, p. 3, col. 1.

———. "City Studies Pioneer Square." *Seattle Post-Intelligencer,* June 30, 1974, sec. D, p. 4, col. 1.

Takami, David. *Divided Destiny: History of Japanese Americans in Seattle.* Seattle: University of Washington Press, with Wing Luke Asian Museum, 1998.

Tanner, J. Renee. Interviews by Mildred Andrews, 1998–2001.

Tanner, J. Renee, Pioneer Square Planning Committee, et. al. *1998 Pioneer Square Plan.* Seattle: Pioneer Square Planning Committee, 1998.

Taylor, Quintard. *The Forging of a Black Community: Seattle's Central District, 1870 through the Civil Rights Era.* Seattle: University of Washington Press, 1994.

Tewksbury, Don. "Pioneer Square Area Determined." *Seattle Post-Intelligencer,* March 24, 1972, sec. A, pp. 1, 5.

Thomson, R. H. *That Man Thomson.* Ed. Grant H. Redgord. Seattle: University of Washington Press, 1950.

Tobin, Caroline. *Downtown Seattle Walking Tours.* Seattle: City of Seattle, 1985.

Tyler, Norman. *Historic Preservation: An Introduction to Its History, Principles, and Practice.* New York: W. W. Norton and Company, 2000.

"Union Passenger Depot, Seattle." *Pacific Building and Engineering Record,* August 11, 1906, pp. 3–6.

U.S. Department of the Interior. See Norris, Frank B.

Vandenbrink, Catherine. Interview by Mildred Andrews, 1999.

A Volume of Memoirs and Genealogy of Representative Citizens of the City of Seattle of the County of King, Including Biographies of Those Who Have Passed Away. New York and Chicago: The Lewis Publishing Company, 1903.

Wakefield, Arthur F., ed. *Highest Office Building in the World Outside of New York City: History of Construction of the 42 Story L. C. Smith Building.* Seattle: Deluxe Publishing Company, 1914.

Warren, James R. *King County and Its Queen City.* Woodland Hills, Calif.: Windsor Publications, 1981.

———. *King County and Its Emerald City.* Rev. ed. of *King County and Its Queen City.* Seattle: American History Press with Museum of History and Industry, 1997.

Warren, Pearl. Interview by Mildred Andrews, 1992.

Washington State Department of Transportation. *King Street Station Historic Structure Report,* vol. 1–2. Seattle: Otak, March 1998.

Washington Writers Project of the WPA. *Washington: A Guide to the Evergreen State.* Portland: Binford and Mort, 1941.

Watson, Kenneth Greg. *Sons of the Profits.* Seattle: Nettle Creek Publishing Company, 1967.

———. *A Change of Worlds.* Gallery guide to exhibit at the Museum of History and Industry, Seattle, 1999.

"What Will Mr. Yesler Do?" *Seattle Post-Intelligencer,* July 1, 1889, p. 4.

Widner, Abbie. Correspondence, March 1905.

Manuscripts Collection. Eastern Washington Historical Society, Cheney Cowles Memorial Museum, Spokane.

Wing Luke Asian Museum. "Denshō Project." Seattle, Wash.: Wing Luke Asian Museum, 1999. Digital sound, video, and written word archive.

———. "If Tired Hands Could Talk—Stories of Asian Garment Workers." Seattle: Wing Luke Asian Museum, 2001.

Wing, Warren. *To Tacoma by Trolley: The Puget Sound Electric Railroad.* Edmonds, Wash.: Pacific Fast Mail Press, 1996.

———. Interview by Mildred Andrews, 1999.

"The Wings of the Phoenix." *Seattle Post-Intelligencer,* June 19, 1889, p. 4, col. 1.

"Work Starts on Occidental Mall." *Seattle Post-Intelligencer,* October 9, 1973, sec. A, p. 3.

Wright, Nancy Allison. "Glory Days of Vaudeville." *Columbia,* fall 1988, pp. 3–9.

Yari, Doris. Interview by Mildred Andrews, 1999.

CONTRIBUTORS

MILDRED TANNER ANDREWS is an award-winning author specializing in Northwest social history and historic preservation. A Seattle native, she holds a doctorate from the University of Washington and has served on the faculties of Northwest colleges and universities. Since the early 1980s, she has written six published books and curated several exhibitions on topics ranging from significant legacies of Washington women to regional church, school, and business histories. She serves as women's history editor for historylink.org and as a consultant for regional historic preservation projects, including several in Pioneer Square.

MARC BLACKBURN is a park ranger with the National Park Service. From 1993 to 2002, he was stationed at the Seattle Unit of Klondike Gold Rush National Historical Park and is currently working as an interpretive specialist in Idaho at Nez Perce National Historical Park. A transplant from Northern California, he earned a bachelor of arts degree from the University of Puget Sound. After receiving a doctorate in modern American military history from Temple University in Philadelphia and teaching in the Seattle area, he began his career with the park service, which provides a unique opportunity to preserve the historical resources and heritage of the Pacific Northwest.

DANA COX became involved with Seattle history while living on Maynard Avenue in the International District/Chinatown. His curiosity about Doc Maynard and that neighborhood's Asian history led to freelance tour guiding and eventually a fifteen-year stint at Pioneer Square's Underground Tour. As the Underground Tour's resident historian, he had the opportunity to investigate various layers of Pioneer Square history. This led him to become a researcher, tour guide, and lecturer with the Northwest Gay Lesbian Transgender History Museum Project (NWGLTHMP), a group which, besides having an impressive acronym, gives historic walking tours of Pioneer Square and collects oral histories and archival material.

LEONARD GARFIELD has been exploring Northwest history since 1985, as architectural historian for the Washington State Office of Archaeology and Historic Preservation, as manager of the King County Office of Cultural Resources, and as the current executive director of the Museum of History and Industry in Seattle. Since 1990, he has taught an introduction to historic preservation planning at the University of Washington and is a past president of the Washington Trust for Historic Preservation.

KARIN LINK has been involved in historic preservation in Seattle since the late 1970s. She is a coauthor of *Impressions of Imagination: Terra Cotta Seattle,* a collection of essays that describe downtown's terra-cotta–clad buildings. She holds master's degrees in architecture and historic preservation from the University of Oregon and a bachelor of arts degree from Barnard College of Columbia University. She has worked in preservation architecture for a number of firms located in Pioneer Square. She has also done preservation-related research for the National Park Service and her own firm, Thomas Street History Services.

INDEX

Page numbers in **boldface** type indicate illustrations.

Aaron, Peter, 162

Abbott Hotel, 52

ABC Junk Company, 155

Ace Café, 127

Ace Hotel Building, 119

A Contemporary Theater (ACT), 148, 168

Action/Better City, 178

Adler and Sullivan, 58

African Americans in Seattle, 27–28, 40, 68, **78**, 95, 97, 99, **100**, 129, 131, 155, 172

African Methodist Episcopal Church, 99

Aguinaldo, Emilio, 88

Alaska, 38, 70, 80–83, 88, 91, 93

Alaska Building, **59**, **60**, 60, 195

Alaska Club, 60

Alaska Marine Ferries System, 157

The Alaskan Intelligence Bureau, 87

Alaskan Way (formerly Railroad Avenue), 62

Alaskan Way Viaduct, **136**, 136, **157**, 194, 202

Alaska Steamship Company, 70, 82

Alaska-Yukon-Pacific Exposition (1909), 58, 76–77, 92, 104

Alaskeros, 126

Aleutian Islands, 88

Alhadeff, Kenny, 141, 154

Alhadeff Charitable Foundation, 14

Alhambra, 146

Alki, 12–15, 26

Allen, Paul, 78

Allied Arts of Seattle, 177, 187; Pioneer Square Committee, 178, 181

America Is in the Heart (Bulosan), 150–51

American Federation of Labor (AFL), 102, 124

American Indian Women's Service League, 153–54

American Institute of Architects (AIA), 51, 178, 196

American Messenger Company, 139, **140**, 195

American Railway Union, 67

Amtrak, 79

Anderson, A. C. (and family), 18

Anderson, Ernestine, 155

Anderson, Jim, 167

Anderson, Ralph, 6, 55, 155, 175, **176**, 179, 186–88, 190, 194–95

Anderson, Stuart, 158

Anderson Koch and Duarte, 195

Andrews, C. L., 67

Andrews, Mildred Tanner, 165

Angeline, Princess (Kickisomlo Cud, daughter of Chief Seattle), 23–24, **24**

Angry Housewives, 169

Annie E. Casey Foundation, 140

Anthony, Susan B., 35

Anti-Chinese Riot, 32–33, **32**

Arctic Building, 112, 123

Arctic Club, 104, 112

The Argus, 70

Areaways, 196

Arlington Hotel, 171

Armbruster, Kurt E., 70

Arts community, x, 150, 154–56, 159–69, 199

Artspace Projects, 199
Asian trade and Seattle, 68–69, 91
Astaire, Adele, 146
Astaire, Fred, 146
Astoria, Ore., 10
Australia, 16

"Bachelor problem," 28–29, 38, 96
Bachelor's Hall, 27
Bagley, Clarence, 19, 21, 44–45
Bailey Building. See Broderick Building
Bailey Gatzert Elementary School, 127, 151
Baillargeon, Bill, 187
Bainbridge Island, 11
"The Ballad of the Pergola," 19
Ballard, 22
Ballast Island, 22, **23**, 37
Bancroft, A. L., 37
Bank of America, 25
Barbary Coast, San Francisco, 170
Barbas, Pete, 155
Barry, Lynda, 163
Barrymore, John, 146
Barton, Clara, 88
Bassetti, Fred, 175, **176**
Battle of Seattle, 19–21, 26
Beacon Hill, 68, 74, 102
Beat Generation, 152
Beaton, Wellford, 71
Bebb, Charles, 58, 196
Bebb and Gould, 196
Bebb and Mendel, 58–60, 111, 182, 196
Beck, Dave, 124–25
Bee, Kenny, 171
Beer and Culture Society, 178
Beige Room (cabaret), Los Angeles, 171
Bell, Laura Keziah, 13
Bell, Lavinia, 13
Bell, Mary Virginia, 13
Bell, Olive Julia, 13
Bell, Sarah Ann (Mrs. William), 13
Bell, William Nathaniel (and family), 12, 13, 15
Bella Union, 147

Bellingham, 63, 64, 78
Belltown, 119, 198
Benson, George, 79
Berner, Richard, 70
Bernhardt, Sarah, 146
Bishop, Anna, 27
Bizzarri brothers, 160
Black, Alan, 55, 175, 186–87
Black Angus restaurant chain, 158
Black Bear factory, **104**
Blackchapel, 68, 96–97
Black Diamond, 30
Black Tuesday (October 29, 1929), 118
Black Manufacturing Company, 134
Blair, Francis, 171–72
Blake Island, 11
Blethen, Alden, 70
Blue Banjo, 136, 155, **158**
Blue collar labor, ix, 3, 5, 16, 31–32, 38, 63, 66–67,
    72, 74, 95, 105–8, 113–14, 122–33, 149, 150
Blue Moon and Sue Isaac, 173
Blue Ox Lodge, 119–20, 128
Boeing, William E., 111
Boeing Company, The, 111, 129, 132, 157
Boone, William E., 43, 44, 50, 52–53, 55, 186
Boren, Carson Dobbins (and family), 13, 15, 18
Boren, Gertrude Lavinia, 13
Boren, Louisa. See Denny, Louisa Boren
Boren, Mary (Mrs. Carson), 13, 15
"The Boss Sport." See Considine, John
Boston Globe, 146
Boutsinis, Dimitriou, 155
Boutsinis, Gus, 155
Bowery District, N.Y., 170
Bowman, Shelly, 173
Box-house theaters, 97–98, 143–45, **144**
Bradford, Gigi, 161
Brainerd, Erastus, 86–88, 91
Brainerd, Mary B. (Mrs. Erastus), 88–89
Braman, Dorm, 183
Brandenfels, Kathryn S., 100
Brasserie Pittsbourg, 157, 159, 191
Bread of Life Mission, 119, 20

"Bridge Between Cultures" (Weller Street pedestrian bridge), 166
Bridges, Harry, 124
Briggs, B. F., **26**
British Royal Air Force, 129
Brittania Tavern, 155
Broadway High School, 151
Broderick, Henry, 97, 140, 145, 195
Broderick Building, **115**, 153
Broshears, Catherine. *See* Maynard, Catherine Broshears
Brown, Beriah, 80
Brown, Edmund ("Doc"), 115
Bryan, William Jennings, 83
Bryant, Anita, 172
Buddhist *fujin kai* (women's organizations), 99
Bud's Jazz Records, 12, 154
Buerge, David, 7, 9, 11, 14
Bulosan, Carlos, *America Is in the Heart*, 150–51
Bumgardner, Alan, 175, **176**
Burke, Marvin, 175, 186
Burke, Thomas, 31, 32, 63–65, 74, 112
Burlington Northern Railroad, 75
Burnham and Root, 50
Burns, Marsha, 162–63
Butler Building (Butler Hotel), 50, 54, 95, **115**, 116, 122, 193, 199
Buttnick, Harry, **108**, 108–9
Buttnick, Meta Bloom (Mrs. Harry), 109
Buttnick, Sam, **108**
Buttnick Manufacturing Company, 134, **134**
Byelorusse, 108
Bystrom and Greco, 158

C. C. Filson Company, *134–35*
Cable cars, 41, 57, **115**
Cadillac Hotel, 56–57, **57**, 202
Cafe Paloma, 160
Cairncross and Hempelmann, 199
Callahan, Kenneth, 150
California gold rush (1849), 145
California Tavern, 160
Campbell, Elsie, 115

Camp Lewis, 88, 113
Canadian Pacific Railroad, 31, 62, 82
Cannery Workers' and Farm Laborers Union (CWFLU), 125–26
Cape Horn, 27
Capitol Brewing Company. *See* Jackson Building
Carl, Kevin, 166
Carmack, George Washington, 80, 91
Carnegie, Andrew, 36
Carr, Walter, 160–61
Carrollton Hotel, 126
Cascade Hotel. *See* Olympic Block
Cascade Tunnel, 65
Casey, James (Jim), 139–40, 189, 195
Casino, the, 171
Casual Labor Office, 139
Cedar River Water Supply System, 47
Central Association, 177–83; *Newsletter*, 178
"Central Business Plan" (1963), 177, 182
Central School, 29
Central Tavern, 160, 167, 169
Century 21 Exposition (Seattle World's Fair, 1962), 155
Chadwick, Harry, 70
Chafe, William, 133
Chan, Jeff, 152
Chaney, John, 196
Chapman, Faye (Sister Faye), 119
Charleston, S.C., 176
Charleston (the dance), 114
Chauncey, George, 170
Chen Cheong, 33
Cherry Grove, Illinois, 12
Chi Chi (cabaret, Palm Springs, Ariz.), 171
The Chicago Record's Book for Gold Seekers, 84
Chicago School (of architecture), 50, 52, 55
Chicago World's Fair, 66
Chief Seattle Fountain, 9, 154
Chilkoot Pass and Trail, Alaska, 82
Chin, Chun Hock, 31
Chin, Frank, 152
Chin Gee Hee, 30, 31, 33, **69**
Chin Gee Hee Building, 117
China, empress of, 109

Chinatown, 31, 33, 106–8, 117; Old Chinatown, 107, 117, 130

Chinatown-International Historic District, 107, 119, 184

Chinese and Chinese Americans, 30–33, **32, 40**, 69, 95, 106–7, **107**, 109, 116–17, 130

Chinese Exclusion Act of 1883, 32, 107

Chinook (language), 12, 13, 23–24, 29

Cimbre's (later the 107 Club), 172

Cipra, Peter, 158

City Club, 95, 167; City Club Building, 181

City Hall Park, **111**, 128, 194

City Loan Pavilion, 158–59

City Mission, 99

Civil Aeronautics Authority, 130

Civil War, 21, 28

Clairmont & Company, 43

Clancy brothers, 98

Clark, E. A., 17

Clark, William, 10

CleanScapes, 166, 200

Cleaver, June, 132

Cleveland High School, 174

Clinton, Gordon, **158**

Coast to Coast, 45

Coliseum, 146

Collins, Diana (Mrs. Luther), 12

Collins, Lucinda, 12

Collins, Luther M., 12

Collins, John, 42, 43, 54

Collins, Stephen, 12

Collins Building, **45**, 198–99

Colman, James M., 29–30

Colman Building, 88, 181

Colman Dock, 29, 152

ColorOne Photographic and Digital Imaging, 99

Columbia (ship), 10

Columbia and Puget Sound Railroad, 30

Columbian, 15

Columbia River, 10

Columbia Street Station, 62, 71, **71**

Columbus Tavern, 171

Combined Asian American Resource Project, 152

Commercial Street (now First Avenue South), 18, 25, 38–41, **39**

Commission houses, 71

Committee of Thirty-three, 156–57

Communist Party, 121–22, 124, 127–28, 150; of the United States of America, 128

Compass Center (Lutheran), 119, 202

Comstock, Nelson, 55, 187

Conklin, Mary Ann (Madame Damnable), 18

Conner, Elizabeth, 165, 199

Considine, John, **98**, 98–99, 143–49, 168, 171

Considine, John, Jr., 146

Considine, Tom, 98

Considine Building, 98

Contemporary Crafts Gallery (Manolides Gallery), 155

Coombs, Samuel, 11, 33

Cooper and Levy Pioneer Outfitters, 84, **85**

Corbett-Fitzsimmons fight, 144

Corona Building, 58, **59**, 60, 198

Cort, John, 145, 149

Costigan, Amnee, **158**

Cotterill, George, 102

County-City Building, **111**, 112, 129

Court in the Square, 195

Court of Seattle (gay organization), 172

Coxey, Jacob, 67

"Coxey's Army," 67, **67**

Cracker Barrels, the, 171

Craven Image, 169

Crystal Theater, 145

Cuba, 88–89

Cud, Chewatum (Betsy), 23

Cud, Kick-is-om-lo. *See* Angeline, Princess

Cud, Mamie, 23

Cultural tourism, 6

Cumming, Bill, 150

Curtis, Edward, xv

D'Agostino, Fernanda, 166

Dado, "Speedy," **125**

Daily Bulletin, 72

Daly, James, 158

Daniels, Kevin, 78

Danz, John, 147

Das Gasthaus, 158

Davidson, Sam, 163

Dawson City, Yukon, 82, 88, 91, 145

Dearborn, Henry H., 72, 77

de Barros, Paul, 155

DeCano, Peo, 126

USS *Decatur*, 21

Democratic Party, 118, 123–24

Demography: African Americans, 27–28, 95, 129,
  138; Asians, 97, 133–34; Canadians, 107; Caucasians,
  138; Chinese, 31, 34, 95, 106–8, 116; Filipinos, 126,
  150–51; Germans, 107, 111; Greeks, 116; Italians,
  116; Japanese, 95, 106–8, 126, 116, 131–33, 151–52;
  Jews, 37, 108, 126–27; male predominance, ix, 3,
  28–29, 38, 96, 191; Native Americans, 7, 10, 138,
  153–54; racially segregated and integrated areas
  (1969), 138; Scandinavians, 95, 107, 116, 119, 153

DeNeuf, Emil, 52, 197

Denny, Arthur Armstrong (and family), 12–15, 18,
  21, 25, **26**, 29, 34, 41, 111

Denny, Charles, 26

Denny, David Thomas (and family), 12–15, 20, 21,
  33, 36

Denny, Emily Inez, 20

Denny, Louisa Boren (Mrs. David), 13, **14**, 15, 20,
  33, 36

Denny, Louisa Catherine, 13

Denny, Margaret Lenora, 13

Denny, Mary Ann Boren, 13, **14**, 111

Denny, Rolland Hershel, 13, **26**

Denny Hill, 106

Denny Party, 3, 13, 25

Denny's Island, 14, 15, 40

Derig Hotel, 57. *See also* Cadillac Hotel

deSoto, Alexander, 99

Devin, William, 130

de Voe, Bill, 171

Dewey, George, 88

Dexter Horton Bank, 25, **26**, 55

Diebenkorn, Richard, 163

Discovery (ship), 10

Djijila'letc, 9, 10, 14

Dolan, Ed, 144

Dollhouse, the, 172

Donation Land Law of 1850, 11

Dore, John, 122, 124

Dorian Society, 172

Dorpat, Paul, 40

Double Header Tavern, 171, **171**

Downey/Monson Associates, 195

Downtown Seattle Association (DSA), 177

Downtown Transit Tunnel, 79

Drexel Hotel, 44, **45**

Duncan, George, Sr., 140

Duncan & Sons, 140

Duniway, Abigail Scott, 35

Duwamish Indians, 3, 26; ancient heritage of, 7–12;
  assimilation with newcomers, 12–17, 21; treaties and
  exile, 18–21; cultural retention, 19–24, 154; tribal
  council, 12, 153

Duwamish River, 7, 14

Duwamps, 15

Duyungan, Virgil, 126

Dynamics, the, 155

Eagle Hall and Casino, Grays Harbor County, 144

Eagles' Auditorium, 135

Eames and Young, 60

Earl Layman Clock, **186**

Earp, Wyatt, 99, 165

Earthquakes, 194; (1949), 6, 135, **135**; Nisqually (2001),
  6, 57, 135, 168, 169, 200, 202

Eastern European immigrants, 67, 108–9, 198

Ebony Council, 172

Eckstein, Minna Schwabacher, 135

Eckstein, Nathan, 135

Eddie Bauer Inc., 134

Edison's Unique Theatre, 145

Edwards, Frank, 116, 121–22

Edwards, Myrtle, 136

Elks Hall, 88

Ellensburg (fire), 43

Elliott, Eugene Clinton, 148

Elliott Bay, 10, 14

Elliott Bay Book Company, 26, 160–62, **160**, **186**, 187

Elroy's, 155

"Empire Builder." *See* Hill, James J.

Empty Space Theater, 168

Ephrata, 198

Estes, David, 172

Evans, Dennis, 163

Evening Post (New York), 35

Everett, Julian F., 58

Everett, 63, 78

Everett Massacre, 152

Exact, 13

SS *Excelsior*, 80

Executive Order 9006, 131

F. X. McRory's Steak, Chop and Oyster House, 159, 195

Facts for Klondykers, 87

Fairhaven and Southern Railroad, 64

Fair Housing and Employment Ordinance, 172

Fairmont Olympic Hotel, 26

Fajans, Michael, 165

Falk, Dennis, 172

Falls, Greg, 168

Falls, Jean (Mrs. Greg), 168

Farley, Jim, 124

Farris, Linda, 162–63

Father's Day picnic, 135

Fat Tuesday, 167

Fecker, Jack, 155

Federal Emergency Trades Council, 113

Federal Tax Reform Act of 1975, 194

Federal Theater Project, 128

Felker, Captain Leonard, 17

Felker House, 17, 18

Fields, W. C., 146

Filipino Cannery Workers' and Farm Workers Union, Local 18257, **125**, 126

Filipinos, **125**, 125–26, 131, 150–51

Finocchio's (cabaret), San Francisco, 171

Firland Sanatorium, 140

First and Cherry Building, 195

First Avenue South, **48**, **96**, 156–57, **175**, 193

First Avenue trolley, 79, 193–94

First Editions (gallery), 162

First Presbyterian Church, 100

First Thursday Gallery Walk, 163

First Washington Infantry Regiment, 88–89, **89**

Fisher, Elmer, 49–52, 182, 188, 197

Florence Crittenden Rescue Circle, 99

Flynn, Elizabeth Gurley, **149**

Ford, Gerald R., 93

Fort Lawton, 113

Fortson, George, 89

Fortson Square, 89, **116**, 172, 199

Fortymile mining camp, Yukon, 80, 82

Foster, Bob, 167

Foster, Don, 162–63

440, the (cabaret), New York, 171

Frances Harper Unit, WCTU, 99, **100**

Frankenthaler, Helen, 163

Franklin, 30

Frantics, the, 155

Fraternal Order of Eagles (FOE), 147–49

Frederick and Nelson's, 22

Freeborn, Steve, 169

Freeman, Jacquetta, **158**

Freeman, Tiny, 167

Free Speech Corner, 127, 149, 152

Friedlander, Polly, 138, 156, 192

Friends of Post Alley, 166

Front Street (now First Avenue), 18, 41–43, **42**, 49

Frye, George F., 111

Frye, Louisa Catherine Denny (Mrs. George), 89, 111–12, 117

Frye Hotel (Frye Apartments), **59**, 60, 89, **111**, **116**, 117, 129, **130**, 138, 158, 181, 202

Frye Opera House, 42

Furth, Jacob, 46

Furuya, Masajiro, 108

Furuya's Bank Building, 108

*G. O. Guy's Drugstore, 98, **116**, 130, 144*

Gaggin and Gaggin, 109

Garden of Allah, 171–72

Gardner, Ann, 163

Garrett-Schafer Building, 179. *See also* Jackson Building

Gates, Bill, 78

"Gateway to the Orient," 25

Gatzert, Babette Schwabacher (Mrs. Bailey), 36, 37

Gatzert, Bailey, 18, 37

Gay Business Council (later Greater Seattle Business Association), 172

Gay Community Center, 173

Gay Pride Week, 173

Gayrilla theater, 173

Geise, John, 155

Gentlemen's Agreement of 1907–8, 107

Gill, Hiram, 101–3, 112

Gilman, James, 31

Ginsburg, Allen, 152

Glad Tydings Temple, 119

Globe Building, 53, 55–56, **56**, 155, 160, 168, **186**, 186–87

Globe Hotel, 56

Glover, E. S., 37

Gold Coast Restaurant, 158

Gold Creek, Montana, 30

Golden Horseshoe, 172

Gold Medal Coffee, 135

Goldsmith Building (now Court in the Square), 196

Gorilla Room, 169

Gottstein, Kassel, 141

Gottstein, Meyer, 86, 141

Gould, A. Warren, 112, 196

Gould, Carl, Jr., **158**

Graham, Billy, 193

Graham, Lou (aka Dorothea Ohben), 97

Graham Plan (John Graham and Co., *Pioneer Square Redevelopment*), 180–83, **180**

Grand Central Bakery, 160, 187

Grand Central Building, **48**, 55, 109, 159, 162, **187**, 187–88, 191

Grand Central Station, New York City, 72

Grandma Fay, 13

Graves, Morris, 150

Gray, Captain Robert, 10

Great Depression, 118–19; and Filipino community, 125–26; and Japanese community, 126–27; and labor unions, 124–26; and politics, 118, 121–25, 127–28, 149; and relief programs, 119–21, 128–29, 150; and self-help organizations, 120–24

Great Fire of 1889, 5, 43–47, **43, 44,** 50, 51, 53, 62, 156, 174, 181, 205

Great Houdini, 147

Great Northern Railroad, 62, 81, 82, 86; Asian and Alaskan trade, 68–70; Seattle wins terminus, 63–66; strike, 66–67; tunnels, 65–66, **67**, 79

Great Northern Silk Express, 68

Great Northern Steamship Line, 69

Great Northern tunnel, 72–73, **73**

Great White Fleet, 92

Green, Roger, 32–33

Green River, 11

Greenwich Village, New York, 142, 198

Greg Kucera Gallery, 163

Gregory Broderick Smith Real Estate, 141, 203

Groening, Matt, 163

Grose, William ("Bill"), 27–28, **34**

Grose, Sarah (Mrs. William), 27

Ground Zero, 169

Grunge, 169

Guy, G. O., 98

Gypsy Rose Lee. *See* Havoc, Rose

Haglund, Ivar, 119

Hambach Building, 196

Hanford Building, **59**

Hanson, Mayor Ole, 114

Harbor Island, 14

Harbor Light Building (Leighton Center), 119, 199

Harmon, Kitty, 161

Harper's Weekly, 28, 32, 46

Harriman, Edward Henry, 70, 77, 78, 106

Harris, Alfred, 163

Harris, Ken, 135

Harrison, Benjamin, 24, 95

Hartford Building, **59**

Hauberg, Anne Gould, **158**

Havana, Cuba, 88

Havoc, June, 146

Havoc, Rose (Gypsy Rose Lee), 146, 172

Hawthorne, Julian, 53

Hay, Marion E., 76

Hayes, Randy, 162

Hayes, Rutherford B., 39

Heap of Birds, Edgar, *Day and Night* (public artwork), 154

Heart Mountain Relocation Camp, Wyoming, 133

Helen's Pup Tavern, 159

"Here Come the Brides," 28–29

Heritage Building (formerly Wax and Raine Building), 195

Hetherington, Clements and Company, 56

Hetherington, James W., 56

Highway 99 (Pacific Coast Highway), 117, 139, 157

Hill, James Jerome, 5, **63**, 78; "Empire Builder," 62–63, 68–70, 75–77; and Seattle, 63–66, 70–77, 106; and strike, 66–67

Hill, Joe, 149, 153

Hillside Improvement Company, 103

Hinterberger, John, 159, 166

Hinton, Hotcha, 171–72

Historic Seattle Preservation and Development Authority, 57, 202

Historic Sites Act (1935), 176

Hitler, Adolf, 127

Hoge Building, 15

Holm, Bill, 190

Home Guard (Seattle), 32–33

Homestead claims, 12, 14–16; platting of, in Seattle, 18

Honolulu, 16

Hoover, Herbert, 118, 120

Hooverville, **120**, 120–21

Hop Sing Tong, 117

Horton, Dexter, 25, **26**, 41

Hotel Brunswick, 39

Hotel Seward. *See* Morrison Hotel

Houghton, E. W., 50

House of All Nations, 97

House Un-American Activities Committee (U.S. House of Representatives), 128

Howard, William, **34**

Howard Building, 150

Hudson, John C., Jr., 190

Hudson's Bay Company, 10, 12, 13

Human Immunodeficiency Virus (HIV), 137

Humphrey, Clark, 169

Hunt, Denice, 196

Huntington, D. R., 158

Idaho (ship), 99

"If Tired Hands Could Talk—Stories of Asian Garment Workers," 134

Illahee, 29

Immigrant laborers, 5, 31, 63, 67, 95, 106–8, 124–25

Industrial Workers of the World (IWW; the Wobblies), 105, **105**, 122, 149, 152–53; *Little Red Songbook*, 152

Inez Fabbri Opera Company, 39

Inside Passage, Alaska, 82

Intermela, Julia Benson, 17

International District. *See* Chinatown-International Historic District

International District Station of the Downtown Transit Tunnel, 79

International Ladies Garment Workers Union (ILGWU), 103, **103**, **104**, 134

International Longshoremen's and Warehousemen's Union (ILWU), 124, 151

International Order of Good Templars; Grand Templar of the United States, 102

Interurban Building, **3**, 53–54, **54**, **55**, 111, 130, 181, **192**, 195, **206**

Interurban depot, **55**

Ishii, David, 152, 162

Isley, Hewitt, 191

Israel, Sam, 163, 197–99

Itoi family, 126–27, 132

IWW Hall, 152

J. M. Frink Building. See Washington Shoe Building

J & M Cafe, 167

Jackson Building (aka Capitol Brewing Company Building, formerly Garrett-Schafer Building), 155–56, 162, 174, 179, **179**, 185–86

Jackson Square, San Francisco, 178

Jackson Street, 41, 96, 193

Jackson Street Regrade (1907–8), 74, **75**, 105–7

Jacobs, Orange, 62

Japanese-Americans, xi, 67, 95, 106–7, 126–27, 133–34, **133**, 158; and World War II, 131–32, **132**, 139, 151–52

Japanese Community Center, 108

Japanese Hotel and Apartment Operators Association, 132

Japanese-Protestant *fujin kai* (women's organizations), 99

Japantown, 106, 127

Jazz Alley, 155

Jefferson, Thomas, 10

Jews, 37, 108, 126–27, 135, 141, 197–98

Johanson, Martin, 119, **119**

John Graham and Company, Architects, 180

Johns, Jasper, 163

Johnson, J. Michael, 156

Johnson, Lauralee, 167

Johnson, Robert Leroy ("Yankee"), 167

Jolson, Al, 146

Jones, Grant, 138–39, **139**, 175, 186, 195

Jones, Ilze, 138–39, **139**, 156, 166, 175, 186, 188, 195, 203–4

Jones, Johnpaul, 186

Jones, Quincy, 155

Jones & Jones Architects and Landscape Architects, 138–39, 153, 156, 159–60, 166, 186, 188, 195–96, 204

Journal of Occurrences, 10

Juneau, Alaska, 82

Junior Cadillac, 155

Justen, William, 198

Kalama, Wash., 30

Kaplan Warehouse, 165

Karlstrom, Otto, 119

Kate (G. W. Carmack's Indian wife), 91

Kerouac, Jack, 152

Kime, Kristopher, 167

King, Billy, **159**, 166

King, William Rufus Devane, 18

King County, establishment of, 18

King County Arts Commission, 167

King County Courthouse, 44, **45**, 112, 172, 187, 193

King County Domed Stadium. *See* Kingdome

King County welfare office, 123

Kingdome, 6, 142, 192, **193**, 200, **201**, 203

King Street Station, 60–61, **61**, 72–74, **74**, **75**, 78, **79**, 96, 117, 129–31, **131**, 200

King Street Wharf, 30, 37, 44

Kipling, Rudyard, 45

Kissel, Francois, 157–59

Kissel, Julia, 157

Klondike gold rush, 5, 52–53, 70, 170; impacts on Seattle, 81–87, 89–93, 96, 142, 179–81, 187; stampede of 1897, 80–81

Klondike Gold Rush National Historical Park, Seattle unit (aka Klondike Museum), ix, 93, 202

Klondike Gold Rush National Historical Park, Skagway, Alaska unit, 93

Klondike Grubstakes, 87

Klondike Information Bureau, 85, 86

"Klondike Kate." *See* Rockwell, Kate

"Know Your Seattle Day," 174

Koch, Jerry, 155

Korn, Moses, 49

Korn Building, 49, **52**, 53, **191**

Kovalenko Hale Architects, 191, 199

Krivanek, B. J., 165

Kucera, Greg, 163–64

Kunishige, Frank, xv

Label, Abie, 138

Labor unions, 150; American Federation of Labor, 124; Cannery Workers and Farm Laborers Union, 125–26; Industrial Workers of the World (IWW, Wobblies), 105; International Ladies Garment Workers Union, 103–4; International Longshoremen's and Warehousemen's Union, 124, 151; Japanese Hotel and Apartment Operators Association, 132; Lady Barbers Union, 103; metal trade unions, 113; Musicians Mutal Protective Union, 147; Railroad Brotherhoods, 66–67; Seattle Central Labor Council, 101; shipyard unions, 113–14; Sleeping Car Porters Club, **78**; Teamsters Union, 124; Waitresses Union, 103; and Seattle General Strike (1919), 113–14

Labuznik (formerly Prague Restaurant), 158

Ladies' Library Association, 36

Ladies' Relief Society, 36

Lady Barbers Union, 103

Lakeside School, 160

Lakeview Cemetery, 24

Lamphere, Phyllis, 183

Lampman, Dell, 144

Landes, Bertha Knight, 115

Langill, Norman, 167

Larsen, Richard, 197

Latimer, H., **26**

Latimer, Norval H., **26**, 55

Law and Order League (Seattle), 35, 98

Layman, Earl, 191, 194

Leary, John, 18, 40

Leary, Mary, 36

Leave It to Beaver, 132

Leavitt, H. L., 147

Left Bank, Paris, 142

Lehman, Hans, **158**

Leong, Jim, 164

Lerner, Barron H., *Contagion and Confinement*, 137

Lewis, Meriwether, 10

Lichtenstein, Roy, 162–63

Lincoln, Abraham, 29

Little Egypt, 144

Little Red Songbook, 152

Longshore Union Hall, 126

Look Magazine, 151

Lopes, Manuel, 27

Louisa C. Frye Associates, 112, 117

Louisa C. Frye Hotel. *See* Frye Hotel

Low, Alonzo, 13

Low, John, Jr., 13

Low, John Nathan, 12–14

Low, Lydia Colborn (Mrs. John Nathan), 13

Low, Mary, 13

Low, Minerva, 13

Low-Income Housing Institute (LIHI), 202

Low- and middle-income housing, xi, 139, 196, 202

Lowman and Hanford Stationers, 40

Lowman Building, 161, 181

Luke, Wing, 135

Lushootseed language, 9, 19, 154

Lynching of 1882, 33–34, **34**

Lyric Theatre, **143**, 149

M. and K. Gottstein's Wholesale Liquors and Cigar, **86**, *141*

Mackensay Real Estate Services, 203

Madame Damnable. *See* Conklin, Mary Ann

Madame Peabody's Dancing Academy for Young Ladies (aka the Dance), 171

Magnuson, Warren G., 124

USS *Maine*, 88

Major Property Owners Group (MPOG), 203

Makah Indians, 22

Makers Architecture and Urban Design, 193–94

Manila Bay, Philippines, 88

Manolides, Jimmy, 155

Manolides Gallery (aka Contemporary Crafts Gallery), 155

Maple, Jacob, 12

Maple, Samuel, 12

Mariners, 200

Markovitz, Sherry, 163

Marshall Building. *See* Globe Building

Marshall-Walker Block. *See* Globe Building

Martin, Clarence, 123

Martin Smith, Inc., 141

Masin, Ben, 141

Masin, Bob, 141

Masin, Eman, 141

Masin's Furniture, 141

Maslan, Michael, 162

Mason, Skookum Jim, 91

Matthews, Mark, 100

Matthews, Tia, 169

Mattie's, 171

Maud Building, 91

Maynard, Catherine Broshears (Mrs. David), 18, 26–27

Maynard, David S. ("Doc"), 15–16, **15**, 18, 21, 25–27, 39

Maynard, Lydia (Mrs. David), 26–27

Maynard Building, 181, **182**, 195, **195**

McBean, J. A., 74

McBride, Ella, xv

McCarthy era, 150

McClure's Magazine, 101–2

McCough, James, 43

McCoy's Firehouse, 160, 171, 202

McEldowney, Mia, 163

McGonigle, Joe, 167

McGonigle, Mary (Mrs. Joe), 167

McHugh, Mick, 159

McKay, Donald, 42, 55

McKesson-Robbins Building, 195

McKinley, William, 88

McNaught, James, 27

McNeil Island federal penitentiary, 125

McPhee, Bill, 80

Meany, Edmond, 55

Meany, Stephen, 55

Mellon, Charles S., 71

Mendel, Louis, 58, 196

Mercer, Alice, 21

Mercer, Asa Shinn, 28

"Mercer Girls," 28–29

Merchant's Cafe Building, 27, **52**, 52–53, 126, 151, 190–91, **192**

Meredith, William, **98**, 98–99

Merrill Place, 168, 196

Methodist Episcopal Church, 35

Metropole Building, 130, **147**

Metropolis, the, 169

Metropolitan Police Museum (Seattle), 34

Metropolitan Transit Authority (Metro), 79, 193

Meyers, Vic, **116**, 122

Mighetto, Lisa, 69

Miike Maru, 69

Mill Street (now Yesler Way), 16–18, 33, 38, 41

Millenium Tower, 141

Miller, Dick, **158**

Millionair Club, 119, **119**

Milwaukee, Minneapolis and St. Paul Railroad, 62

"Mineral Palace," **65**

Minidoka Relocation Center, Idaho, 132

Minnehaha Saloon, 97

Missionaries, 10

Missions, 99, 119–20, 138, 202

Mitchell, Dany, 159, 166

Mocambo, 172

Montana, Ruby, 167

Montgomery, Marcia Babcock, 69

Moonlight Serenaders, **125**, 126

Moose Hall, **128**

Moran, Robert, 27, 45, 47, 86–87

Moran Brothers Shipyards, 67, 87, 92, **92**

Morgan, J. P., 70, 75

Morgan, Murray, *Skid Road*, ix, 101–2, 122, 124, 139

Morrison Hotel, **111**, 112

Mothers' Congress, 102

Motherwell, Robert, 163

Muckilteo, 18

Mudhoney, 169

Mumford, Esther Hall, *Seattle's Black Victorians*, 27

Municipal Art Commission, 178, 181

Municipality of Metropolitan Seattle (Metro), 79

Murphy, Ron, 188

Musicians Mutual Protective Union, 147

Mutual Life Building, 51, **89**, **102**, 155, **158**, 181, 195, **197**

Nakamura, Yukio, 139

Nakano, Kenichi, 199

National Advisory Council on Historic Preservation, 176

National Endowment for the Arts, 161

National Historic Landmarks Program, 176

National Historic Preservation Act, 176–77

National Labor Relations Board, 124

National Park Service, 93, 140, 176

National Register of Historic Places, 176–77, 184

National Trust for Historic Preservation, 176, 200

Native Americans, 7–24, 26, 153, 190. *See also* Duwamish Indians

NBBJ (Naramore Bain Brady and Johanson), 195–96, 200

U.S.S. *Nebraska*, 92

Nelsen, Ibsen, 175, **176**

Neltner, Ned, 155

Nestor, John, 42

Never Touch Me Saloon, 68

Newcastle, 30

New Deal, 118, 123, 128

New England Hotel, 122

"New gold rush era," xi

New York, Alki, 12

New York Building, 53

The New York Times, 146

Nihonmachi ("Japantown"), 108

Nippon Kan Theater Building, 108

Nippon Yusen Kaisha (Japanese Steamship Line), 69

Nirvana, 168–69

Nisqually, 10, 12–13

Nitze-Stagen, 78, 200, 203

No Boundaries, Inc., 203

Nome, Alaska, 145

Nomura, Gail, 133

Nootkan Indians, 22

Nordstrom, John, 91

North American Transportation and Trading Company, 70, 82

Northcoast Electric Company, 196

Northcoast Building (now Court in the Square), 196

Northern Club, 101–2

Northern Hotel. *See* Terry-Denny Building

Northern Pacific Railroad, 30, 31, 40, 62–66, 80, 82, 86

Northern Securities Company, 70, 75

Northwest Area Music Hall of Fame, 155

Northwest Bookfest, 161

Northwestern Drug Company, 56

Northwest Gay Lesbian Transgender History Museum Project (NGLTHMP), 170, 173

Northwest School (of art), 150

Norwegians, 63

O'Brien, John, 136

Occidental Hotel, **40**, 40, 41, **44**, 51, 54–55. *See also* Seattle Hotel

Occidental Mall, 192

Occidental Park, **3**, **153, 154**, 156, 158–60, 173, 185, 187, 197; **188**; pergola, 188, 189, 201

Occidental Square parking lot, **190**, 193

Odd Fellows, **14**

Ohben, Dorothea Georgine Emile (Lou Graham), 97

Okada, Frank, 151, 163

Okada, John, *No-No Boy,* 151–52

OK Cafe, 139, 159

O.K. Hotel, **108**, 109, **121**, **168**, 169, 202

Okuba, Sam, 109

Old Boston Hotel, **121**

Olin, Laurie, 138

Olmstead, Roy, 114–15

Olson/Walker Architects, 195–97

Olvera Street, Los Angeles, 178

Olympia, Wash., 10, 15

Olympia Brewery, 112

Olympic Block, 181, **182**, 185, 191, 194

Olympic Hotel, 177

107 Club, 172

One Reel Vaudeville, 167

Ordway, Elizabeth ("Lizzie"), 29

Oregon and Wash. Station. *See* Union Station

Oregon Improvement Company, 30, 37

Oregon Territorial Legislature, 18, 26

Oregon Territory, 11

Oregon-Washington Railway, 77

Oriental Building, 115

Ormsky, Butch, 155

"The Orphan Home," 36

Orpheum Theater, 145

Orpheum Vaudeville Circuit, 146

Osgood, Frank, 40, 41

Otani, Valerie, 166

Our House Hotel and Restaurant, 27, **121**

Our Lady of Good Help Catholic Church, 24, 38, 44, 97

Ozark Hotel fire, 138

Ozark Hotel Ordinance, 138

Pacific Coast Coal Company, 72

Pacific Coast Highway (Highway 99), 117, 139, 157

Pacific Coast Steamship Company, 82

Pacific Trail Sportswear, 134

Palm Garden, 145

"Panic of 1893," 57, 66, 83

Pantages, Carmen, 146

Pantages, Pericles ("Alexander"), 145–46

Pantages Vaudeville, 146

Pantages Vaudeville Circuit, 146

Parkinson, John, 50, 53–54, **54**

Parkinson and Associates, 53

Parnell's, 155

Pasco, Duane, 153–54

Patterson, Daniel J., 77

Paulson, Don, *An Evening in the Garden of Allah*, 170–71

Payne, Benjamin, 33, **34**

Pearl Harbor, Hawaii (1941), 129, 131

Pearl Jam, 168–69

Peavy, Linda, 17

Pennock, Bill, 124

Pennsylvania Station, New York City, 177

Penthouse, the, 155

People's Theater, 98, 143–44

Pergolas. *See* Occidental Park; Pioneer Place; Washington Street Boat Landing

Pete's Poop Deck, 155

Pettyjohn, Elroy, 155

Philippines, 88–89, 91, 125–26

Phinney and Jones Building. *See* Butler Building

Piazza San Marco, Venice, 61, 72

Pier 46, 203

Pier 48, 157, 203

Pierce, Franklin, 18

Pike Place Market, 156, 167, 178, 180, 193, 198

Pike Plaza Project, 180

Pilchuck glass, 163

Pinnell, John, 29

Pinto Pony, Ruby Montana's, 167

Pioneer Banque, 155

Pioneer Building, 17, 50, **51**, 139, 155, 157, 181, 188–89, **189**

Pioneer Library Association, 27, 36

Pioneer Place, **x**, 50–52, **65, 89**, 185; Chief Seattle fountain, **182**; pergola, **xiv**, 9, 58, **58**, 93, 156–57, 178, 181, **182**, 188–90, **191**; Tlingit totem pole, **90, 91**, 91, 190; underground comfort station, 193, 194

Pioneer Place Park. *See* Pioneer Place

Pioneer Square Annex Theater, 168

Pioneer Square Association, 177, 192

Pioneer Square Community Association, xii, 165, 177

Pioneer Square Community Council, xii, 177; Open Space Committee, 197

Pioneer Square Community Development Organization (CDO), 165

Pioneer Square Historic District (aka Pioneer Square Preservation District), 7, 177, 182–85, 191–92, 194, 196, 203; maps, **vii, 184**; visions for future development, 202–5, **202, 206**. *See also* Pioneer Square Special Review District; Pioneer Square/Skid Road Historic District

Pioneer Square Historic District Plan (1974), 193–94, 196, 202

Pioneer Square Historic Plan Update, 196, 200

Pioneer Square History Project, ix–xii

"Pioneer Square Pals," **166**

Pioneer Square Plan, (1998), xii, 119, 165, 188, 200–201, 203

Pioneer Square Preservation Board, 184, 194, 202

Pioneer Square Properties, 203

Pioneer Square Public Arts and Legends Program, xii, 165, 201

Pioneer Square Public Spaces Forum, 165

"Pioneer Square Rehabilitation Economic Study," 179

Pioneer Square/Skid Road Historic District, 175, 183, **184**

Pioneer Square/Skid Road National Historic District, 184

Pioneer Square Special Review District, 184–85, 192

Pioneer Square Theater, 168

Pittsburgh Lunch, 157

Plummer, Charles, 27

Plummer's Hall, 27

Plymouth Congregational Church, 27

Point Elliott Treaty, 18, 21

Poll, Harry, 167

Poll, Stan, 167

Pontius Building, 43

Population of Seattle, 3–6, 21, 37, 70, 105, 113, 129, 142–43. *See also* Demography

Populists, 83

Portage Magazine, 140

Porter, Francis, 46

Port Gamble, 25

Portland, Ore., 13, 29, 30, 45, 77

SS *Portland*, 80–81, 83

Port Madison, 25

Port of Seattle, 76, 157, 203

Post Building, **40**, 166

Post-Intelligencer. See *Seattle Post-Intelligencer*

Potlatch, 9, **104**, 104–5

Prague Restaurant (aka Labuznik), 158

Prefontaine, Father Francis Xavier, 24, 38, 44

Prefontaine Building, 181

Prefontaine Place, 24, 165, 181

Presidents of the United States, the, 168

The Press-Times, 86

Progressive movement, 76

Prohibition, 35, 102, 112–15, 126; blue laws, 154

Prohibition Party, 102

Prosch, Thomas, 31, 46

Prose, Francine, 161

Prostitution, 18, 29, 68, 96–103, 130

Prowda, Sherry, 161

Public Safety Building, 100, 137; drop-in clinic, **137**

Puget Sound Interurban Railway, 53, **77**, 77–78

"Purity Squad," 112

Puyallup, 78

Puyallup Fairgrounds, 132

"Queen City of the Northwest," 25

Queen of the Pacific, 31, **81**

Quitzlitza (aka Anne Tuttle), 22

Railroad Avenue (now Alaskan Way), 31, **64***, 64–65,*
    75, **121**

Railroad Brotherhoods, 66–67

Rainier Brewery, 112, 167

Rainier Club, 72

Ralph Anderson and Partners, 188

Rasmussen, James, 12, 19, 22

Rauschenberg, Robert, 162

Ravensdale, 30

Ray, Emma (Mrs. Lloyd), *Twice Ransomed, Twice Sold,*
    99, **100**

Ray, Lloyd, 99

Recreational Equipment Inc., 134

Red Cross Society, 89

Red River Valley, 63

Reed, Charles A., 72

Reed College, Portland, Ore., 152

Reid, Larry, 163, 169

Renton, 30, 78

Reynolds, George B., 33

Republican Party, 70, 118, 122–23

Richardson, H. H., 50

Robertson and Blackwell, 52, 197

Roblee, Robert, 138

Rockefeller, John D., 78

Rockwell, Kate (aka Klondike Kate; Queen of the
    Yukon), 145–46, 158

Roe, JoAnn, 149

Rogers, John R., 88

Rogers, Will, 146

Roman Catholic, 10, 11, 38, 44

Ronald, J. T., 96–98

Roosevelt, Franklin D., 118, 123, 131, 132, 151

Roosevelt, Theodore, 75

Rosco Louie Gallery, 163, 169

"Rosie the Riveter," 132

Ross, James D., 122

Rothenberg, Susan, 163

Rousch, Jeff, 141

Royal Canadian Mounted Police, 83

Ruffner, Ginny, 163

Ruggles-Lucknow Building, 195

Rutten, Joe, 155

Ryan, Claude, 139

Ryther, Noble, 99

Ryther, Olive ("Ollie"; "Mother Ryther"), 99

Ryther Child Home, 99

Safeco Field, 6, 79, 113, 120, 200

Saftig, Marguerite, 91

St. Michael, Alaska, 82, 88

St. Paul, Minn., 62, 70, 72

Sale, Roger, *Seattle: Past to Present*, 25, 64

Salish, 8

Salmon Bay Charlie, 22

Salsbury, Allen, 155, 179

Salsbury, Jean Claire, 156

Salvation Army, 100, 119, 127, 143

Samis Foundation, 54, 198, 203

Samis Land Company, 198

Sanderson, Caroline, 36

Sanderson Building. *See* Merchant's Cafe Building

San Diego Padres, 200

San Francisco, 3, 16, 29, 30, 37, 41, 43, 45, 46, 80, 88, 152

Santa and his reindeer, **91**

Santos, Pedro, 126

Sasaki and Associates, 195

Sato, Norie, 163

Saturday Evening Post: "Four Freedoms" articles, 151

Saunders, Charles W., 50, 182

Saunders and Lawton, 60, 196

Save Our Children Crusade, 172

Sayre, Willis, 27

Scandinavian National Bank, **87**

Scandinavians, 87, 95

Schmechel, Donald, 184

Schwabacher, Babette, 37. *See also* Gatzert, Babette Schwabacher

Schwabacher, Minna. *See* Eckstein, Minna Schwabacher

Schwabacher Brothers and Company, 37, 41

Schwabacher Brothers Grocery, 130, 135

Schwabacher Hardware Company, 84, 120, 129, **182**, 196

Schwabacher Hardware Company Warehouse, **121**

Schwabacher's Dock, 44, 45

Schwantes, Carlos, 67

Seafirst Bank, 25

Seahawks Stadium, 3, 79, 193, 200–201, 203

Seattle: building and land use codes (first), 46–47; naming of, 15; platting of, 18

Seattle, Chief, 7–12, **11**, 15, 21–22, 154

Seattle and Montana Railroad, 64

Seattle and Walla Walla Railroad, 29, 30, **30**

Seattle Art Museum, 164

Seattle Arts and Lectures, 161

Seattle Arts Commission, 164–65, 178, 181

Seattle Benevolent Society, 99

Seattle Building Department, 185

Seattle Camera Club, xv

Seattle Center, 15

Seattle Central Labor Council, 101

Seattle Chamber of Commerce, 85–86, 104, 112, 124–25, 174

Seattle Children's Home, 36

Seattle Chronicle, 33

Seattle City Charter, 21, 36

Seattle City Council, 98, 102, 177–78, 183

Seattle City Hall, 38, **94**, 97, 112, 193–94

Seattle City Light, 116, 122

Seattle College (now Seattle University), 150

Seattle Community Capital Development Corporation, 202

Seattle Counseling Services for Sexual Minorities, 172

Seattle Daily Journal of Commerce, 95

Seattle Daily Press, 45

Seattle Daily Times, 83

Seattle Department of Construction and Land Use (now the Department of Planning and Development), 198, 203; CityDesign, 203–4

Seattle Department of Neighborhoods, 194

Seattle Electric Company, 77

Seattle Exchange, 15

Seattle Federation of Women's Clubs, 102

Seattle Fire Department, 33, 44, 57

Seattle First National Bank, 25, **102**

Seattle General Strike (1919), 114, 149

Seattle Guide, 156

Seattle Health Department, 120

Seattle Hotel (formerly the Occidental Hotel), **51**, 95, 177, 181, 185

Seattle Indian Center, 153

Seattle Indian Services Commission, 153, 172

Seattle Lake Shore and Eastern Railroad (SLS&E), 31, 62, 64, 65

Seattle Magazine, 153

Seattle Motorcycle Club, **vi**

Seattle National Bank Building. *See* Interurban Building

Seattle Office of Historic Preservation, 191, 194

Seattle Office of Urban Conservation, 194

Seattle Order of Good Things. *See* Fraternal Order
    of Eagles
Seattle Park Department, 178
Seattle Planning Commission, 175, 178
Seattle Police Department, 33–34, **94**, 98–99, 101, 112,
    114–16, 140, 170, 172, 200
Seattle Post, 40
Seattle Post-Intelligencer, 40, 43, 70, 73, 80, 86, 95,
    98, 98–99, 108, 119, 123, 128, 145, 149, 162–64,
    175, 190, 192
Seattle Public Library, 36, 151
Seattle Public Schools, 29, 38, 114, 127, 129, 133, 151, 161
Seattle Quilt Building, 53
Seattle Star, 19
Seattle Steam Plant, **71**
Seattle Street Railway System, **40**, 41
The Seattle Times, 69, 70, 85, 100, 102, 116, 135, 139,
    159, 166–67, 178, 197
Seattle Trust and Savings Bank, 187
Seattle Weekly, 163–64
Seattle World's Fair, 180
Second Avenue, **115, 116**
Second Avenue Extension, **116**, 117
Seidelhuber Iron and Bronze Works, 189, **191**
Seller Building, 196
Semple, Eugene, 74
Sephardic Jewish community, 198
Seven Gables (movie theater chain), 147
Seward Hotel. *See* Hotel Seward
Shelly's Leg, 173, **173**
Sher, Ron, 161
Sherman Anti-Trust Act, 75
Simmons, Michael, 21
Simon, Aurelio, 126
Simons, Langdon, **158**, 178
Simonson, Rick, 160–62
The Simpsons, 163
Sims, Patterson, 164
"Sinking Ship" garage, 55, 177, 181, **185**, 193–94
Sires, David, 33
Sister Faye's Mission, 119
Siwash Indians, 97
Skagway, Alaska, 80–81, 68, 87

Skid Road, ix, xi, 68, 87; hillside where logs were skid-
    ded, 5, 16; name for district south of Yesler Way,
    96, 100. *See also* Mill Street; Yesler Way; Pioneer
    Square/Skid Road Historic District
Skid Road Theater, 167
Skinner and Eddy Shipyards, 113, 120
Skolnik, Arthur ("Art"), 157, 192, 194
Skyway Luggage, 134
Sleeping Car Porters Club, **78**
Slemmons, Rod, 106–7, 146
Smith, Burns Lyman, 111
Smith, Edmund, 107
Smith, Greg, 141
Smith, Henry, 7, 19
Smith, H. Martin, Jr., 140
Smith, Kiki, 163
Smith, Leonard P., 140
Smith, Lyman Cornelius, 109–11
Smith, Mickey, 141
Smith, Ursula, 17
Smith Corona typewriters, 109
Smith Cove, 64, 124
Smith Tower, **3**, 109–10, **110, 111**, 124, 198
Smith Tower Annex (aka Interurban Building), 111
Snoqualmie (fireboat), 57
Snoqualmie Hall, 27
Snoqualmie Pass, 26
Snyder, Gary, 152–53
Soap Lake, Wash., 198
Social Security, 123, 129
Social services and public health, 136–39, 196–97
Sone, Monica, nee Kazuko Itoi, *Nisei Daughter*, 126
Sound Transit, 78–79, 200
South Downtown (SoDo), 74, 106
South End Steam Baths, 170
Space Needle, 133
Spanish-American War, 88–89; economic impacts in
    Seattle, 91–92
Special Review districts, 184. *See also* Pioneer Square
    Historic District
Speidel, Bill, *Doc Maynard, Sons of the Profits*, 6, 50,
    156, 174, 183, **183**
Speidel, Julie, 163, 174

Speidel, Shirley, 156, 175

Speidel, Sunny, **156**, 174

Spokane, 43

Spring Hill Water Company, 41, 47

Squire, Watson C., 32, 39, 41, 109

Squire-Latimer Building. *See* Grand Central Building

Squire's Opera House, 39, **39**, 55

Stagen, Frank, 78

Stalin, [Joseph], 128

Standard Theater, 145

Starbuck, Susan, 128

Starr, Jackie, 171

Star Theater, 168

State Building, 130

Steele's Landing, 29

Steel Lake, 135

Steinbrueck, Victor, 6, 174–76, **175**, **176**, 183–84, 191

Stem, Allen H., 72

Sterling (movie theater chain), 147

Stetson and Post Mill, 67

Stevens, Isaac, 18–20

Stevens Pass, 66

Stickney Murphy Architects, 195, 198

Stickney Murphy Romine Architects, 198

Stine, Sue, 73

Stone and Webster, 77

Stonewall Riots, Greenwich Village, New York, 172

Streetcars, **40**, 41, 57, 79, 95, **115**, 121, 129

Street people, 138

Strong, Anna Louise, 114

Stuck Junction (now Auburn), 31

Suiter, John, 152

Sullivan, Louis, 58–60

Sullivan, Tim, 146

Sullivan, William, **34**

Sullivan/Considine Vaudeville Circuit, 146

Sunset Magazine, 72

Suquamish Indians, 7, 11, 21

Suquamish Reservation, 21

Su-quattle, 17

Su-quattle, Susan, 17, 22

Swedes, 43, 63, 119

Tacoma, 29, 30, 45, 62, 77

Tagish Indian, 91

Tanner, Renee, xii

Tashiro, Billee (Mrs. Juro Yoshioka), 133

Tashiro, Kanjiro, **133**

Tashiro Hardware Building, **133**, 165

Tashiro-Kaplan Building, 133, 165, 199

Taylor, Quintard, 95

Teamsters Union, 124, 127

Teen Dance Ordinance, 169

Tenderloin. *See* Skid Road

Terminal 46, 203

Territorial University, 25, 28, 38. *See also* University of Washington

Terry, Charles Carrol, 13, 14, 26

Terry, Lee, 12–14

Terry-Denny Building (aka Northern Hotel), 170, 181, **182**

Third Alliance Music, 155

Thompson, Mary, 97

Thomson, Reginald Heber, 65, 71, 74, 105

Tidelands, reclamation of, 65, 72, 74–75, 77, 106

Tilikums of Elttaes, 104

Timberlake, Marvin, 158

Tlingit Island of Tongass, Alaska, 91, 154

Togetsu Restaurant, 158

Tomita, Teiko, 133

Toner, Harry, 155

Toner, Wally, 155

Torrefazione Italia, 160

Totem poles: Pioneer Place, **90**, **91**, 91, 190; Occidental Park, **153**, 154

Traditions and Beyond, 153

Trattoria Mitchelli, 159, 195

Travelers Aid Society, 73

Travelers Hotel, 138–39, **139**, 195, **196**

Travelers/Post Mews Building, 139, 195, **196**

Traver, Bill, 163

Treaty of 1846 (between the U.S. and Britain), 11

Treaty of Paris (Spanish-American War), 88

Triangle Hotel and Bar, **5**

Troetsche, Carl, 55, 187

Trotskyites, 127

Tsimshian tribe, 190

Tsonoqua, 153

Tuberculosis, 136–37

Tucker, Sophie, 146

Tumwater Tavern, 155, 179

Turkish Baths, 170

Tuttle, Anne (aka Quitzlitza), 22

Uhlman, Wes, 173, **183***, 185, 192*

Underground Seattle, 49–50, 120, 174, 183, 186, 188

Underground Tour, 50, 120, 156, 158, 174, **183**, **185**

Underground Tour Museum, ix

Underwriters' Inspection Bureau of San Francisco, 46

Unemployed Citizens League, 122, 124

Union Gospel Mission, 202

Union Pacific Railroad, 62, 70, 77, 82

Union Record (labor daily), 114

Union Station, 61, **61**, **76**, 76–78, **79**, 96, 129, 131, 193–94

Union Station Associates, 78, 200

United States Bicentennial, 193

Union Trust Building, 186

United Parcel Service (UPS), 139–40, 189, 195

University of Washington, 25, 28, 38, 93, 125, 151; Department of Architecture, 175; Northwest Collection, 188–89

University of Washington Press, 151–52

Upper Green and White River Indians, 11

Urban renewal, 6, 177–83

U.S. Dept. of Housing and Urban Development (HUD), 138

U.S. Navy and Seattle, 92

U.S. Xpress Enterprises, 189

Uysal, Sedat, 160

Van Asselt, Henry, 12

Vancouver, British Columbia, 80

Vancouver, Captain George, 10, 11

Vancouver, Wash., 10

Vandenbrink, Catherine, 165

Vaudeville, 142–49, **146**

Velvet Elvis Theater, 169

Verona (ship), 152

Vietnamese in Seattle, 159

Vieux Carre, New Orleans, 142, 176

Villard, Henry, 30–31, 62–64, 70

Volunteer Park, 89

Voyage of Discovery, 10

Vulcan Northwest, 78, 200, 203

Wa Chong Company, 31

Waitresses Union, 103

Wakamatsu, Mr., 127

Walker, Burke, 168

Walker, Olson, 191

Walker Building. *See* Globe Building

Wappenstein, Charles W. ("Wappy"), 101

Warhol, Andy, 162

Warren, Pearl, 153

Washington, George, 40

Washington Building, 181

Washington Cigar Store, 149

Washington Commission for the Humanities, 161

Washington Commonwealth Federation, 123

Washington National Guard, 45, 88

Washington Old Age Pension Union, 124

Washington Post, 146

Washington Shoe Building, 53, 164, **199**

Washington State Convention and Trade Center, 192

Washington State Department of Transportation, 202

Washington State Intertribal Council, 153

Washington Street Boat Landing, *157,* 188, 193

Washington Territory, creation of, 18

Washington Woman Suffrage Association, 35, 102

Waterfall Park, 195

Waterfront Streetcar. *See* First Avenue trolley

Wax and Raine Building. *See* Heritage Building

Wayside Mission Hospital, 99–100

Webster and Stevens, 189

Wehn, James A., 11

Weller Street pedestrian bridge, ("Bridge Between Cultures"), 79, 165–66

Wells, MacIver, 172

Wessel and Lieberman, 162

Western Avenue, 156

Weyerhaeuser, Frederick, 70

White, Richard, 6, 55, 153–55, 162, **162**, 175, 186–87, 194

Whitechapel, 68, 96–97

White Pass Trail, Alaska, 82

White River Valley, 20, 77–78, 156

Wichern, Peter, 172

Wickersham, Albert, 182

Widner, Abbie, 97

Wilkes, Charles, 10

Will, Bill, 199

Willamette Valley, 13

Willcox, William H., 53

Willwerth, Cliff, 165, 198

Wilse, Anders B., 23

Wilson, Clodall, 156

Wilson, John L., 70

Winchell, Walter, 148, 171–72

Windsor Hotel (renamed Globe Hotel), 56

Wing Luke Asian Museum, 134

Winters, Terry, 163

Wittler Block. *See* Cadillac Hotel

Wobblies. *See* Industrial Workers of the World

Wolf, Hazel, 122, 128

Wong, Shawn, 152

Woodbury, Charles J., 35

Woman suffrage, 34–36, 102

Women's Christian Temperance Union (WCTU), 35, 99, 102

Women's labor unions, 103, 133–35

Workers' Alliance, 122, 124, 128

Working men's hotels, xi, 109, 126, 138–39, 150–51, 195

Works Progress Administration (WPA), 123, 128, **128**; Federal Art Project, 150

World Trade Center, New York City, 202

World War I, 92, 113, 121, 140, 149

World War II, 181; and Filipinos, 131, 150–51; and home front in Seattle, 129–30, 134, 171, 198; Japanese American internment and military service, 131–32, 151–52; postwar return to "normalcy," 132–34, 151–52; and women's employment, 129, 132–34

Wright, Nancy Allison, 145

Wright, Virginia, 162

Wyckoff, Louis, 33–34

Wyman, Helen Marie, **158**

Yakama Indians, 20

Yari, Dean, 158

Yari, Doris, 158

Yesler, Henry Leiter, 3, 15–17, 21, 22, 29, 32, 33, **34**, 36, 48–49, 50, 51, 111, 188

Yesler, Sarah Burgert, 16, 17, **17**, 22, 27, 33, 35, **35**, 36

Yesler Building, 51, 156, **182**

Yesler Corner, 49

Yesler house (pioneer home), **17**, 22, 34, 35

Yesler-Leary Building, **40**, 41, 48, 53

Yesler mansion, **36**, 44

Yesler's cookhouse, 16, 17, 51

Yesler's mill, 3, 15, 16

Yesler's Pavilion, 27, 32, 35

Yesler's Wharf, 16, 27, 37

Yesler Way, 5, 100, **113**, **192**. *See also* Mill Street

Yoshioka, Juro, 133

Young Women's Christian Association (YWCA), 73

Yukon, Canada, 80–86, 90–91, 93

Yukon River, 88

Zeitgeist, 160

Zen Buddhism, 172

Zioncheck, Marion, 122–24